How to Be a Perfect Stranger

No Longer Invisible

NO LONGER INVISIBLE

Religion in University Education

DOUGLAS JACOBSEN

and

RHONDA HUSTEDT JACOBSEN

OXFORD
UNIVERSITY PRESS

OXFORD
UNIVERSITY PRESS

Oxford University Press is a department of the University of Oxford.
It furthers the University's objective of excellence in research, scholarship,
and education by publishing worldwide.

Oxford   New York
Auckland   Cape Town   Dar es Salaam   Hong Kong   Karachi
Kuala Lumpur   Madrid   Melbourne   Mexico City   Nairobi
New Delhi   Shanghai   Taipei   Toronto

With offices in
Argentina   Austria   Brazil   Chile   Czech Republic   France   Greece
Guatemala   Hungary   Italy   Japan   Poland   Portugal   Singapore
South Korea   Switzerland   Thailand   Turkey   Ukraine   Vietnam

Oxford is a registered trademark of Oxford University Press
in the UK and certain other countries.

Published in the United States of America by
Oxford University Press
198 Madison Avenue, New York, NY 10016

© Oxford University Press 2012

All rights reserved. No part of this publication may be reproduced, stored in a
retrieval system, or transmitted, in any form or by any means, without the prior
permission in writing of Oxford University Press, or as expressly permitted by law,
by license, or under terms agreed with the appropriate reproduction rights organization.
Inquiries concerning reproduction outside the scope of the above should be sent to the
Rights Department, Oxford University Press, at the address above.

You must not circulate this work in any other form
and you must impose this same condition on any acquirer.

Library of Congress Cataloging-in-Publication Data
Jacobsen, Douglas G. (Douglas Gordon), 1951–
No longer invisible : religion in university education /
Douglas Jacobsen and Rhonda Hustedt Jacobsen.
p. cm.
ISBN 978–0–19–984473–9 (hardcover : alk. paper)
1. Church and college—United States.
2. Universities and colleges—United States—Religion.
3. United States—Religion.   I. Jacobsen, Rhonda Hustedt.   II. Title.
LC383.J33 2012
378′.071—dc23
2011047153

ISBN 978–0–19–984473–9

3 5 7 9 8 6 4 2
Printed in the United States of America
on acid-free paper

Contents

Preface vii

PART ONE: *Religion in the Context of University Education*

1. No Longer Invisible 3
2. The History of Religion in American Higher Education 16
3. Trail Markers in a Time of Transition 31
4. A Framework for Better Questions 46

PART TWO: *Six Sites of Engagement*

5. Religious Literacy 59
6. Interfaith Etiquette 73
7. Framing Knowledge 92
8. Civic Engagement 107
9. Convictions 123
10. Character and Vocation 137

Conclusion: Religion and the Future of University Education 153

Acknowledgments 158

Notes 161

Index 183

Preface

THIS BOOK IS about religion and undergraduate education at America's thousands of colleges and universities. Its main argument can be stated simply: Paying attention to religion—which we define broadly to include traditional religion, spirituality in its many different forms, and life's big questions of meaning, purpose, character, hope, and ethics, whether or not they are formulated in religious language—has the potential to enhance student learning and to improve higher education as a whole. We also think that religion is educationally unavoidable. Religion is a part of the real world that demands objective analysis and critical study, and questions and concerns related to religion (defined broadly) appear in almost every academic field of study. There was a time, not very long ago, when religion was all but invisible in the educational programming of most colleges and universities. That time is past; religion is no longer invisible. This book provides a map of how colleges and universities across the country are re-engaging religion and how they can do that more intelligently and effectively. This is not a compendium of answers, but an invitation for educators to look more closely at a facet of life that is too big and important to ignore.

The two of us have been thinking and talking about religion in higher education for a long time. One of us studied psychology as an undergraduate and later went on for a doctorate in the social foundations of education from Temple University; the other earned an undergraduate degree in philosophy and then completed a doctorate in religious studies at the University of Chicago. Our first real disagreement—which took place long ago on a train from Belfast to Dublin in Ireland—was about which field of study, psychology or philosophy, had contributed more to the advancement of human understanding. We have now been married for thirty-five years, and we have been debating—and learning from each other—about matters of psychology, philosophy, religion, and education the entire time. We wrote our first joint essay on the topic of religion in higher education about twenty years ago, and ever since then we have been asking if and how religion can play a constructive role in advancing the work of higher education.

During the last four or five years, we have discussed this topic with literally hundreds of faculty, students, college administrators, student-life professionals, chaplains, and leaders of various national organizations dedicated to the support and improvement of higher education in America. This book is the result of what we have heard.

To some degree, the present volume is a sequel to our 2008 publication entitled *The American University in a Postsecular Age*. That earlier work was an edited volume illustrating the many different ways that educators are already thinking about religion and its connections with higher education. Contributors included sociologists like Robert Wuthnow from Princeton, political scientists like John DiIulio from the University of Pennsylvania, national higher educational leaders like Lee Shulman, then president of the Carnegie Foundation for the Advancement of Teaching, and religious studies scholars like Mark Edwards from Harvard and Amanda Porterfield from Florida State University. By bringing together the work of these experts, who represent a wide array of subject areas and viewpoints, that book was intended symbolically to set the table for "a more comprehensive and connected conversation [dealing] with religion in its entirety—including its personal and social dimensions, values and ideas, subjective and objective characteristics, and potential for good or ill."[1]

During the last several years, we have used *The American University in a Postsecular Age* as a starting point for conversations at dozens of colleges and universities. All told, we visited more than fifty campuses, ranging from Brown University to Brigham Young, Vassar College to Cal State Bakersfield, MIT to Ave Maria, Penn State to Pepperdine, the University of Miami to Pacific Lutheran, Yale to USC, and the United States Air Force Academy to Soka University (a Buddhist-influenced school in southern California).[2] The purpose of these visits was not to catalogue everything we saw—we are not anthropologists or sociological researchers—but to learn how people thought and talked about religion and its connections with higher education. Our methodology was to ask the best questions we could, to listen carefully to the responses we were given, and then to reformulate our own thinking so that our next round of conversations might be even more productive. And those subsequent conversations were often suggested by individuals at the last school we visited, who frequently told us quite clearly who we simply *had* to talk to next. Over time this process helped us learn how to ask better questions and to clarify our rhetoric in ways that facilitated meaningful discussion rather than fruitless, conceptually confused argument.

All of that trekking across the country obviously took considerable time and money, and we are grateful to the Lilly Endowment for providing the needed funds. We are also thankful that our liaison there, Christopher Coble, was sometimes willing to take on a role analogous to that of a baseball manager.

A few months into the process, one of us started getting antsy to begin writing this book, and Chris told us to close our laptops and not even consider writing for at least two years. "Just listen," he said. "Don't jump to conclusions. Take your time." So we did, and we learned a great deal more than we ever could have predicted.

One of the lessons we had to learn over and over again was how much our own religious dispositions and habits of thought shaped the way we saw things. Both of us are lifelong Protestants, but when we began our campus visits, we were quite confident that as scholars we could bracket any Protestant intellectual biases we might have. We quickly discovered, however, that our Protestant biases (or perhaps more accurately our Protestant habits of thought and practice) went deeper than we knew, and people pointed them out to us more often than we'd like to admit. Eventually, slowly, we became more religiously, spiritually, and secularly multilingual, but it took effort. We also realized we were not alone. Religious or secular convictions and ways of life haunt everyone's thinking and acting, and that means any comprehension of the place of religion in higher education requires a heightened self-awareness from everyone, along with more sensitivity to the ways in which various religious or religion-like frames of cognition, affectivity, and action (of which we are often only partly conscious) shape us as individuals, educators, and students.

This book is divided into two sections. The first part describes the context of American higher education as a whole and the changing place of religion within it. The initial chapter discusses religion's recent "return" to higher education, arguing that religion's current visibility does not represent a movement back toward the past but is actually something quite new (which is why the word "return" is in quotes). Religion in America today is not the Protestant monolith it once was—it is much more diverse—and religion's boundaries have become fuzzier than ever before, making it hard to differentiate between religious and nonreligious life stances. These changes make it impossible to keep religion out of higher education, even if that might be the preferred goal for some people. The second chapter is a historical overview of religion in American higher education that provides some of the background information necessary to grasp the uniqueness of the contemporary situation. The third chapter analyzes several "trail markers" that colleges and universities developed during the late twentieth century as religion was beginning to become more visible on campuses once again. We consider these trail markers to be important, although ultimately inadequate, ways of addressing the complexity of religion that exists within higher education today. The fourth chapter proposes a new and more comprehensive framework for understanding religion in the contemporary era, a framework for asking better questions about how religion and higher education are intertwined.

②   The second half of the book is organized around the six key topics or questions related to religion and higher learning—six sites of engagement where religion and higher learning overlap—that we think all colleges and universities need to address. These essays are not attempts to spell out what educators or institutions must do. Instead they are intended to help colleges and universities engage in more productive discussion, debate, planning, and assessment related to religion's presence—sometimes hidden, but increasingly visible—within the goals and practices of contemporary American higher education. In terms of specific topics, we start with what is perhaps least controversial—the need for religious literacy in a religiously diverse world—and then move on to discuss interfaith etiquette, religion and the framing of knowledge, religion and civic engagement, the place of convictions in the process of teaching and learning, and the practical concerns of character and vocation.

It should be clear by now that we are not arguing that higher education should somehow submit itself to the teachings of traditional religion. This book is not about the eternal truths of heaven; it is about the place of religion in the rough-and-tumble educational realities of the here and now. Our argument is educational, not religious: that giving more careful and nuanced attention to the religiosity (or spirituality) that is *already present within* the enterprise of higher learning will benefit colleges and universities and improve the education they offer to students.

No Longer Invisible

PART ONE

Religion in the Context of University Education

I

No Longer Invisible

DRIVE NORTH FROM the Mason-Dixon Line past the Civil War fields of Gettysburg, Pennsylvania, and about two hours later you reach a place called "Happy Valley," home of Pennsylvania State University. Penn State's mammoth presence dominates the sparsely populated valley, and it offers nearly everything that one might expect from a fine public university: incredible facilities, world-class scholars, smart students, and an amazingly loyal body of alumni. Like every university, Penn State has its warts and blemishes. In 2009, for example, the university had the dubious honor of being listed in *The Princeton Review* as the number-one party school in the nation, and more recently the school's reputation has been tarnished by an ongoing investigation into allegations of child sexual abuse by an assistant football coach—revelations that led to the dismissal of both the university president and Penn State's longtime football coach, the late Joe Paterno, fondly referred to as "JoePa" by Penn State fans.

What most people don't know about Penn State is that the school is also at the cutting edge of higher education's new engagement with religion. The most visible symbol of this engagement is the massive Pasquerilla Spiritual Center (PSC), located prominently on the campus. Constructed in 2003 and funded entirely by private donations, the center has a 750-seat worship hall that can be reconfigured in minutes to suit the needs of any of the campus's various religious communities, and the building includes office space for all of Penn State's more than sixty student religious (and secular/ethical) organizations, including the Atheist/Agnostic Association. The programs of the PSC are overseen by the Center for Ethics and Religious Affairs (CERA), which says that its goal is to provide "a welcoming, safe, inclusive environment for the Penn State community to explore a multitude of faith traditions in a compassionate, open-minded setting," an environment "that stretches beyond tolerance to a genuine appreciation of and respect for religious and spiritual diversity." Proselytizing is explicitly forbidden, and all PSC-supported programs (whether student-led or university-sponsored) are supposed to "support students' commitment to academics, to self, and to family."[1]

As a public institution, Penn State is committed to the separation of church and state, but no tension is assumed to exist between that commitment and the religious and ethical work of the PSC. There was a time in the past when Penn State, like many other public universities, had an ordained Christian chaplain on campus, but that office was eliminated in the 1960s. The PSC today is directed by Bob Smith, a non-ordained former social worker who defines his responsibility as making sure that everyone, regardless of their faith or lack of faith, feels at home and is treated equally, both at the PSC and on the campus as a whole. Smith sees the PSC as a bold experiment in public higher education, and he is not alone. In our conversations with directors of religious or spiritual life at colleges and universities all across the country, Penn State was repeatedly cited as among the vanguard when it comes to dealing with religion in public higher education.

Like many cutting-edge initiatives, it took significant efforts to get the PSC and CERA off the ground, and the one person who did more than anyone else to make it happen was Coach Joe Paterno. Paterno, a devout Catholic who was known for running a genuinely character-building football program, cajoled the president into approving the project, and he and his wife contributed more than a million dollars toward its construction. In a turn of events worthy of a Greek tragedy, the PSC also became one of the primary places where students congregated to sort through their confusion, disappointment, and anger about the sexual abuse scandal involving the former assistant football coach and the university's subsequent decision to fire Paterno along with the university president. The PSC helped to organize a massive candlelight vigil for the victims of the abuse, and when Paterno died of cancer three months later, the PSC, for the first time in its history, was the site of a funeral service. More than 40,000 Penn State students, staff, alumni, and friends filed through to pay their respects before the local Catholic bishop performed the actual service. According to Smith, many members of the campus community expressed their appreciation that the PSC was there to be a place of spiritual hope and healing during a troubled period in the school's history.[2]

Religion's New Visibility

Religion, as we discuss it in this book, encompasses all of the concerns and activities associated with the PSC at Penn State. It involves traditional religiosity such as that represented by the Catholic, Protestant, Jewish, and other student religious organizations housed in the center, but it also relates to "big questions" (questions of meaning and purpose) and deep moral concerns, whether these matters are expressed in explicitly religious language or not. Religion is about how people relate to God or the "higher power(s)" of the universe, but it is also about how people relate to each other, especially when words fail but sympathy and support still need to be expressed. And religion is about the values that we live by as individuals and as groups. There was a time in the not-too-distant past when this whole jumble of concerns was metaphorically swept under the rug at most colleges and universities, which tended to operate on the assumption that religion was a purely personal concern that had little or nothing to do with higher education. That is, however, no longer the case. Religion has once again become visible on campuses, and colleges and universities, both public and private, are grappling with how to proceed.

Growing out of these developments, the question that has driven our research and reflection is this: How is religion present within higher learning, and how might educators maximize the cognitive, social, and personal dimensions of student learning by paying more attention to the inherently religious or spiritual dimensions of higher education? One of our earliest findings was that many educators do not know where to start when such a question is asked. Many people acknowledge that religion and spirituality are somehow relevant to educational processes, but most don't know how to talk about it. The conversation about such matters is dominated on many campuses by the extremes: by convinced believers championing traditional religion, on the one hand, and by emotivists of vague spirituality, on the other. Conversations with those in either camp tend to be not particularly fruitful. The first defines religion too narrowly to take into account the diversity of faith that exists within higher education; the second defines the topic so loosely and individualistically that there is little to do other than swap personal stories. The goal of this book is to chart a middle ground where religion can be discussed critically and intelligently (in other words, in the natural language of the academy) so that the multiple connections between religion and higher education can be identified and analyzed.

We are not suggesting that colleges and universities need to *add* religion to the already overloaded list of concerns they are supposed to address. Religious and spiritual matters are already embedded in the work that colleges and universities do. The goal is to become more aware of and attuned to what is already going on, and the potential gains are enormous. Giving more careful attention to religion (broadly construed) has the possibility of enhancing the work of higher education in untold ways, because religion is inextricably blended into the key dispositions that drive learning itself—the mixing of critical thinking with hope, the awareness of difference, the ability to wonder and to see the world in new ways, the skill of focusing on one thing at a time, and the blending of the personal with the impersonal. Attending to religion can enliven all of these dimensions of higher learning; ignoring religion undermines them.

That said, we are not at all suggesting that religion itself is somehow above criticism. At colleges and universities, religion should be subjected to the same critical inquiry that is directed at every other topic of study in the academy. Religion is not an unmitigated good; it can be a repository of evil as well. But that is precisely why religion needs attention. It has too much power to be ignored, and it is too enmeshed in life to be treated as irrelevant to the choices people make and the ways in which societies organize themselves.

If any particular event signaled a sea change regarding the place of religion in university education, it was a conference that took place at Wellesley College in September of 1998. The theme of the meeting was "Education as Transformation: Religious Pluralism, Spirituality, and Higher Education," and the organizers assumed that it would be a relatively modest gathering of administrators and academicians. That assumption was mistaken. More than 800 people showed up, representing 350 institutions of higher learning, including the Ivy League, some of the nation's most elite liberal arts colleges, and a variety of research universities. The hypothesis of the conference was that religion and spirituality are inseparable from learning. Education itself, the conference proclaimed, is a spiritual journey, an inherently transformative experience.

Just as religion was beginning to re-emerge as a significant concern within higher education, it also resurfaced with deadly violence in society as a whole when religiously motivated terrorists attacked the World Trade Center and the Pentagon on September 11, 2001. Across the nation, people asked how this could have happened. How could the American government and its intelligence-gathering organizations have so completely misunderstood the world situation? How could the negative consequences of religion have been so overlooked? Religion could no longer be ignored—not by politicians or the military, and not by the academy. Although many scholars had dismissed religion as tangential to the quest for geopolitical understanding, that attitude was changed in a day. Like everyone else in the nation, educators had received an unwelcome wakeup call. It was time to start taking religion more seriously, and it was time to learn how to "manage" religion on campus more effectively. This was a matter of national security and political necessity; it had to be done. What might have been a gradual process of re-engaging religion on campus suddenly became a matter of grave urgency.

The recent "return" of religion to higher education—in both the Wellesley sense and in response to 9/11—is a complex phenomenon. On the one hand, the return of religion simply means that religion is more visible, less private, and more integrated into the learning process than it has been for years. It now pops up regularly in the courses and academic journals of history, anthropology, sociology, psychology, politics, science, literature, and virtually every kind of professional study. Religion is now the hottest topic of research for the American Historical Association, nudging out "cultural history" for first place,[3] and the American Psychological Association recently stated that it wants more attention given to religion and spirituality, because these factors "are under-examined in psychological research both in terms of their prevalence within various research populations and in terms of their possible relevance as influential variables."[4] The same kinds of developments are evident in other disciplines as well.

It is important to note, however, that the religion that is "returning" to university life and learning is not the old religion of the past. The word "return" accordingly needs to be used with care. Religion in America has undergone a significant transformation in the last ten to fifteen years, and the primary difference is that it has become much more diverse, so diverse that we prefer to use the term "pluriformity" to underscore the expansiveness of current options. This pluriformity has two sides. One side represents traditional, "organized" religion, and the main change here is that the range of organized religions in America has increased exponentially. College and university students now attend classes not just with Catholics, Jews, and Protestants (and many different kinds of secular individuals), but with Muslims, Hindus, Jains, Buddhists, Zoroastrians, Wiccans, Sikhs, and members of other religious communities and subcommunities. This development alone would call for rewriting the rules of engagement with religion on campus.

The other side of today's religious pluriformity, however, makes things even more complex and confusing: The boundary line between what is and what is not religion has become thoroughly blurred. If secularity is like freshwater and religion is like saltwater, life in America is now thoroughly brackish. More and more people are cobbling together their own unique combinations of religious ideas, practices, experiences, and core values from a variety of religious and nonreligious sources. The term "spirituality" is sometimes used to describe this new do-it-yourself style of faith. Some people who consider themselves "spiritual" are also traditionally religious, but many of them are atheists, agnostics, or self-proclaimed skeptics. To be spiritual, understood in this sense, is to have deeply held convictions, and anyone can have those kinds of heartfelt allegiances. This new ambiguity about what counts as religion or spirituality makes it virtually impossible to keep religion out of higher education, because no one knows exactly where to draw the line indicating that one person's convictions count as religion while those of someone else do not. To say that religion has "returned" to higher education is thus something like saying that dinosaurs have returned to earth in the form of birds. Birds are the evolutionary descendants of dinosaurs, but they are hardly the same animals, and American religion today is a very different animal than it was in the past.

Three Stories from Boston

The multifaceted and complicated character of religion in higher education today can be illustrated by stories from three universities in the academically rich and culturally diverse city of Boston. The first comes from the Massachusetts Institute of Technology. MIT was begun in 1861 as a polytechnic institute, and founder William Barton Rogers defined the school's purpose somewhat inelegantly as "the teaching, not of the minute details and manipulations of the arts, which can be done only in the workshop, but the inculcation of those scientific principles which form the basis and explanation of them, their leading processes and operations in connection with physical laws."[5] MIT is a practical, scientific place where religion, while never being entirely ignored, has never been central. The campus is graced with a beautiful prayer chapel, and religion courses have been taught for decades, most notably by the prolific author and spiritually eclectic Huston Smith who chaired the philosophy department from 1958 to 1973. But the university has no formal religious connections, and it never had any officially designated overseer of religious life on campus until the fall of 2007 when it appointed Robert Randolph to be "chaplain of the institute."

MIT, like most universities, is awash in students of faith, and the main administrative task of the new chaplain is to coordinate the work of the twenty-two unpaid associate chaplains who serve the religious needs of the student body, representing all of the world's major religions and a dozen different versions of Christianity. But since MIT always had religious students on campus, why appoint a chaplain in 2007? In short, MIT needed a chaplain because meeting the religious needs of individual students—something religious volunteers could do—was no longer enough. What matters now is helping students learn how to conduct themselves in a world inhabited by many different kinds of secular and religious people. Randolph explains; "The biggest challenge...is simply keeping people talking to each other, so that the stereotypes that operate, and have operated for far too long out there, are not allowed to reimpose themselves." Randolph says that getting Muslims and Jews and Hindus and Christians and everyone else to be comfortable with each other is the most important religious work he does. He notes: "In [twenty-five] years [these students] are going to be decision-makers in wider worlds than we can imagine. And having some appreciation and understanding of these different religious communities and traditions will serve them well. That's the goal; that's what we're trying to do."[6] In Randolph's opinion, the very future of the world may hinge on the interfaith friendships that are born at MIT and the skills of religious etiquette that are developed there.

A second story: The same year that MIT appointed its first official chaplain, an interesting debate about religion and education was taking place next door at Harvard University. The focus at Harvard was on the classroom, and specifically on general education requirements, the package of courses that every student is required to take in order to graduate. A faculty task force, chaired by the Pulitzer Prize-winning literary scholar Louis Menand, recommended the addition of a new general education requirement in an area of study the committee called "reason and faith." The rationale was straightforward: "Religion is a fact of twenty-first-century life," and a Harvard education should recognize its presence. The committee noted that 94 percent of Harvard's incoming students say they discuss religion frequently or occasionally, and 71 percent attend religious services. The new requirement was designed to make a place in the curriculum where students could "sort out the relationship between their own beliefs and practices, the different beliefs and practices of fellow students, and the profoundly secular and intellectual world of the academy itself." The courses that would fulfill this requirement were supposed to be scholarly and not "prescriptive," and the goal was to help students "understand the interplay between religious and secular institutions, practices, and ideas" in order to become "more self-conscious about their own beliefs and values" and "more informed and reflective citizens."[7]

Dissent erupted almost immediately. Some members of the faculty detected a weakening of Harvard's commitment to hardheaded, rational, empirically based learning. The evolutionary psychologist Steven Pinker was particularly outspoken, asking why the university would waste its time on the "ignorance and irrationality" of religion at a time when "the rest of the West is moving beyond it." He further wrote that "[u]niversities are about reason, pure and simple," and "faith—believing something without good reasons to do so—has no place in anything but a religious institution."[8]

The final resolution of faculty debate was to require a course called "culture and belief" instead of "reason and faith." The redefined course was still supposed to provide space within the curriculum for students to reflect on "cultural issues of concern or interest that are likely to arise in students' own lives," but religion, defined as a "cultural issue," became only one potential topic of study.[9] This outcome disappointed many Harvard watchers, including Lisa Miller, the religion editor of *Newsweek*. In a multipage article entitled "Harvard's Crisis of Faith," she opined: "[T]o dismiss the importance of the study of faith—especially now—out of academic narrow-mindedness is less than unhelpful. It's unreasonable."[10]

A third story comes from Boston College, a Catholic university. It was founded by the Jesuits in 1863. Its history largely mimics the history of Catholic higher education in America as a whole. During its first hundred years, Boston College was a solidly Catholic institution serving an almost entirely Catholic student body. Like many religiously affiliated schools, it was also frequently in debt. But in the 1960s, things began to change. Over the years, American society had become much less stridently Protestant and more welcoming toward Catholics, and the Second Vatican Council of the Catholic Church (1962–1965) had redefined Catholic structures to make them more open to non-Catholic ideas and ideals. In fact, one of the most famous documents of the council affirmed that "nothing genuinely human" is foreign to Catholic Christianity.[11] The religious and cultural walls that had formerly separated Catholics from other Americans were dissolving. Boston College, like many other Catholic colleges and universities, concluded that the maintenance of a distinctively Catholic identity was no longer the institution's main concern. Quality of education became the goal. The school, accordingly, opened its doors to everyone, sought federal aid, expanded its donor base, and changed its faculty hiring patterns. Today Boston College is one of the most financially solid and academically respected institutions of higher education in the country, and until very recently it had a relatively low-key approach to its Catholic identity.

Then, during spring break in 2009, various examples of religious art—most notably crucifixes—suddenly appeared in many of the campus's classrooms. The walls had been bare when faculty and students left, but they were festooned with religious icons when they returned. Reactions were mixed. Some individuals were disturbed, or even irritated, by the new art work. Amir Hoveyda, a professor of chemistry, said, "For [eighteen] years, I taught at a university where I was allowed to teach in an environment where I felt comfortable…[then] without any discussion, without any warning, without any intellectual debate, literally during the middle of the night during a break, these icons appear." Dan Kirschner, a professor of biology who is Jewish, had to take on "three hands" to express his consternation: "On the one hand, BC wants to be all-inclusive. On the other hand, they do things like this to make people feel not included. On the other hand, it is a Catholic university."[12] Many faculty and students were confused about what message the university was trying to communicate.

Speaking on behalf of the administration, Reverend Jack Dunn, chair of the campus committee on Christian art, said that, far from wanting to offend anyone, the newly installed crucifixes were intended to send a message of welcome. Drawing on the writings of Pope John Paul II, Dunn explained that the crucifix should be seen as a "sign of God, who has compassion on us, who accepts human weakness, who opens to us all, to one another, and therefore creates the relation of fraternity." Dunn added that the crucifix is simultaneously "an invitation to love, and an invitation to faith.… One is not required to respond, one can decline, and one can have many reasons for declining the invitation, but to imply that a Jesuit and Catholic university is not free to offer this invitation is simply an impossibility."[13]

Clearly, the crucifix is a symbol of Catholic identity, and a Catholic university like Boston College has a legal right to display it. Doing so may be an act of simple honesty about who they are. But can it function as a sign of compassion and a source of fraternity? Can a very specific religious symbol like the crucifix draw people together, or does it inherently divide? More broadly, does making the campus a place of welcome for everyone mean that religion has to be kept out of sight, or might the public acknowledgment of an institution's religious (or nonreligious) orientation be a necessary first step toward putting everyone at ease—a way, so to speak, of naming the elephant in the room?

These kinds of questions about religion can be aimed at many colleges and universities, not just at Catholic institutions like Boston College. In the recent past, institutions have often assumed that the only valid model for accommodating diversity on campus, especially religious diversity, is the model of the public square—a place where everyone has equal status and standing. No one is special; everyone is similarly ordinary. But Boston College and other American colleges and universities have begun to ask whether a hosting or hospitality model might provide a better alternative for their campuses. When people or institutions act as hosts, they welcome others positively into their space and try to make them feel not simply "at home," but rather like honored guests. Hosting implies a difference between residents and guests—insiders and outsiders—raising the specter of discrimination, but it also has the potential to offer something more humane and thoughtful than the hustle, bustle, and jostling for space that define the public square. Whether Boston College's new crucifixes communicate good hosting of a diverse college population is an open question. Crucifixes aside, the notion of hosting may be worthy of consideration by any university looking for a way to alleviate the alienation of a purely "public square" approach to campus life.

Defining Religion

All three Boston stories are about "religion," but religion is notoriously difficult to define. In many traditional societies, both ancient and contemporary, there is no separate word for religion. Religion is simply "the way" of that society, a reflection of reality itself. The *tao* of Chinese traditional religion refers to the way things are, the natural harmony that exists among all living (and nonliving) things, and it also refers to the way that things are supposed to be. The *tao* is inextricably part of life. It cannot be isolated, and it emphatically cannot be named. It simply is what it is. In the Western tradition, religion has been construed differently. Rather than being part of the natural world, religion is seen as bringing order to the natural world and as tapping into spiritual power that comes from beyond the natural world. More recently, in the modern era of the last several centuries, religion has come to mean a single facet of life that exists separately from the rest of ordinary, nonreligious, secular life.

It is this last assumption, in particular—belief in a neat distinction between the sacred and the secular—that has become increasingly problematic in recent years. Neither religion nor secularity seems to be staying in its defined place. The two now overlap, interact, and sometimes even merge.[14] This new reality can be described metaphorically by picturing organized religion as one mountain and secularity as another, with almost everyone now living somewhere in the religio-secular valley that lies between them. In this valley, every person is to some degree simultaneously secular and religious.[15]

Those at the extremes, both secularists and religionists, would prefer to depopulate this middle valley where religious and secular impulses overlap. For example, the outspoken atheist Sam Harris has argued that moderate religious views and religious tolerance are some of the "principal forces driving us toward the abyss," because they mask the horror of real religion, which in his view is necessarily literalist, irrational, and evil.[16] As far as Harris is concerned, the religious half of the religio-secular valley is nothing more than a dangerous delusion. On the opposite mountain, untold numbers of fundamentalist Christians, Muslims, Hindus, Jews (and other religions as well) are convinced that "real" religion has nothing at all to do with the kinds of middling and mixed views that prevail in the valley of religio-secular experience. For them, any kind of "compromise with the world" is as wrong as the most extreme forms of secular atheism. Still, it seems a simple acknowledgment of reality to say that most Americans today experience the world as a place where religion and secularity mix.

A generation or two in the past, life was different. Back then, most Americans knew what religion was. It meant believing in God or gods; it meant going to church, synagogue, or temple; and it meant living in accordance with the moral dictates of one's particular community of faith. That is no longer an adequate description. All the things on that list still count as religion, but religion overflows those old containers. Now, many individuals who never enter a church or other sacred building say they are religious or spiritual, and even the most devout believers tend to pick and choose which rules and doctrines really matter.

Religion today is much more personal and interpersonal, and less institutional and theologically dogmatic, than it was in the past.[17] A friend of ours illustrates this contemporary approach. She wanted to join a church and was deciding between two options: One was a congregation of the United Church of Christ, often called the most liberal and progressive denomination in the country; the other was an independent Pentecostal church that was fundamentalist in its theology and right wing in its politics. But our friend found them to be "actually very similar"; she said both congregations were filled with friendly people, and both worship services "gave [her] spirit a lift." She was not concerned in the least that the two churches have historic religious beliefs and practices that are miles apart. What mattered was how she experienced the churches. This kind of religious subjectivity and choice has a long history in the United States, with roots in the so-called "Great Awakening" of the mid-1700s and the "Second Great Awakening" of the early 1800s, but the trends have accelerated in recent decades, making religion ever more difficult to define in terms of beliefs and organization. More and more, religion is a matter of personal preference and affectivity.

Simultaneously, religion has become more political. When running for president in 1960, John F. Kennedy famously pledged that his religion would have nothing to do with how he behaved in office. Kennedy was going out of his way to assuage Protestant worries because he was only the second Catholic to ever be seriously considered for the highest office in the land. But politicians in general avoided religion during these years, and even ordinary citizens typically kept their faith and politics in separate compartments. That is no longer the case. In court-ing religious voters, politicians now routinely explain how their faith and religious values will guide them in office. Citizens, too, see religious overtones (positive or negative) in many pieces of legislation that are ostensibly about other matters such as civil rights, health care, international relations, or local zoning laws. It is this new sensitivity to religion (or religious-like concerns) in public life that has fueled the culture-war mentality that still infuses much of American politics.

Given the breadth of what religion has become—ranging from traditional "organized" religion to personal spiritual preferences to public values and politi-cal wrangling—some scholars have suggested that the word "religion" itself has lost its usefulness and that a new vocabulary needs to be developed for naming the various attitudes and activities that the word "religion" is sometimes used to describe. The well-known Canadian Catholic philosopher Charles Taylor, for example, uses the term "fullness" (instead of "religion") to describe the human quest for "life [that] is fuller, richer, deeper, more worthwhile, more admirable, [and] more what it should be."[18] The Jewish social commentator and moral phi-losopher Susan Neiman, author of *Moral Clarity: A Guide for Grown-Up Idealists* (2008), suggests that the phrase "gratitude for Being itself" might be a better term for religion at its best: "an experience not simply of pleasure, but of silent celebration. These are feelings that enlarge us, and make us better than before."[19] But religion also has its negative side, and some scholars today would prefer to name that negativity more directly. They see religion as an illusion or simple prej-udice or a mask for power over others or a destructive cognitive "meme" that has infected human thinking.[20] More neutrally, the sociologist Thomas Luckmann proposed the term "invisible religion" as a name for the many different ways in which people think, act, and feel religiously outside the boundaries and control of traditional, institutional religion. This kind of "invisible religion"[21] is a widespread phenomenon that applies to many people who might never use the word "reli-gious" to describe themselves, including many people who might label themselves as secular or even atheistic.[22]

Although we sympathize with those who are looking for new terms to describe the broadly varied phenomenon of religion, we think there is wisdom in retaining the word and using it in the singular. However diverse the referents of religion might be, they are all interconnected. Understanding those interconnec-tions (and understanding religion's complex relationship with secularity) is part of what scholars around the world are busily investigating.

But what is this thing—religion—that is being investigated? In our own use of the term we lean in the direction of Paul Tillich, who more than half a cen-tury ago defined religion as "ultimate concern," a definition that encompasses the experiences of all humans, however traditionally secular or religious they may be.[23] Following Tillich, this book uses the word "religion" to refer to all the different ways in which human beings seek to understand the world and order their lives in light of what they believe to be ultimately true, real, and important. Religion in this sense of the term includes all the ideas, values, rituals, and affections that people reference when they are focusing on "things that really matter."[24] Obviously, this will differ from individual to individual and from society to society—what one person or culture considers religious, another may not—but that fluidity of meaning itself is one of the key characteristics of religion as it exists in the world today.

The "Soul" of Higher Education

The well-known educator Ernest L. Boyer, who served as U.S. commissioner of education in the 1970s and was later president of the Carnegie Foundation for the Advancement of Teaching, once commented that "today we are rediscovering that the sense of the sacred is inextricably interwoven with the most basic of human impulses." In that light, he suggested that while "no school should impose religious belief or practice…it's simply impossible to be a well-educated person without exploring how religion has shaped the human story." Going further, he asked whether it might even be necessary to move beyond merely studying religion and actively engage "the sense of the sacred" itself.[25] Some educators are troubled by that kind of suggestion. Anthony T. Kronman, a self-described secular humanist and the former dean of Yale Law School, is one of them. Now teaching in Yale's undergraduate Directed Studies Program, Kronman says that what colleges and universities need is a revival of the humanities, not more interaction with religion or the sacred. He argues: "The crisis of spirit we now confront is a consequence not of the death of God, but of man. It is the forgetfulness of our own humanity.…[I]t is not God that needs to be remembered. It is man. Only the recollection of humanity is an adequate response."[26]

Kronman makes a valid point—higher education is a human endeavor, not a divine one—and yet his own use of the term "crisis of *spirit*" points beyond academic business as usual toward something deeper, toward something that "really matters." Other intellectuals also reach for spiritual metaphors in describing the goals and purposes of higher education. In her book *Not for Profit* (2010), for example, Martha Nussbaum uses the language of soul to describe the current woes of higher education, saying "we seem to be forgetting about the soul, about what it is for thought to open out of the soul and connect person to world in a rich, subtle, and complicated manner." Soul is a religious word. In traditional usage, the soul is the animating force of life that differentiates living things from inanimate objects. "Having soul" or being "soulful" can, however, also mean being sensitive to life in all its many facets—its wonders, its horrors, its joys, its tragedies, its achievements, and its defeats. Soul alludes to the capacity to experience all of these modalities of life with and alongside others. In Nussbaum's usage, soul refers to "the faculties of thought and imagination that make us human and make our relationships rich human relationships, rather than relationships of mere use and manipulation."[27]

The boundaries separating the religious and the secular have become too fluid and porous to sustain the kind of clear distinction between the humanities and religion that Kronman desires, and much the same can be said about religion and learning in general. In the seamless fabric of human experience and knowledge, these matters are interwoven. It makes sense for colleges and universities to examine the many different aspects of reality separately, but higher learning also involves the work of seeing life as a whole and of bringing together knowledge and meaning. That includes religion.

Colleges and universities have many roles. They expand the boundaries of human knowledge and introduce students to the search for truth. They train people for future employment. They provide students with the skills and information that can empower them to become community leaders. They teach people how to see the world in new ways that may differ considerably from the ways in which they were raised. And they also provide opportunities for students to reflect on life in general, asking them not only to analyze reality as it is but to ponder the meaning of the world and what it could become in light of their own deepest values and commitments. These roles point to the very "soul" of why colleges and universities exist: to educate students as *persons* and not just as minds.

There is no question that paying attention to religion sometimes can make the educational process more difficult. Religion can disrupt classroom conversation, exchanges between students can become heated, personal feelings can be interjected into academic debates, and "faith" can sometimes express itself in ways that seem antithetical to critical thinking. But religion can also deepen discussions, connect students more holistically with the process of learning, and force everyone to grapple more realistically with the world as it actually is—a world where religion is no longer invisible.

2

The History of Religion in American Higher Education

TO UNDERSTAND THE distinctive ways in which religion interacts with university education in the present requires some awareness of how it functioned in the past. Over the nearly four-hundred-year course of American higher education, religion has moved from being central to being marginal to being newly relevant. This chapter sketches that history, referencing three broad periods of development that we call the Protestant era, the privatized era, and the pluriform era (see Figure 2.1).

The Protestant era began with the founding of Harvard in 1636 and lasted until roughly 1900. During those two-and-a-half centuries, the words "religion" and "Protestant" were functionally synonymous at most American colleges and universities. Higher education was largely owned (both literally and figuratively) by Protestantism. The second era, the period of religious privatization, began around 1900 (although its roots go back further) and extended through most of the twentieth century. This was a time when religion, though never entirely eliminated from higher education, was increasingly separated from the more public domains of teaching and research and was restricted to the private and academically invisible realm of personal opinion and informal conversation. The privatizing proclivities of this era are still evident in some circles of higher education today, which is not surprising because the breaks between historical periods are rarely sharp and clean. One age is usually still waning as the next one begins. The pluriform era, which began in the late twentieth century, represents a new and very different phase in the history of religion in higher education, when pluralism, rather than Protestantism, defines the lay of the land, and when religion has become quite visible once again. The unique place of religion in higher education today becomes clearer when compared to the characteristics of the preceding historical periods.

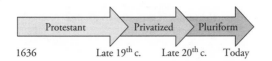

FIGURE 2.1   Three Eras of Religion in American Higher Education

The Protestant Era

The Protestant era of American religion and higher education was a time when all of life, including education, was set within a national culture dominated by Protestant Christianity.[1] Housed in a variety of different denominations, Protestantism defined the ethos of the nation as a whole. It molded public values, shaped public perceptions of the world, and defined the core goals of higher education. Protestantism began as an immigrant faith brought to North America from Europe, but once transplanted, it quickly took on a distinctive American character. Most notably, American Protestantism became a voluntary, pluralistic, and democratic affair, in contrast to the state-controlled established churches of Europe.

Protestantism was, of course, never the faith of all the people, and for those in the minority, it could become oppressive. In the early years of the Protestant era, traditional Native American ways of life were often denigrated; members of smaller religious groups like Quakers, Jews, and Catholics were sometimes abused; and African slaves, who were thought by some to be incapable of conversion, were deemed not only religiously "other" but less than fully human. But Protestantism was also a source of much that was good in the new nation. Perhaps most importantly, Protestantism's emphasis on the individual gave a significant boost to the formulation of American democracy. For Protestants, true faith is a matter of uncoerced choice—in order to be genuine, religion has to be free—and Protestant insistence on the voluntary nature of faith paved the way for the separation of church and state that eventually became the law of the land.

As America settled into a new national context based on principles of religious freedom and church–state separation, education came to play a significant role in the practice of religion itself. Persuasion was the only approved mechanism by which to create and maintain religious communities, and the first Protestant colleges in America (see Table 2.1) were founded, at least in part, as training institutions to provide ministers with those skills of persuasion.

By the early nineteenth century, the religious education of ministers was being transferred to educational institutions called seminaries or divinity schools, and the function of colleges was broadening to include training for leaders of society as a whole. The theological basis for educating non-ministerial students was found in the Protestant notion of vocation: the belief that almost any form of

Table 2.1 Colonial Colleges[2]

Institution	Year Founded	Denominational Affiliation
Harvard	1636	Congregational
William and Mary	1693	Anglican
Yale	1701	Congregational
University of Pennsylvania	1741	Anglican (informally)
Princeton	1746	Presbyterian
Columbia	1754	Anglican
Brown	1764	Baptist
Rutgers	1766	Reformed
Dartmouth	1769	Congregational

work that is moral and serves the needs of humankind can be understood as a religious way of life, a way of doing God's will in the world. When ordinary work is potentially infused with religious meaning and significance, it blurs the line between the ministry (ordained religious leadership) and other vocations, and people could move relatively easily from one to the other. This kind of movement was common: More than a quarter of the nineteenth-century graduates of New England's Protestant colleges—places like Amherst, Williams, and Bowdoin—served as ministers, missionaries, or church-related teachers for at least a while before assuming other non-church-related roles in society.[3]

Character education played a huge role in these early Protestant colleges. They were essentially training institutions for religious and social leadership, and students often were required to take a final capstone course, typically taught by the college president, that summarized all the moral and religious values it was hoped students would internalize before graduating. Learning and character were assumed to intertwine, and the job of the college president was to model the connections of faith, knowledge, wisdom, and moral virtue that students were supposed to emulate. Mentoring of this sort was feasible only because the colleges of the time were so small. Up until the middle of the nineteenth century, higher education was largely reserved for members of the social elite and for those who might aspire to join it. No colonial college ever enrolled more than one hundred students at a time, and as late as 1880, only twenty-six colleges in America had more than two hundred students on campus.[4] In this context, a focus on character and the liberal arts, as opposed to practical skills or job preparation, made a great deal of sense. College education provided an education in moral and intellectual responsibility for those destined to be leaders. It was a privilege with incumbent duties, not a means of personal advancement.

The Civil War was a watershed in American history, and it represented a crucial turning point in the history of American religion. The nation lost some of its perceived innocence during the war, and Protestantism itself was tarnished. President Lincoln famously noted in his second inaugural address that people on both sides of the war "read the same Bible, and pray to the same God; and each invokes His aid against the other."[5] American Protestantism was fractured, and it would never again be the same. In the South, Protestantism was remodeled to align with the myth of the Lost Cause,[6] while Protestantism in the North became more connected than ever with the idea that America as a unified nation was a special, God-blessed place.

During the post-Civil War years, the nation was on the move. The agrarian age was ending, and the industrial boom was underway. A new sense of purpose and progress was in the air, and the demands on education were expanding accordingly. Character and vocation remained central, but useful knowledge and pragmatic skills were blended more and more deeply into the mix, giving rise to a whole new range of institutions designed to educate individuals and to advance democracy. This is when the first women's colleges began and when the first African American colleges and universities were organized for the purpose of "uplifting the race."[7] Also, the first "normal schools" were created to produce teachers for the nation's ever-expanding public school system, and in 1862 the Morrill Land Grant Act provided funding for a new public university system dedicated to the advancement of learning and the common good. Although Protestantism had fractured, the moral ethos of Protestantism—its generalized biblical vision of life—continued to function as a kind of de facto religious point of reference for all of these schools. Most Americans remained confident that Protestantism was still the best and highest expression of religion the world had ever seen.

Protestants themselves also remained firm believers in the importance of higher education. They supported the institutions that were already in existence, and different Protestant churches continued to create their own explicitly church-related institutions during this post-war period. Some Protestant groups established ethnic denominational colleges, hoping to preserve old-world ways of faith while simultaneously training the children of immigrants for success in a new land. Examples include St. Olaf College in Minnesota, which served Norwegian Lutherans, and Hope College in Michigan, founded by and for Dutch Calvinists. Another new kind of Protestant college was the evangelical "Bible school" or "Bible College," organized to prepare ministers and missionaries for the tasks of home and foreign missions. Protestantism was not the only educationally active religion during the post-Civil War years, however. Catholics began the task of building a separate non-Protestant educational infrastructure for themselves, a comprehensive system that extended from grade school through college, and these were also the years when Jewish efforts in American higher education began.

It is impossible to provide one blanket description that covers all the various nineteenth-century American colleges. Many of them were academically respectable institutions; many were not. Some endured; a good number did not. Some were "private" institutions, and others were "public," but the distinction between public and private was not very clear, and it meant much less than it does today. Most of the new schools were, like their predecessors, quite small, but some universities grew to have enrollments in the thousands. The one thing almost all of these schools shared in common—except for those that were Catholic or Jewish—is that every one of them was still discernibly Protestant in ethos and orientation. This was so much the case that even "state schools" frequently required students to attend chapel services that functioned in a thoroughly Protestant manner.

By the end of the nineteenth century, the Protestantism of the nation was no longer the same kind of Protestantism that had given birth to American higher education during the colonial period. American Protestantism had been stretched and pulled and heated and cooled in many different ways, but some themes remained consistent nonetheless: belief in God, reliance on the moral teachings of Jesus, an emphasis on the individuality of faith, and confidence in the superiority of Protestant Christianity when compared to all other religions. Perhaps most importantly, the development of character was still a predominant concern. In the Protestant view, a college education came with responsibilities. Higher education was supposed to make its recipients better people, better able to discern and advance the common good. Many other elements of the old Protestant model of higher education have passed away, but this ideal remains a central theme in the rhetoric of higher education even today.

A Century of Religious Privatization

Over the course of the twentieth century, religion in American higher education was increasingly privatized. At most colleges and universities, religion was slowly withdrawn (or withdrew) from the more public domains of education and came to be seen as a personal matter that faculty and students, if they so desired, could address on their own terms outside the academic framework of the institution. The move toward privatized religion accelerated during the 1960s, with religion becoming an almost exclusively personal concern on most campuses by the 1980s and 1990s.[8]

This privatization of religion has often been told as a narrative of secularization,[9] as a story of religion's slow exile from the academy.[10] No one has told this story better or more convincingly than the former University of Notre Dame historian George Marsden, whose magisterial treatment of the topic, *The Soul of the American University,* is subtitled "from Protestant establishment to established nonbelief." Marsden's focus is on what he identifies as the "pace-setting American universities" (places like Harvard, Yale, Princeton, Johns Hopkins, the University of Michigan, and the University of California), and he says that all of these schools changed from being visibly Christian (meaning Protestant) at the beginning of the twentieth century to being stridently secular or nonreligious by the late twentieth century.[11]

This trajectory of religious "decline" or secularization (with the image of a "slippery slope" frequently invoked by those lamenting it) is not necessarily wrong, but it overemphasizes particular elements of what occurred. For the most part, religion was not pushed out of the academy; instead, the privatization of religion on campuses was often religiously motivated. In fact, the privatization of religion, when viewed from some perspectives, is a religious step forward. Most obviously, it opened up space for greater religious inclusivity. As the dominance of Protestantism in higher education waned, it became easier for people of other religions to feel comfortable on American college and university campuses. At the beginning of the twentieth century, Catholics and Jews (members of the two largest non-Protestant religious communities in the nation) were still barred from many colleges and universities, but by the 1960s and 1970s, they were welcomed at nearly all institutions of higher learning.[12] Even so, there is a Protestant irony in this development. The pathway to academic acceptance for any religious person was the privatization—read "individualization"—of that person's religious identity. This is a natural stance for many Protestants, but it is decidedly foreign to the practices of many other religious traditions.

Various factors combined to encourage the privatization of religion in higher education. One of the most important was the massive upheaval that divided American Protestantism in the early years of the twentieth century into two camps, with fundamentalism at one end of the spectrum and modernism at the other. Fundamentalists took a stand against what they saw as the modern "apostasy" of the sciences, while the more liberal or modernist wing of the Protestant movement embraced the new findings of science as the equivalent of religious revelation. The most famous symbolic event in this conflict was the Scopes trial in 1925. John Scopes, a high school teacher in Tennessee, was charged with teaching evolution in his science class in violation of state law. Scopes was found guilty and assessed a $100 fine, but old-fashioned religion was the big loser in the court of public opinion. By the end of the trial, the Bible-believing, fundamentalist Protestantism embodied by William Jennings Bryan, whose testimony spearheaded the prosecution's case against Scopes, appeared out of sync with modern culture. The news coverage of the trial made fundamentalists into laughingstock among the cultural and intellectual leaders of the nation. By the late 1920s, many fundamentalist Protestants began to separate themselves from mainstream culture in an effort to maintain their religious views and way of life. They created their own independent world of private institutions, including not only new churches, but also schools, radio stations, and publishing houses. Their withdrawal from higher education dramatically altered the face of religion in the mainstream academy.[13]

The fundamentalist departure is only half the story. The modernist or liberal Protestants who remained connected with higher education were themselves in the process of redefining Christianity in ways that made it more private. In particular, liberal Protestants welcomed the distinction between facts and values that some academics were beginning to make. From their perspective, issues of factuality belong in the sciences, and it is not the job of religion to pontificate about facts. The job of religion is to add values: ethics, meaning, significance, and wonder. One consequence of this division of labor was that liberal Protestantism was forced ever more deeply into the private world of personal opinion, because liberal Protestants themselves often disagreed vehemently over which values to espouse. Perhaps no one grasped this situation better than the Harvard psychologist William James, who opined early in the century that religion, in the modern sense of the term, should be defined as "the feelings, acts, and experiences *of individual men in their solitude*, so far as they apprehend themselves to stand in relation to whatever they may consider the divine" [emphasis added].[14] Although the Social Gospel movement that was popular during the early years of the twentieth century provided an alternative and more communal option for liberal or progressive Protestants, it never became a major force in American higher education. It was the individualism of liberal Protestantism that provided the enduring influence.

A second, quite different, nudge toward privatization came from the American adaptation of the German university model. The German version of higher education placed a new emphasis on research and discovery (*Wissenschaft*), in addition to the development of character (*Bildung*). Its goal was to balance both purposes of higher education, but in the pragmatic context of American democracy it was *Wissenschaft* that quickly assumed the leading role. Concerns about character were never entirely jettisoned, but the discovery and dissemination of new knowledge became the central rationale for creating a new group of research *universities* that saw their work as decidedly different from that of *colleges* devoted to teaching and learning. The first school to be founded on the basis of this new vision of higher education was the Johns Hopkins University launched in 1876. The new educational ideal was formalized in 1900 when the Association of American Universities was created, an organization self-defined as including the best of the best American institutions of higher learning. It did not take long for the "university ideal" of research and scholarship to become the benchmark for higher learning in general, the standard by which quality was measured at all universities and colleges.

The new German-inspired model of the university was not at all antithetical to religion, at least not at first. However, as more and more emphasis was placed on research and on new scientific discoveries, it became increasingly unclear where religion fit and what its proper role might be in terms of creating knowledge and building character. The eventual consensus was that religion really did not fit anywhere, and it was especially unfit for the classroom or laboratory. Religion was not a science, and attempts to make the study of religion more scientific usually succeeded only in making it less appealing to students. An even more basic question had to do with use of time: Should the tasks of the academic workday include religion? The general agreement was that they should not. Time in the laboratory and the classroom was to be spent creating and disseminating knowledge, and time for religion should be made somewhere else. Religion and character were still considered important by many leaders in higher education, but they were matters to be dealt with by individuals on their own time or in dialogue with their religious communities, not within the teaching and research settings of the university.

A third force diverting higher education away from religion arose from the business community, especially the new breed of industrial philanthropists who emerged in the latter years of the nineteenth century and took it upon themselves to support higher learning. The founding of new universities became a kind of competitive sport among the business magnates of the time. Leland Stanford (railroads) founded Stanford University, and Benjamin Duke (tobacco) founded Duke University. Somewhat less egoistically, John D. Rockefeller (oil) gave his money to the geographically named University of Chicago. But the story was the same everywhere. Flush with money, private universities set out to become the best educational institutions possible, competing with each other for top ranking just as their financial supporters competed with each other for status in the world of business and finance. Historian Mark Noll notes that the entrepreneurs who started these universities "were not paying for moral uplift but for the means to advance a vision of the good life that increasingly stressed the powers of free choice and the pleasures of personal consumption."[15] These philanthropists expected to be in charge, they assumed their friends should be on the board of trustees, and they wanted their university presidents to think like them. During the first half of the nineteenth century, almost every college president had been a member of the ordained clergy, but few presidents of the nation's new research universities were cut from that cloth. Most of them were scholars and academic entrepreneurs who applied a pragmatic, businesslike logic to the work of the academy.

Not everyone was sanguine about the waning of religious influence in higher education, and many mechanisms were explored to keep religion visible on campus, ranging from endowed professorships in biblical studies to the "great books" curriculum that included many Christian classics of Western culture. But the over-all trend was toward the increasing privatization of religion on campus. Given the larger social developments of the era, this development seemed perfectly sensible to most people. American society as a whole was becoming more specialized, and life was being sliced up into different, separate realms of activity and expertise. Religion represented one sector of life and scholarship another, and it seemed reasonable for the two to be kept mostly apart.[16]

This pragmatic separation of religion from the classroom received a huge boost after World War II, when higher education began to boom. Before World War II, the percentage of Americans who attended college or university was still relatively low, around 10 percent. This represented a significant increase over the 3 or 4 percent who pursued higher learning in 1900, but it was nothing like the explosion in numbers that was about to take place (see Figure 2.2). The initial trigger for the boom was the G.I. Bill that provided tuition reimbursement for any military veteran who wanted to go to college, but once that generation had experienced the benefits of higher education, they were convinced that their children should have the same opportunity. By 1975, roughly a quarter of all eighteen-to-twenty-four-year-old Americans were involved in higher education, and a college or university degree was becoming a prerequisite for most of the nation's better-paying jobs. Today, nearly half of all young adults undertake at least some study at the college or university level.

This incredible expansion of the student population produced a commensurate multiplication of institutions. Roughly 1,000 colleges and universities existed in America in 1900; today there are about 4,500 (see Figure 2.3). Higher

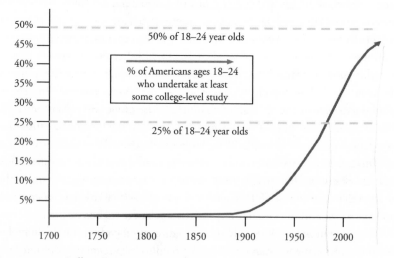

FIGURE 2.2   College/University Attendance in the United States, 1700–2010

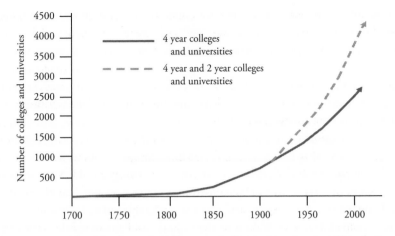

FIGURE 2.3 The Number of Colleges and Universities in the United States, 1700–2010

education in America is now a gigantic industry, embodied in a vast menagerie of schools, including a variety of elite public and private research universities, many different state schools and community colleges, and a wide range of private higher educational institutions, some of them profit-making but most of them nonprofit. In 1900, most students were enrolled in private universities or colleges. Today, two out of every three students attend public, state-funded institutions. In the emerging world of public-dominated higher education, job preparation became increasingly central, pushing aside not only religion but also the liberal arts. Campus communities (including faculty, students, and staff) also became ever more religiously and secularly diverse, making the privatization of "personal" matters like religion the easy default position for maintaining civility on campus.

The same trends were visible outside the bounds of higher education; all of American society was moving in a similar direction. In the two decades following WWII, America was proud to be a "melting pot." It was assumed that all Americans, regardless of social, ethnic, or religious identity, were slowly blending together to create a single homogeneous American culture. What mattered in melting-pot America was being "nice," without being extreme. Religion, as long as it didn't become fanatical, was part of that niceness. During these years, President Dwight Eisenhower famously commented that America made "no sense unless it is founded in a deeply felt religious faith, *and I don't care what it is*."[17] And this is when Will Herberg wrote his widely acclaimed book, *Protestant, Catholic, Jew*.[18] Herberg argued that whatever differences might have existed among America's Protestants, Catholics, and Jews in the past, those differences no longer really mattered. Instead of being a Protestant nation, America had become a "Judeo-

Christian" country where Catholics, Jews, and Protestants were all equals. In this new America, religion in general was good and morality was expected, but personal religious preferences were to be kept to oneself.

Most Americans perceived this new public ethos of religious moderation as nothing more than being polite, but by the early 1960s, some intellectuals began to suspect that religion was not merely becoming more private and more polite; it was also becoming much less powerful. The trend toward secularization was obvious in Europe, and many scholars assumed that America would eventually follow the European lead. Peter Berger, one of the leading proponents of this new theory of inevitable secularization, predicted that American society would eventually free itself "from the domination of religious institutions and symbols." As he observed the trends of the time, Berger speculated that "probably for the first time in history, the religious legitimations of the world have lost plausibility not only for a few intellectuals and other marginal individuals but for broad masses of entire societies."[19]

Those who accepted the theory of secularization as an accurate predictor of the future thought that higher education had a responsibility to prepare students for a world in which religion would soon be a nonfactor. Some people thought that learning how to think about the deepest values of life without recourse to religion was an educational necessity. This thoroughly secularist perspective of higher education was never adopted universally across the academy, but it was widespread, and its increasing prominence was what led George Marsden to argue in 1994 that "nonbelief" had become the established faith of higher education.

While Marsden was documenting higher education's trend toward nonbelief, however, other scholars were beginning to detect signs that the privatization of religion in America may have passed its peak. As early as 1970, Peter Berger retracted some of his claims about secularization, arguing in *A Rumor of Angels* that symbols of transcendence continued to abound in modern society, even though some forms of religion were on the decline.[20] When Protestant evangelicals (the offspring of early twentieth-century fundamentalists) began to re-enter American politics in the form of the Moral Majority (later the Religious Right) in the mid-1970s, when the Islamic Revolution took place in Iran in 1979, and when Polish Catholics united with workers in the Solidarity movement that helped end communist rule in Poland, the predictive power of secularization theory seemed to dissolve. Rather than disappearing, religion was becoming more visible, and privatization ceased to be an adequate strategy for either society or higher education.

Religious Pluriformity

The religion of contemporary America is pluriform, more complex and multifaceted than it has ever been before. It is not just that religion has become more pluralistic—that more of the world's religions are now represented in the

American population—but also that the notion of religion itself has undergone a major restructuring. Being religious used to mean being part of a historic religious community, but most Americans now assume that a person can be spiritual or religious to varying degrees without any connection to a particular religious group. The differences between religious and nonreligious lifestances are not always obvious, and the line between public and private has also become blurred.

This new, foggy pluriformity of religion in American society did not emerge overnight. The massive social upheaval of the 1960s paved the way, creating a milieu in which inherited notions of social and religious authority could be cast aside and new pathways for being religious and nonreligious could be forged. Huge social movements for civil rights and equality challenged older patriarchal and hierarchical notions of religion, and they also spawned their own egalitarian and justice-oriented religious alternatives. Changes in immigration laws made it possible for many more Asians to move to America, bringing their Asian religious traditions (Islam, Hinduism, Buddhism, and others) with them. The Second Vatican Council sent a shock wave through American Catholicism, updating Catholic faith and practice, and leading some Catholics to lose faith in their church and others to become more active. The religious and political resurrection of conservative, evangelical Christianity also reshaped the landscape, invigorating traditional Protestantism. All of America's religious communities have been reconfigured in recent decades, often becoming more fluid and flexible than before, but sometimes becoming more distinctive and dogmatic. The number of people who identify themselves as nonreligious has grown, and nonbelief has become more acceptable—although many nonbelieving, nonreligious individuals now consider themselves to be "spiritual." Whatever spin is put on this complicated set of developments, one thing is clear: Religion in America today is not the old religion of nineteenth-century Protestantism, nor is it the privatized faith of the twentieth century. Religion as it is present in twenty-first-century America is something quite different.

The same cultural shifts that were reshaping American religion were simultaneously having an effect on colleges and universities. Some of the core orientations of higher education were being modified, and some of these changes—even though this was not their conscious intent—paved the way for colleges and universities to re-engage religion. Three almost totally unrelated developments were especially significant in this regard: (1) the rejection of epistemological objectivity and the embrace of multiculturalism, (2) the growth of professional studies, and (3) the turn toward student-centered learning. None of these changes was undertaken with the goal of pushing colleges and universities toward a new engagement with religion, but they made it easier for religion to slip back into some of the public domains of higher education almost without notice.

Multiculturalism and the rejection of objectivist epistemology: Starting in the mid-1960s, scholars in a variety of disciplines began to question the objectivity of knowledge. Much of what appeared to be fair and objective scholarship began, on closer inspection, to look as if it was laden with bias. Women saw male prejudice; African Americans saw racism; postmodernists and post-colonialists saw issues of power and control everywhere. Once articulated, these criticisms stuck, because even a cursory examination of older scholarship showed that the criticisms had some validity: Intellectual prejudice is everywhere. Just as troubling was the dawning realization that there was no easy cure. Prejudice is built into the work of scholarship. People are the products of the cultures, communities, families, and the times in which they live. They have feelings, they have values, they have likes and dislikes, and they have both blind spots and areas of hypersensitive awareness because of who they are and how they have lived their lives. Subjectivity and finitude infuse everything people know or think they know, and there is no way around it.

Multiculturalism has become the term used to name this awareness of the finitude and particularity of knowing, but multiculturalism does not imply that there are no ways of making judgments about the relative intellectual worth of differing perspectives. Peer review and evidence-based reasoning remain central to the scholarly process in all fields of study. But the role of interpretation and the importance of personal and social influences are now widely acknowledged. Who one is as a person—what one has experienced, the different forms of intelligence one possesses, the angle from which one approaches an issue, the cultural grid through which one sees the world, and one's religious or spiritual convictions—affects one's work as a scholar, teacher, and student. In acknowledgment of that reality, most colleges and universities have begun to emphasize the multifaceted nature of learning and the importance of epistemological diversity within the scholarly community. Exposure to a variety of alternative perspectives or "ways of knowing" is now considered a sign of good teaching and scholarship.

Professional studies: A second recent development in higher education centers on the growth of professional and applied programs of study. Today, a majority of the courses offered at colleges and universities are in fields of study like business, health, engineering, and education. By their very nature, these fields of study focus on human behavior. Human behavior requires making choices, and choices involve ethics, that is, judgments about which options are better or worse. Almost all programs of applied study have accordingly decided that discussions about ethics and professional behavior need to be included in their curriculums. Giving space to reflect on these kinds of moral and ethical concerns necessarily brings the personal values of both students and faculty into play. Do their own natural inclinations agree with the ethical norms of the field? What existing attitudes or practices might need to be modified to bring them into line with the rules of the profession? Or, more critically, do the norms of the profession seem right? Is it ever appropriate—or even morally required—to disregard some rules of one's profession some of the time? People in all of the applied fields of study must wrestle with these kinds of questions, and higher education has a responsibility to help students acquire the needed skills of reflection.

Student-centered learning: A third major shift in higher education has been the move from professor-centered teaching to student-centered learning. Up until the 1970s, college students were often treated as empty vessels that professors were supposed to fill with knowledge. The focus was on teaching: Professors communicated what students had to know. But the amount of intellectual material available in the world today is overwhelming, and the educational focus has shifted toward student learning. Rather than simply pouring information into students, learning occurs when students understand and use information, developing the intellectual skills and habits to access and digest the ever-expanding storehouse of knowledge that is available to them. A student-centered approach also recognizes that people learn better, and retain what they learn longer, when they have an active role in the learning process, connecting new information and insights with other things they already know or believe or have experienced. In other words, learning is maximized when students bring themselves wholeheartedly into the learning experience, and for many students, religion is part of who they are.

None of these three developments was initially connected to religion, but religion was invisibly bundled up inside each of them. Religious perspectives are unavoidably intertwined with multiculturalism and epistemological pluralism; the divergent ways that people make sense of reality are often influenced by their own religious or religion-like views of the world. Similarly, questions of ethics or professional conduct open the door to religion, because religious beliefs, values, and habits of behavior shape how people define what is good and right action. Finally, student-centered learning contains an implicit receptivity to religion, because respecting the autonomy of students as learners necessarily entails some degree of respect for the religious identities and the spiritual quests of those students. If the world as a whole had continued to become more and more secular, the religious implications of these three developments may never have become particularly obvious. But because religion has instead become increasingly more visible in society as a whole and on campuses, these three developments began to function like huge cracks in the dam of privatization, allowing religion at first to trickle and then to cascade back into the "public" work of colleges and universities.

One facet of higher education's focus on student-centered learning is especially relevant: Today, it is often students themselves who are asking to have more attention given to religious and spiritual matters. According to the Higher

Education Research Institute (HERI) at UCLA, 80 percent of today's first-year students say they have "an interest in spirituality," 76 percent say they are on a "search for meaning and purpose in life," 64 percent say their "spirituality is a source of joy," and almost half (47 percent) say it is essential or very important to "seek out opportunities to help me grow spiritually."[21] Students do not want colleges and universities to take on the role of "church" and supply religious answers to life's questions, but many students do expect their undergraduate experience to help them think more clearly, feel more deeply, and consider more responsibly the broad questions of life. These questions no longer necessarily come pre-labeled as religious, but they are functionally religious because they focus on ultimate concerns: how to make sense of the world, what to hope for, who to care about, how to script one's own life, where to place trust, and what really matters.

Nearly everyone in America now rubs shoulders every day with people of differing faiths and lifestances. Students know this. They know they live in a religiously pluriform world, and they are trying to figure out the implications. This means that, perhaps for the first time in American higher educational history, the push for talking about matters of religion and spirituality and answering questions about human purpose and meaning is coming from the bottom up, rather than from the top down. Paying attention to religion in higher education today is not at all a matter of imposing faith or morality on anyone; it is a matter of responding intelligently to the questions of life that students find themselves necessarily asking as they try to make sense of themselves and the world in an era of ever-increasing social, intellectual, and religious complexity.

3

Trail Markers in a Time of Transition

THE COMPLEXITY AND ambiguity of contemporary America's pluriform religion have become fodder for the entertainment industry, including its dramas and comedies. In one episode of the TV series *Gilmore Girls*, a college student named Rory, about twenty years old, and her mother Lorelai, in her mid-thirties, are asked to be godparents for the children of a friend, and the friend's minister questions them about their faith.

LORELAI: Well, um, religion. But, you know, I can't speak for Rory, but I have a strong belief in good. You know, over evil. I mean, if I was asked to choose a side.
RORY: I read *The Lion, the Witch and the Wardrobe*.
LORELAI: I have a Bible. Although I may or may not have accidentally given it to Goodwill, because I'm remodeling. But, Goodwill is a religious organization. I think. But even if it's not. Good. Will. It's in the ballpark.
RORY: I buy tons of Girl Scout cookies.[1]

This riff from *Gilmore Girls* makes us laugh because it is an accurate reflection of the world in which we all now live. Lots of people no longer know what religion means, or at least people don't know how to talk about it. The twentieth-century privatization of religion has left everyone out of practice, and inarticulate awkwardness abounds. But religion itself has also become a more slippery concept, which means that the topic has become more complex at the same moment in time when fluency has declined. The result: When the subject of religion arises, many Americans feel as if all they have available to them is what T. S. Eliot once described as verbally "shabby equipment always deteriorating in the general mess of imprecision of feeling."[2]

Talking about Religion on Campus

Ask any group of professors or college students to describe religion and how it affects life on campus, and their responses will vary widely. Some of the professors and administrators with whom we spoke expressed very precise views about religion, including several faculty members (from both public and private institutions) who emphatically told us that "real" religion meant "having a personal relationship with Jesus Christ" and that everything else was simply mistaken human opinion. Partly because they are in the majority, Christians in America often speak with great confidence. When we spoke with devout members of non-Christian groups, they almost always framed their comments less forcefully, starting with some kind of qualification like "from my point of view" or "in my tradition" or "where I come from" before saying religion is this or is that.

Others, both Christian and not, spoke more generically of religion in terms of core beliefs: "It's having a worldview that guides my thinking about, well, everything." But some educators were clearly irritated with that kind of emphasis on belief, and in a group discussion at one institution, an exasperated Jewish faculty member finally nearly shouted: "Religion is what you do, how you live. It doesn't have anything to do with belief! Who cares what you believe? Religion is about how you treat others, the contribution you make. Everything else is beside the point!" At another campus, a professor defined religion as being similar to ethnic identity, something that is more or less inherited at birth: "I was raised Catholic....For me, religion is a given, like ethnicity. It is part of me whether I like it or not. My students are the same. They can't help it if they were raised evangelical or Jewish or Catholic or whatever. It's just who they are, and who I am. It's just a fact."

A number of professors and administrators told us, sometimes quite proudly and sometimes almost in embarrassment, that they were simply nonreligious. Several took care to clarify that they weren't opposed to religion, but they just didn't get it. Others, falling back into clearly nonacademic rhetoric, declared that religious people just seemed goofy. One professor signaled a halt to the conversation just as it was about to begin so he could let us know in advance that, in his view, religion was "all that garbage my church tried to teach me in Sunday school when I was a kid." He added, "I got over it and I want my students to get over it too." But the point of view expressed by another professor from the same institution was almost the opposite: "I think of religion as the inner core of my being, it's who I am and what I really care about. It's very personal. It's what makes life meaningful. And I want to help my students make meaning in their lives too." Professors and administrators, just like their students, cover the gamut of viewpoints when it comes to religion.

On some private campuses, uneasiness about religion is rooted in lingering institutional memories of religion as educationally oppressive. At a number of casually church-related schools, there is a vague recollection of ancient heresy trials and of people losing their jobs (sometimes accurately remembered, but sometimes not) for saying the wrong things, with a corresponding expression of relief that ties with the founding religious organization have been weakened or severed over time. In settings like these, the primary concern is often that re-engaging religion might open the door for new threats to academic freedom. Even at public institutions and private schools that have never been associated with any church or religious community, some professors worry that talking about religion poses a threat to the quality of education on campus; they fear it may undermine the Enlightenment's emancipation of higher education from religion's oppressive grip. Religion's "return" to higher education makes all of these people uneasy. It is out of keeping with the way they were trained in graduate school and socialized into the academy. It just feels wrong. Even today, graduate education (especially at the doctoral level) encourages students to bracket any personal feelings or values they might have about the subjects they are studying and not to deviate from the methodologies that have been developed in the discipline. For individuals nurtured into the academy by way of this regimen, the reappearance of religion in higher education can seem like a bizarre intrusion into a world where, to them, it simply has no place.[3] Perhaps it is no surprise that the number of overtly negative expressions of concern about religion seemed to correspond to the status of the institution involved. The more a college or university saw itself as being or striving to be elite, the more nervous the professors at that institution seemed to be about re-engaging religion. This pattern was consistent across the institutions we visited, and, although our conclusion is based on impressions rather than statistics, recent quantitative studies seem to confirm this correlation.[4]

We also discerned some generational differences in the attitudes of the faculty with whom we spoke. Most notably, older faculty tended to be cooler in their response to religion than younger faculty, but younger faculty were more cautious in what they said, especially in public conversations. Our hunch is that older faculty who were introduced to the academy during the height of religion's privatization have simply internalized that attitude, making it part of how they "naturally" see the world. Younger faculty often seem more attuned to the pluriform religious realities of today and to the need for colleges and universities to pay attention to those realities, but they also feel caught between the demands of "making it" in their disciplines (i.e., satisfying the expectations of older faculty) and "being themselves." In group meetings held on various campuses, junior faculty were almost always less forthcoming than their senior colleagues. But not infrequently when we met with the same junior faculty in one-on-one conversations, they talked with great enthusiasm about hoping to bring matters of meaning and purpose into their classes—and even their academic work—at some point in the future when they felt more secure in their positions. Once again, our observations about generational differences are impressionistic. However, a recent study conducted by Elaine Ecklund of Rice University provides evidence that younger faculty—at least those in the sciences—are more positively predisposed toward religious and spiritual concerns than their older colleagues.[5]

Talking about religion with students is generally more straightforward than talking with professors, and it is easier to get a conversation going. In fact, many students said it was their professors' hesitations about discussing religious and spiritual issues that seemed odd to them, not talking about religion itself. Students told us repeatedly that including religious or spiritual concerns when appropriate did not in the least "dumb-down" learning, but instead made it more interesting, engaging, and meaningful. One articulate student said that allowing religious or other personal concerns into the classroom "humanizes the discussion," adding that "these concerns seem personal only because the nonhuman is already there, defining most of what we do in any course." A student majoring in sociology said sarcastically that she was tired of hearing professors simply assert "*Durk-whim* said this or that." She wanted a "real conversation" about the issues being studied, not a staged academic debate. However, a significant number of students expressed concerns that "talking about religion or spirituality can make atheists feel uncomfortable," and that was troubling to them. They did not want religion to be a source of distress or division. The classroom, they always insisted, should "be safe for everyone." But they were also convinced that paying attention to personal and religious matters, as long as they were "legitimately connected" (their term) to the subject being studied, was much more likely to enhance than to undermine the learning process.

One of the most interesting events we attended in the course of our research was a path-breaking conference in November 2008 organized by four highly ranked liberal arts colleges: Vassar, Bucknell, Macalester, and Williams. Neither of the words "religion" or "spirituality" was included in the conference title "Varieties of Secular Experience: Pedagogy, Politics, and Meaning in the Liberal Arts," but the purpose of the meeting was to explore ways to include questions about meaning and purpose and, by extension, about religion in academic conversations. The starting point was the word "secular" itself, a term that is now being scrutinized within the academy. In some contexts, "secular" is meant to imply the ability to see the world without blinders (i.e., without the supposedly irrational blinders of religion) and thus to see the world as it really is. But scholars are raising questions about that meaning of the term. Talal Assad and Charles Taylor (among others) have suggested that there is no such thing as "secular" in the singular; there are only secularisms, or different ways of construing the world nonreligiously in contrast to different religious perspectives.[6] This explains the employment of the plural "*varieties* of secular experience" in the conference title, which is also a play on William James's classic text *The Varieties of Religious Experience*.

One of the conference organizers was Sam Speers, director of religious and spiritual life at Vassar, who explained that giving more attention to "the religious life of undergraduates" was one important way to help students better understand the "contested secular ethos in which they learn."[7] Conference organizers shared the assumption that the secular myths developed during the era of religion's privatization were no longer adequate in addressing the educational needs of students. The goal was not at all to legitimate religion in contrast to secularity, but rather to acknowledge the currently contested character of both religion and secularity and to open up new space for students and faculty to explore how both secular and religious frames of interpretation shape questions of meaning, purpose, and politics. This was not a conference about answers, but a conference for asking questions. It also functioned as a public acknowledgment of the thinness of academic vocabulary when it comes to talking about these kinds of "big questions," and how much richer it needs to become in order to connect with the full spectrum of human experience.

Dealing with Religion in a Time of Transition

Given the pluriformity of religion today, it is no wonder that colleges and universities are uncertain about how to talk about it and respond to it. We are living in a time of transition. The old rhetoric of religious privatization no longer works, but new and better ways of addressing religious concerns and questions have not yet been clearly formulated. The challenges are immense. The range of religious views in the contemporary college and university world is simply stunning. Most large campuses have student populations that include conservative Protestant creationists and earth-worshipping Wiccans, spiritually inspired vegans and hijab-wearing Muslims, social-justice religious activists and right-wing religious ideologues, spiritual atheists and "believers" who are no longer sure they believe in God, new converts who want to share their faith with everyone, and students who have grown up religious but know practically nothing about their own faiths. And all of that just scratches the surface. Many questions naturally emerge from this scene: What should be allowed in the classroom and what should not? What has the most potential to offend, and how can such offense be avoided? What limits should be put on discussions to keep them from getting out of control? What rules should guide student interactions? How should faculty respond to religious comments by students? Should faculty themselves ever reveal their own religious or spiritual convictions?

Some professors and administrators would still much prefer to avoid encountering these questions. Several years ago, the philosopher Richard Rorty proclaimed that "religion is a conversation stopper" and that "the claims of religion need, if anything, to be pushed back still further, and that religious believers have no business asking for more public respect than they now receive."[8] Increasingly, however, those kinds of sentiments seem like relics from the past, leftover attitudes from an era that is passing away. But even among educational leaders who are open to a new engagement with religion, there is concern. Most of them think that religion is tricky stuff and that keeping religion under control needs to be a priority. The image of a power-generating nuclear reactor comes to mind: Adding religion to a classroom can generate significant energy, but there is always fear of a meltdown. Religion has to be engaged, but it also needs to be safely contained.

Faced with those kinds of concerns, educators have, over the last two or three decades, developed a kind of corporate wisdom about how to proceed. For the most part, the results represent tactical thinking—that is, guidance about how to respond to religion in the immediate, if and when it happens to appear—and four tactics have become particularly prominent. We call them "trail markers" because they direct faculty members and other educators toward safe ways of negotiating the mine-filled maze of religion on campus. These four trail markers are:

- Spirituality (versus religion)
- Teaching *about* religion (versus teaching religion itself)
- Difficult dialogues
- Big questions

The first two markers indicate forks in the road—where one pathway or another has to be chosen—and only one of them is safe. The last two are more like traffic information signs, warning educators and students that there are risks associated with the journey ahead.

Individually and together, these trail markers have significant merit. They point toward genuine issues, and they have served the academy well during the closing years of the twentieth century and early years of the twenty-first, when patterns of religious privatization have been declining and the new realities of religious pluriformity have been gaining ground. They are no longer adequate by themselves to guide higher education's new engagement with religion, and they will need to be transcended in the future—the academy today needs a more strategic and proactive stance toward both religion and secularity—but a brief examination of the strengths and weaknesses of these markers provides a good summary of where many colleges and universities currently find themselves as they try to adjust to the new visibility of religion on campus.

Trail Marker 1: Spirituality (Versus Religion)

The sign that directs educators toward spirituality and away from religion is probably the most commonly posted of the four trail markers. It is intended to draw a sharp line of distinction between traditional organized religion and "spiritual-ity," which is construed as a more personal, less institutionalized way of creat-ing meaning and relating to the transcendent. In this scheme of things, religion is considered to be particular, whereas spirituality is universal. Religion is about being a member of one specific religious tradition rather than any other, and it involves responsibilities that are tied to membership in that particular group: attending religious services, affirming the group's beliefs and rules, and deferring to the religious authorities who are honored in that tradition. Spirituality, by con-trast, is both more nebulous and more accessible to everyone. Spirituality is about self-discovery and self-expression, about authenticity, compassion, respect for others, and the freedom to explore any number of potentially life-enriching ideas and ways of life. Religion is taught by churches, synagogues, and temples, whereas spirituality is what people discover or decide on their own about truth, goodness, meaning, and what really matters.

In the typical division between religion and spirituality, spirituality often comes across as the more attractive option. The calculus is easy. All of the more restrictive or negative ways of relating to the transcendent or of addressing things that really matter are assigned to the religion side of the page, while most of the more positive and liberating connections are attributed to spirituality. Thus, reli-gion is said to be about rules and restrictions, while spirituality is about the free-dom to be oneself. A clear example of this way of dividing attributions between religion and spirituality was provided in a television interview about the behav-ior that nearly ended the presidency of Bill Clinton. When his former White House intern was asked by Barbara Walters if she felt she had sinned, Monica Lewinsky famously replied, "I'm not very religious; I'm more spiritual." In one of our campus visits, a student served up an expanded version of the Lewinsky analysis, saying, "In college, I'm spiritual. I think something more is there, but I'm not religious—at least not now. I mean, this is college. Religion is for later when I am not having fun."

The distinction between religion and spirituality can be parodied, but the underlying difference is real, and it can serve as an important guideline for edu-cators. Religion is about being part of a group or not being part of that group. Religion has boundaries. Overt expressions of religion are worrisome, because they have the potential to divide and to prompt disagreement. With this in mind, it makes sense to articulate careful rules of engagement in advance of any con-versation that includes religion. The same concern may not apply to spirituality, however, because it is assumed that everyone has a spiritual story to share, some-thing that explains who they are and what they care about. Rather than being contentious, sharing spiritual stories can be invigorating both personally and aca-demically. A student from an elite liberal arts college explained to us why she thought religious views should be welcomed into classroom discussions, and what she described was an attraction to individual narratives: "The idea that our personal stories have value is radical. To think that our stories have academic or moral significance is energizing. It helps us make sense of theories. It is liberating."

The guideline of religion versus spirituality can be helpful as a general rule of thumb, but the distinction can become problematic. Although religion and spirituality can be separated conceptually, in real life the two are frequently intertwined. For example, no one questions that Mother Teresa served as a modern-day icon for both religion and spirituality. By almost any measure, she was a spiritual giant, a saint. She poured her life into serving the poorest of the poor in Kolkata, India, trying to ensure that sick people left to die in the streets and small children left destitute in the slums would be treated with love and dignity. But much of her spiritual strength derived from religion, from the fact that she was intent on being obedient to the teachings of Jesus (and the Roman Catholic Church) as literally and completely as possible. She knew exactly what was expected of her, and she held to those views even when they seemed antithetical to human freedom or authenticity—and even when, as chronicled in her own writing, she was wracked by doubts amid the seeming silence of God.[9] Her goal was to live in accordance with vows prescribed by religion, which meant that her spiritual fulfillment was not a matter of self-discovery or happiness, but rather about denying herself in order to help those in much greater need. She was simultaneously a spiritual/religious saint and a thoroughgoing spiritual/religious dogmatist. To ascribe some of her traits to spirituality and others to religiosity is a false dichotomy.

While they may not be saints, many contemporary college and university students have spiritual and religious profiles that are as intertwined as Mother Teresa's. The overlap between religion and spirituality in the lives of college students can be inferred from data gathered by the Higher Education Research Institute (HERI) at UCLA. Based on a survey of more than 100,000 first-year students, the HERI researchers found that "students who are strongly religious also tend to be highly spiritual."[10] This does not mean that students automatically merge religion with spirituality. Indeed, we spoke with a few students who self-consciously chose to be spiritual rather than religious, and they explicitly associated their choice of spirituality with notions like quest or compassion, while they associated religion with commitment or assurance. But for many other students, spirituality and religion are two ways of naming the same cluster of personal concerns: the desire to have a sense of grounding in their lives, to be kind and caring, to be connected with God and/or the sacred, and to be moral but not judgmental.

The religion-versus-spirituality guidepost can be helpful in many circumstances, but it seems clear on closer inspection that it is not the fork in the road it purports to be. Rather than being about a fundamental difference between something called religion and something called spirituality, the distinction seems more like a pragmatic guideline for interpersonal communication. The old adage that "stories unite while doctrine divides" conveys this sentiment. Interfaith conversations that focus on the telling of personal stories (spirituality) are more likely to be cordial and constructive than dialogues or debates about doctrine (claims about religious truth); in fact, exchanges about doctrine are often set up to highlight conflicts rather than to point out areas of consensus. While argument may, on occasion, be a helpful tool for education, the effective exchange of ideas does not require the creation of conversational winners and losers. When it is used well, the trail marker of spirituality versus religion signals a healthy awareness of the fact that religion is potentially divisive, but when it is used too woodenly, this trail marker can become educationally counterproductive.

Trail Marker 2: *Teaching* about *Religion* (*Versus Teaching Religion Itself*)

Another important trail marker within higher education communicates that there is an important difference between teaching *about* religion and teaching religion itself. The assumption is that teaching *about* religion is a religiously neutral activity, whereas *teaching religion itself* is an exercise in indoctrination, with students being told what they ought to believe and how they ought to act. Defined in this way, the first option is deemed educationally permissible, while the second option is inappropriate unless a student has freely chosen to affiliate with a particular institution for the purpose of religious instruction.

Teaching *about* religion involves describing the objective characteristics of a religion's history and development, its formally stated doctrines, the institutions that preserve it, and the practices required of its adherents. All of this can be studied "from the outside" without requiring anyone to engage religious topics on a personal level. It is this commitment to objectivity that turns the task of teaching *about* religion into an appropriately academic field of study. Many professors of religious studies (professors who teach *about* religion) would also say their courses help students develop an important intellectual skill: the ability to observe and evaluate religion dispassionately. In a world where religious passions sometimes lead to violence, learning how to make such assessments is obviously important.

The problem, however, is that the distinction between teaching about religion and teaching religion itself can be hard to maintain in practice. Good teaching about religion sometimes seems to require going beyond merely teaching *about*. Take, for example, the contemplative practices and meditation techniques that are so important to many religions. Is it sufficient merely to describe these activities from the outside, or does effective teaching require that students—many of them with no comprehension of what sitting in silence and meditating might entail—be asked to try meditating themselves? And if students are asked to meditate in this way, is this still teaching about religion, or does it become teaching religion itself? The same principle applies to all sorts of religious activities and experiences. One religious studies professor (from a public university) told us that, while trying to avoid teaching religion itself, she once developed an elaborate "procrastinators anonymous" in-class activity for the purpose of nonreligiously simulating the religious experience of having "hit bottom." She said that exercise had worked reasonably well, but she added that in many cases nonreligious parallels of religious experiences are hard to identify. Thus, when teaching about Buddhism, the same professor said she simply asked students to experiment with Buddhist meditation using the book *Miracle of Mindfulness* by the well-known Buddhist writer Thích Nhất Hạnh as a guide. This too worked relatively well too, and no one seemed offended by having been "forced" into a religious act against their will.

Other faculty with whom we spoke had different stories to tell. One professor of Hindu studies who is herself Hindu (and also teaches at a public university) told us that she requires students who enroll in her introductory-level course to participate in a workshop on Hindu dance "because this is the essence of the tradition." Students cannot understand Hinduism, she said, without experiencing dance. But recently some of her students refused to take part, protesting that she was essentially requiring them to worship a Hindu deity. Many professors would agree with her students, convinced that any exercise requiring students to "internalize" a specific experience of religion through active participation in the rituals or practices of that religion goes beyond what should be allowed in the classroom. There are similar differences of opinion with regard to religious ideas. Some teachers think that genuine understanding of a religion requires developing a sense of respect and empathy for the doctrines and teachings of that religion. But one faculty member told us quite forcefully: "My job is not to teach students respect and empathy for any religion. My job is to teach students how to distance themselves from religion and to view it as objectively as possible."

However, objectivity is an elusive goal, even if words like respect and empathy are eliminated as educational outcomes. Every act of teaching—whether the course is about religion or anything else—requires making choices about what topics to include, what metaphors to use in introducing new concepts, and how to explain the subject being studied. All of this involves interpretation, and interpretation is never purely neutral or objective. No two professors teach about religion exactly the same way. Each professor has a unique view about what is most essential and what most needs to be emphasized, and pedagogical choices can result in wide variations in the presentation of the same religion in different classroom settings. When people within a religious tradition do this kind of interpretation of their own religion, it is usually called "theology," which most people see as the essence of "teaching religion itself." But when professors do something very similar regarding someone else's religious tradition, it is usually just called "good teaching," even though the activities are almost identical. Viewed in this light, the claim that teaching *about* religion is inherently more "objective" than teaching religion itself becomes difficult to sustain.

The distinction between teaching *about* religion and teaching religion itself can also become blurry because students insist on making it that way. Regardless of the intentions of the instructor, many students who enroll in college or university courses on religion do so precisely because they are self-consciously evaluating or re-evaluating their own spiritual and religious commitments, and they want to explore their options. These students want classes about religion to be fair and objective (i.e., fact-oriented), but often they are also looking for space to reflect personally on the material. They want the study of religion to include perspectives from the outside (*about* religion), but also from inside religion itself. Sometimes professors seem clueless about this double-sided student motivation. One professor who teaches a course on religion, death, and dying told us that everything in his course was presented solely in the mode of "teaching about religion," and nothing else was allowed. A few minutes later, he confided that nearly everyone who signed up for the course was a person dealing with a recent encounter with death—a near-death experience, a life-threatening disease, or the loss of someone they loved—and that many students ended up crying in his office as they wrestled through their personal questions and pain. Yet, this professor remained adamant that none of this had anything to do with teaching or practicing "religion itself."

There is no question that the difference between teaching *about* religion and teaching religion itself remains an important trail marker for higher education. It stands as a bulwark against using the podium as a pulpit and the classroom as a setting for conversion. In rare instances, there are professors who disdain that distinction. We spoke with one professor of Catholic studies who said he taught Catholic theology from a Catholic perspective, and it was his right to do so even though many of his students were not Catholic. From his viewpoint, students wanting to hear another perspective or to criticize Catholic theology were welcome to sign up for someone else's course. This one-sided manner of "teaching religion itself" is, however, very rare. Even when teaching theology (the religion-related academic discipline that comes closest to teaching religion itself), and even when teaching theology in church-related schools or seminaries, most professors present a variety of perspectives on a given religious doctrine and tell students that ultimately what they believe is theirs to decide. Old-fashioned religious indoctrination is almost nonexistent, even at the most conservative church-related colleges and universities.

Trail Marker 3: Difficult Dialogues

The term "difficult dialogues" functions something like the Hollywood sign that looms impressively above the Los Angeles basin, illuminating a region within higher education where emotionally charged encounters might occur and offering a not-too-subtle warning that some precautions may be in order. The "difficult dialogues" marker acknowledges that there are large swaths of life that are hard to corral into the kind of dispassionate, objective, and safe discussions that colleges and universities typically prefer. The "difficult dialogues" approach assumes that, if everyone involved in such dialogues is warned in advance, and if educators are trained in the handling of conflict, these kinds of conversations can produce meaningful learning and help promote civic tolerance and understanding.[11]

Religion is not the only topic that makes dialogue difficult. Race, ethnicity, gender, politics, and differences of socioeconomic class can produce just as much tension and conflict. What makes religion so potentially volatile is that differences of religion are often invisible, making it hard to tell in advance how problematic or stress-laden a conversation might become. An additional complication is that many educators are ill-equipped to respond when religious issues do arise. Religious illiteracy and religious inarticulateness remain common within the professorate, a legacy from the prior age of religious privatization. One science professor confessed bluntly that he and his colleagues had no option other than to avoid all discussion of religion in class because none of them "have a clue about religion." He said that "when this stuff comes up in class I just punt."

The phrase "difficult dialogues" gained prominence in 2005 when the Ford Foundation launched a grant program designed "to promote academic freedom and religious, cultural, and political pluralism" by having students "constructively engage with difficult and sensitive topics" that might include "fundamentalism and secularism, racial and ethnic relations, the Middle East conflict, religion and the university, sexual orientation, and academic freedom." The foundation's call for "difficult dialogue" proposals received an overwhelming response, with more than six hundred submissions. Only twenty-seven institutions received grants, but the term "difficult dialogue" was instantly embedded in the lexicon of the academy. Ask an administrator from any public university (and many private schools as well) about the status of religion at their institution, and the strong likelihood is that the reply will include some reference to orchestrating difficult dialogues on campus.

But the way in which the Ford Foundation defined its program may be part of the reason these dialogues were so difficult. Their concern was with public issues—issues that center on or are in some sense linked with politics—and that is potentially volatile almost by definition. It used to be said that politics is "the art of compromise," but few say that now. Today, politics is often more like warfare. The goal is not so much to achieve a workable compromise as to position oneself for the next brutal encounter. Talking honestly and civilly about religion or anything else in conjunction with politics is indeed difficult. When the topic is religion by itself, however, not mixed with politics, the results can be much more varied and often much more positive in tone. This is especially the case if the partners involved in the dialogue have already developed some degree of familiarity with and respect for each other. University chaplain after university chaplain told us that bringing students from various religious groups together to talk about their similarities and differences rarely produced any helpful results if the people involved did not already know each other. Everything tended to remain at the superficial level. But if those involved in the conversation were dorm mates or knew each other from classes or had worked on some kind of school or community project together, then there was a much greater likelihood of constructive and meaningful discourse.

When educators use the word "difficult" to describe an upcoming dialogue on campus, they intend to communicate a realistic warning that the exchange might become tense and testy; it is a way of letting everyone know what to expect. But using the word "difficult" can also become a self-fulfilling prophecy. When it is announced in advance that a conversation will be strained and challenging, such an outcome becomes more likely. It can be taken as a license for ranting. Yet, for many contemporary students, talking about religion is just not that difficult. Perhaps the young are inevitably optimistic, but many of today's students believe that conversations about religion are as likely to be enjoyable as they are to be tendentious. Thus, what some anxious educators might anticipate as a difficult dialogue about religion might be construed by students as an opportunity for "delightful discussion." Although talking about religion can produce tensions, it can also produce serendipitous, positive results. Undoubtedly, educators need to be aware of risks, but flagging them in advance may not be the most effective strategy for constructive interaction.

Trail Marker 4: Big Questions

The sign that reads "big questions" is, like "difficult dialogues," a way of pointing out a large domain within higher education where religion may appear, but in this case the message is much more inviting. The person whose name is most closely associated with this approach to religion in higher education is Sharon Daloz Parks, a former member of the faculty at Harvard and author of the widely read book *Big Questions, Worthy Dreams: Mentoring Young Adults in Their Search for Meaning, Purpose, and Faith*. In her view, big questions are inherently questions about "faith," which she describes as "the activity of seeking and discovering meaning in the most comprehensive dimensions of our experience." Parks, who is a developmental psychologist, says that young adulthood "is rightfully a time of asking big questions and discovering worthy dreams."[12] Although her focus is on traditional-aged college students, Parks is fully aware that big questions present

themselves throughout the life span. Art Chickering, a well-known higher educational theorist who is now in his mid-eighties, concurs, saying that "issues
concerning purpose and meaning, identity and integrity, interdependence, and
interpersonal relationships" are as important for older adults as they are for young
people. He adds, "I [am still] experiencing them powerfully myself."[13]

The rubric of big questions and worthy dreams potentially includes a vast array
of topics ranging from the very personal—Who am I, and what are my bedrock
values, my purpose for living, my "calling" in life, and my responsibilities?—to
the broadly political, including questions about peace and war, the environment,
the common good, and social justice. Answers to these big questions, many of
which have religious overtones, typically come couched in the language of convictions and commitments, rather than facts and knowledge. Big questions ask for
an impassioned response, not a theoretical discussion. In popular parlance, this
translates into material for which the answer will almost always be "No" when
students ask "Is this going to be on the exam?" Yet, how these questions are asked
and answered is a matter of huge consequence for society as a whole. They are not
solely individual concerns; they go to the heart of what it means to be human and
to live well with others.

If there is a weakness in this way of approaching religion, it is that the concerns of traditional religion can easily be caricatured as rote and unimaginative.
Big questions are about the living issues that people confront—the worries and
concerns that people face in their real lives—and not about the theoretical questions and answers provided catechistically by traditional religion. Parks herself
says that one of her main concerns is to help young people "discover a critical perspective that would call into question their inherited, conventional faith."[14] That
is certainly a valid educational goal, and "conventional faith," defined as religion
that is accepted with no personal reflection at all, is deserving of critique. But the
big-questions approach may not sufficiently appreciate the benefits that can result
from staying loyal to the rituals and disciplines of a particular religious tradition,
including such things as prayer, meditation, corporate worship, hospitality, and
food regulations. Scholars from all religious traditions insist that their practices
and rituals, properly performed, are not rote or mindless, but rather involve intro-
spection, self-criticism, and responsibility along with other social and religious
benefits.[15]

During the era of religious privatization in higher education, big questions
were often declared to be pedagogically off limits. They represented matters that
students were supposed to wrestle with on their own or in conversations with their
peers, but not in the classroom. Even at the most traditional liberal arts colleges in
the most humanities-oriented fields of study like literature and philosophy—the
places in the curriculum where the focus on the human is the strongest—many
professors insisted that reflection on the personal implications of the topics being

studied were not part of the course. That attitude is slowly changing, but many professors still get queasy at the thought of allowing "big questions" into the formal educational program. One literature professor at an elite college proudly recounted to a group of us at a recent conference that he saves the most poignant and personally relevant material until the very last minutes of the instructional period, at which point he reads the pertinent passage from the text aloud, tells his students to process the material on their own, and then leaves the classroom.

There are, however, many professors who welcome the introduction of big (or at least less small) questions into the classroom. A professor who teaches at a large state university provided an example of big questions being prompted by material in a standard psychology textbook. He said that the book's discussion of recent research on happiness—especially studies showing that happiness is not dependent on material wealth—inevitably "raises all sorts of questions about the meaning and purpose of life" for his students, usually prompting a rich conversation replete with religious as well as nonreligious comments. The psychology professor's example illustrates one of the great benefits of the big-questions approach: It immediately levels the playing field. Everyone has big questions, whether or not that person self-identifies as explicitly religious, nebulously spiritual, or thoroughly secular.

All four of the trail markers discussed in this chapter have been enormously helpful to higher education during the past few decades as it has inched its way into the new engagement with religion that is now visible at colleges and universities across the nation. However, these trail markers do not offer the kind of comprehensive guidance that now seems to be required. Too much of the terrain where religion and higher education interact is left uncharted. The following chapter fills that gap by providing a broader conceptual map of religion and then using that map to identify six key sites where religion and higher learning unavoidably overlap.

4

A Framework for Better Questions

IT IS A truism within the academic world that it takes a good question to get a good answer, and that observation applies to religion as much as to any other subject of inquiry. In order to promote clearer thinking about the ways in which religion and higher learning overlap, the first step is to ask better questions. One of the things we discovered at the very outset of this project was that asking people about religion in the abstract is not a fruitful way to begin a conversation. Ask people how religion connects to the work of higher education, and they often say things like "Religion is just irrational, and it has nothing to do with higher education" or "Let's just leave religion to the churches and synagogues" or "I teach chemistry, and I am very glad that I never have to think about religion." Those responses make sense because the original question is framed so poorly. It is similar to asking someone to explain what nature has to do with higher education and getting responses like "Nature is about bugs and worms, and it has nothing to do with higher education" or "Let's leave nature to the farmers and hunters."

There was, of course, a time when university professors would have made precisely those kinds of comments about "nature." At the great medieval universities of Europe, for example, professors thought that the study of nature was beneath them. Medieval university education was about God and logic and law, along with the study of human culture at its best. It was most definitely *not* about bugs and worms. But the times changed, the modern sciences emerged, and the questions that are asked about nature became much better formulated: How is the universe structured? What are the characteristics of different materials? How do biological organisms function? What factors drive the process of evolution? Modern scientific questions are directed at specific dimensions of the natural world. All of these dimensions are ultimately interrelated in nature itself, but the relationships among them can only be explored after something is known about the component parts. Intellectually, nature could never have been digested whole. It had to be divided into reasonable, bite-sized pieces in order to be comprehended, and the same principle applies to religion.

Religion as Historic, Public, and Personal

Asking good questions about religion requires a more nuanced vocabulary. In the concluding chapter of our earlier book *The American University in a Postsecular Age* (2008), we suggested that "religion in general" could be divided into three categories—historic religion, public religion, and personal religion. Subsequent conversations have confirmed the usefulness of these three categories and helped us refine our understanding of them. If religion in America today is a "forest," then these three varieties or dimensions of religion can be likened to the undergrowth, the ground cover, and the trees. Historic religion is like the shrubs growing at the eye level of hikers walking through the woods, or like the vines that sometimes hang down into the pathway and whack trekkers in the face. It is the kind of religion that cannot be missed, that comes pre-labeled as Christian, Buddhist, Jewish, and so on. Personal religion is much easier to overlook, something like the ground cover people walk on without noticing. It corresponds to individual questions of meaning, purpose, values, and morality, which are often infused with religion even though its presence is frequently not recognized. Public religion, on the other hand, is like the trees towering over everyone's head; they form a religion-like canopy for society as a whole, including society's presumptions (and arguments) about the common good, about what constitutes proper loyalty to the nation, and about what counts as truth in any given society. The trunks of public religion are all around us, but most people rarely look at the leaves closely enough to identify the various species.

One way to quickly illustrate the helpfulness of this three-part description of religion is to locate the four trail markers (described in the preceding chapter) in relation to the three subcategories of historic, public, and personal religion (see Figure 4.1). In this context, it becomes clear that the main function of the "religion versus spirituality" trail marker is to differentiate historic religion (the "religion" referenced in the pair) from personal religion ("spirituality"), but the religion-versus-spirituality guidepost says next to nothing about public religion. The other trail markers are similarly limited. "Teaching about religion" in distinction to teaching religion itself focuses almost entirely on historic religion. "Difficult dialogues" tend to fixate on matters related to public religion, and the "big questions" approach straddles the public and personal dimensions of religion, but gives scant attention to historic religion. The three-category description of religion proposed here captures the key insights of all four of the trail markers, but also situates them in a more comprehensive framework.

Our description of religion also allows for strategic as opposed to merely tactical thinking with regard to pedagogical concerns and learning outcomes. The

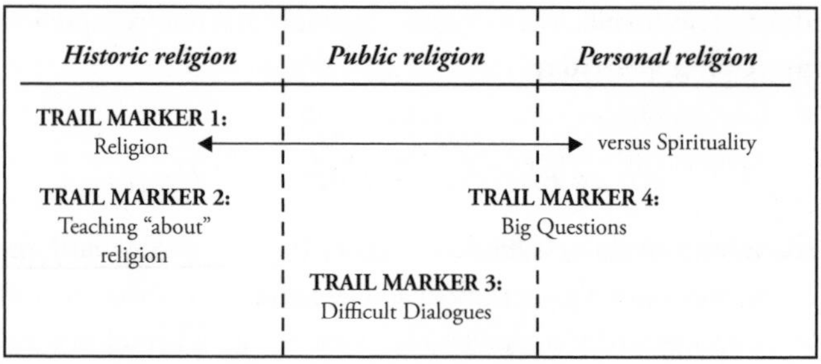

Historic religion	Public religion	Personal religion
TRAIL MARKER 1: Religion ←		→ versus Spirituality
TRAIL MARKER 2: Teaching "about" religion	**TRAIL MARKER 4:** Big Questions	
	TRAIL MARKER 3: Difficult Dialogues	

FIGURE 4.1   The Four Trail Markers and the Three Categories of Religion

trail markers are tactical; they are guidelines for responding to events that have their genesis elsewhere. In contrast, a map of the whole territory allows colleges and universities to think strategically about where and how to engage religion proactively and constructively, whether it enters the conversation unexpectedly or is intentionally introduced.

The three forms of religion (historic, public, and personal) describe the basic grid of religion within higher education, but one additional qualifier helps to complete the picture. Religion, like almost all other human activities, functions in two modes. It involves beliefs (or ideas), and it also involves practices (or behaviors). Separating these two facets of human experience is somewhat artificial, of course, because beliefs and behaviors are almost always interconnected. But prying them apart allows closer attention to be paid to each of them. This is especially important when the topic is religion in the American context, because Americans tend to focus their attention on religious belief. No religious tradition has a stronger emphasis on beliefs than Protestantism, and that Protestant predilection has become part of American culture. It is thus not uncommon for Americans to refer to religiously devout individuals as "believers" and to inquire about someone's faith by asking "What do you believe?" This American propensity to think of religion in terms of ideas rather than practices makes it all the more important to pay special attention to religious practices when reflecting on religion's presence within higher education. In the explanations of historic, public, and personal religion that follow, we will accordingly discuss both beliefs *and* practices.

Finally, it is worth noting that however helpful it is to separate historic, public, and personal religion from each other conceptually, in reality these three modes of religion are frequently interrelated. Religious beliefs and behaviors that have been shaped within a historic religious community may well influence an individual's personal and public religious orientations. Likewise, personal religious convictions can shape decisions about whether to join or leave a historic religious movement and can affect how a person views the culture in which he or she lives. Public religion interacts with both personal and historic religion, because it infuses the whole culture, defining the religious-social medium in which both individuals and religious traditions either languish or flourish.

Historic Religion

Historic religion is religion the way most people have traditionally thought of it. It is religion that names itself and that is organized into observable communities of belief and practice. It includes Judaism, Islam, Christianity, Buddhism, Hinduism, and the host of other named religious traditions that appear in any standard list of the world's religions.

Historic religion is a global presence. About 85 percent of the world's people are adherents of at least one of the world's many historic religions. Globally, Christianity is the world's largest religion, accounting for roughly one-third of the world's population. Islam is the next largest (20–25 percent of the world's population—the estimates vary), followed by Hinduism (around 14 percent) and Buddhism (6 percent or more). About 15 percent of the world's population describes itself as nonreligious. The level of religiosity in America is relatively similar to the rest of the world. According to the most recent survey conducted by the Pew Forum, 83 percent of Americans identify themselves with a historic religious tradition, 16 percent say they are nonreligious (or religiously unaffiliated), and about 1 percent say they "don't know."[1] The main difference is that more than three-fourths of America's population currently identifies as Christian. Followers of all other historic religions together comprise only about 5 percent of the American population.

No historic religion is monolithic. Labels like Christianity, Islam, Buddhism, Hinduism, and Judaism name broad religious traditions, but each of them is rife with its own internal complexities. Christianity can be subdivided into Catholic, Protestant, Orthodox, and Pentecostal camps, and each of those can be further differentiated into various churches, denominations, and movements. Christian beliefs and practices vary widely in America and around the world based on cultural difference and geographic location.[2] The same is true of Islam, which can be divided into Shi'a, Sunni, and other Islamic sub-traditions, each of them more or less prevalent in various locations. Internal diversity is also found within Judaism, Buddhism, Hinduism, and every other formally organized religion in the world.[3]

Part of what sets historic religion apart from public and personal religion is that it is communal. To be a member of a historic religion is to be a member of a group with its own beliefs and practices that have been intentionally handed down from generation to generation through years or centuries or even millennia of time. Historic religions value continuity, and their adherents are expected to change their lives to fit the ideals of that historic religion. Personal innovation is not usually encouraged.

Historic continuity does not mean that the world's historic religions are totally inflexible and unchanging. To the contrary, they are all constantly evolving to meet the needs of their followers, but they usually change incrementally and deliberately. Observing those transformations can feel like watching paint dry. Sometimes, however, changes occur rapidly. In the Catholic tradition, for example, the Second Vatican Council (1962–1965) set aside a spate of old beliefs and practices in a few short years. Whether changes occur quickly or slowly, however, this process of "traditioning"[4] allows historic religions to maintain their identities from generation to generation despite the fact that all of them have modified their ideas and ideals significantly over the years.

In addition to holding particular beliefs, the world's historic religions are also communities of practice. The lives of followers are organized around the community's rituals, ceremonies, yearly calendars of events, and rites of passage, as well as around the religion's moral guidelines and ethical imperatives. Many religious practices, especially those associated with annual celebrations and various rites of passage from birth through adolescence to adulthood and death, generate strongly positive emotions. These are times of fellowship with family and friends, of gift-giving and rejoicing, and sometimes of sadness and consolation, and all of this slowly merges into the affectivity of the religious celebration itself. Most religious traditions also have guidelines about behavior (prohibition of sins or avoidance of taboos) that make people feel good when they follow them and uncomfortable, ashamed, or guilty when they do not. These feelings can remain powerful components of personality even if a person later converts or drifts away from that community. Religion seeps into people; it leaves its mark; and it is not easily discarded. Thus, religious identity is not entirely voluntary; it frequently can be a "given" aspect of identity similar to ethnicity, class, and gender.

Higher education's responsibilities related to historic religion derive largely from this "given-ness" of religious identity. Colleges and universities appreciate that the world is a diverse place, and religion is recognized as an important element in the mix. Many colleges and universities have devoted significant time and energy to implementing programs that help students understand the constructs of culture, race, and sexual orientation, and they are now adding historic religion to that list. Responding appropriately and thoughtfully to the world's religious diversity will require significant reflection and planning, but that task can be simplified by focusing on two specific questions. The first deals with religious literacy: *What should an educated person know about the world's religions?* The second focuses on interfaith etiquette: *What are appropriate ways to interact with those of other faiths?*

Public Religion

"Public religion" is very different from historic religion, but it is religion nonetheless. In the broadest sense, public religion is how a society idealistically "presents itself to itself."[5] Public religion defines what a society takes to be true, provides a rationale for that society's way of life, and enumerates the values that society strives to uphold. Rather than being carried and preserved by an identifiable sub-community in society (as is the case with historic religion), the carrier of public religion is society itself, society as a whole. Everyone who is a member of a given society is a participant in that society's public religion. This does not mean that everyone participates at the same level or that everyone agrees about what the content of public religion should be. But it does mean that, when the subject is public religion, the distinction between being religious and being secular makes no sense. Everyone has a stake in these matters.

In the United States, this blending of the religious and the secular in public religion goes back to the very founding of the nation. From the start, Christian (and specifically Protestant) ideas and ideals have played a large role in American public religion, and so also have Enlightenment appeals to "the Laws of Nature and of Nature's God" and secular appeals to human or humanistic values. Today, the whole spectrum of possible lifestances, from the most conservatively religious to the most progressively secular, continues to contribute to the clamorous dialogue of forming and reforming the ideas, ideals, and ways of life that define American public religion.

Public religion is always contested turf, but there are usually a few relatively fixed points of reference. In America, for example, notions like freedom and democracy are central ideals, and behaviors like reciting the pledge of allegiance and singing the national anthem are powerful rituals. Beyond this limited set of core ideas and ideals, however, there is a great deal of arguing, dispute, division, and rancor. In this regard, public religion is a bit like a rugby game. On the field, people and organizations that champion different public religious views engage each other face to face and shoulder to shoulder in a kind of scrum, trying to push society's core ideas and central values a little bit this way or a little bit that way. In the stands, the rest of the population watches. Some of them are fans of one team or another and others are mere observers, but the results of the game have implications for everyone.

Individuals or groups can resist the dictates of public religion to some degree, but it is hard work and often they will be punished for it. An example is provided by remembering the way communists were treated in mid-twentieth-century America. Communists disputed both democracy and capitalism, two of the main planks of American public religion. Accordingly, they were deemed to be more than merely mistaken in their beliefs and values; suspected communists were denounced as public enemies. Cast in the terminology of public religion, communists were heretics who defied the intellectual and moral norms of the nation's public faith and, for a time, most Americans thought they should be duly punished for that sin. Those who associated with them, even if they were not communists themselves, were often shunned. Eventually, another commitment of

American public religion—a commitment to freedom of thought and speech—enabled the nation to move on.

Americans can have a hard time acknowledging the reality of public religion because they think it is not supposed to exist—at least, not here in America. They know that many societies of the past promoted some form of public religion. The Roman Empire had its cult of emperors, and centuries ago, the Han Dynasty established Confucianism as the public faith of China. Catholic Christianity and later Protestant Christianity served as the official, publicly sanctioned religion of many countries in Europe up through the nineteenth century, and some European nations still support state churches today. In America, however, this is not supposed to be how religion works. The United States is envisioned as a place where religion and public life are separate. After all, the disestablishment of religion that took place at the founding of the nation legally separated religion from *control* by the state and the state from *control* by any specific religious organization. Legally separating church and state is not, however, the same as dismantling public religion. America has never had a formal state religion,[6] but it has had and continues to have a powerfully functioning public religion that exists in the form of an ad hoc cultural framework that is constantly being reaffirmed and challenged at the same time.

The ideas of American public religion—the nation's ongoing public argument about what counts as truth—are evident in a host of settings, from the divergent opinions expressed in newspaper editorials and online blogs to school-board fights about textbooks and whether creationism or "intelligent design" should be taught side by side with evolution in public school science classes. Americans have decidedly different views about whether God (or Gods) exist and about how God (or the Gods), if they do exist, might be connected to events on earth. They differ with regard to beliefs about gender, global warming, and when human life begins. They hold different values related to sexuality, entertainment, politics, the arts, business practices, the Constitution, and personal freedom. These differences sometimes spring prominently into view as they have in recent media debates between the so-called New Atheists (people like Sam Harris, Daniel Dennett, Richard Dawkins, and the late Christopher Hitchens) and various defenders of traditional religion. But many important discussions about public religious ideas—about beliefs that really matter and about what people take to be genuinely true in contrast to mere opinion—occur in less visible and less antagonistic settings, including the classrooms of the nation's colleges and universities. In fact, this is one of higher education's chief roles in society: to vet ideas and to evaluate alternative proposals about what counts as truth or knowledge.

During the era of religious privatization in higher education, there was a tendency to act as if disputes about ideas and values were a matter of evidence and logic alone. The expectation seemed to be that, eventually, better research and improved thinking would produce a fair and objective secular consensus about what was true and not true. But America's shift toward greater social and religious pluralism has shown that to be an unrealistic expectation. Many different individuals and groups now vie with each other, trying to bend public religion this way or that, struggling to get traction for their values and ideas any way they can. This includes voices from the historic religions, but it also includes the voices of many others who want their own personal religious or nonreligious ideas to be reflected in the public beliefs and practices of the nation. Higher education is in the process of adjusting to this newly raucous debate. For colleges and universities, this means helping students develop the ability to scrutinize, dialogue, evaluate, contest, and critique the many different values and ideas that are hoisted up for public inspection in the ongoing negotiation and debate that constitutes American public religion. The central question is about framing knowledge: *What assumptions and rationalities—secular or religious—shape the way we think?*

In 1967, Robert Bellah coined the term "civil religion" as a way of naming the more behavior-oriented side of public religion.[7] Bellah made the case that civil religion was especially important in America because it is a land of immigrants. Without a common ethnicity or a historic sense of peoplehood to bind them together, Americans are literally held together by the values, practices, symbols, and rituals of the nation's civil religion. Whether the focus has been on abolitionism, women's suffrage, temperance, and the Civil Rights movement or more recently on issues like abortion, gay rights, and national health care, the arguments have been cast in the terms of public religion, about who Americans are "as a people"—on what they consider to be right and wrong practices, morally healthy or morally degenerate activities, and appropriate or inappropriate behavior.

The role of colleges and universities in this disputed terrain of public religious practices is complex. On the one hand, America's colleges and universities (along with K-12 public schools) have almost always seen themselves as nurturers of civil religion in the sense of encouraging students to embody American public ideals like democracy, freedom, individualism, fairness, and equality through various forms of civic engagement. On the other hand, campuses have also served as forums for evaluating these foundational American attitudes and activities. In an age of increasing cultural, political, and religious diversity, educational institutions are finding themselves at the forefront of even more complicated conversations about the obligations and ideals that inform civic engagement in America. The key question now being explored is this: *What values and practices—religious or secular—shape civic engagement?*

Personal Religion

Personal religion is unique to the individual. It is an idiosyncratic collection of whatever it is that provides meaning, purpose, grounding, trust, hope, and a sense of wholeness. In the past, this personal dimension of faith was often embedded within the life of a historic religious community, and the term "spirituality" was used to describe how individual members of that community grabbed hold of its ideas and practices, adapting them to fit their own personal needs. That older understanding of spirituality still persists, and various historic religions suggest ways in which their followers can enhance their personal spiritual journeys. In the broader culture, however, it has become common to emphasize the differences between spirituality and historic religion, and many individuals who have no connection with historic religion, including atheists and agnostics, now feel comfortable describing themselves as spiritual.

The distinctiveness of personal religion was highlighted in the groundbreaking book *Habits of the Heart* (1985). One memorable vignette recounts the response of a young nurse named Sheila Larson when she was asked to describe her religion: "I believe in God. I'm not a religious fanatic. I can't remember the last time I went to church. My faith has carried me a long way. It's Sheila-ism. Just my own little voice."[8] The term "Sheila-ism" aptly describes the individualistic religious preferences of vast numbers of contemporary Americans. The old historic religious traditions do not seem to be working for them—at least not as total packages—and so people fashion their own personal bricolages of beliefs and values out of various fragments of historic religion, bits and pieces of popular culture, and, most importantly, their own experiences. The goal of personal religion or spirituality today is not so much to find a changeless refuge in an ever-changing world as it is to recognize and savor those sometimes fleeting moments of wonder and insight that facilitate the resetting of one's inner compass, what the commentator David Brooks has termed a person's "spiritual GPS."[9]

Some leaders of the world's historic religious communities dislike this personal, in-the-moment, choice-oriented style of religion. They scoff at the notion that an individual can craft a personal religious identity. They denounce "cafeteria Catholicism" and every other variety of pieced-together, hybrid faith as not really religion at all—just half-baked, half-thought-out opinions. But that is a minority view. Almost 80 percent of Americans believe it is possible to be a good Christian or Jew without attending church or synagogue.[10] Even if they are members in good standing of their own historic religious communities, many Americans no longer assume that historic religion provides the only way or the best way to be religious. Individualized, freelance religion is considered to be a valid alternative or complement to historic religion, and some would assert that it is actually more "real" than historic religion because it is "authentic" rather than rote and repetitive.

Personal religion is very different from public religion. Public religion operates at the level of society as a whole, which means that competing claims about it are rightly subject to contestation and debate. But personal religion operates on a different plane entirely. Personal religion expresses (or, perhaps more accurately, it *confesses*) the individual's unique take on the world as refracted through his or her own life. It is idiosyncratic in its claims, not universal, and it is not always logical or consistent in configuration. (But then again, Ralph Waldo Emerson, one of the great early American prophets of personal religion once famously said "a foolish consistency is the hobgoblin of little minds."[11]) George Dennis O'Brien, the former president of the University of Rochester, uses the notion of "signature truth"—truth rooted in one's own particularity—to describe what we call personal religion.[12] Marcia B. Baxter Magolda calls it "authoring your life," learning to listen to your own inner voice when making life decisions.[13] And Alexander Astin, Helen Astin, and Jennifer Lindholm talk about personal religion in terms of the "inner lives" of human beings.[14] This emphasis on the inner and individual should not be taken, however, as referring to people in isolation. For the most part, personal religion is, in fact, deeply interpersonal. Just as individuals develop many of their attitudes, affections, and affinities from the people that mean the most to them, so too personal religion is often acquired, shaped, and sustained by friends, family, lovers, and neighbors.

Like all forms of religion, personal religion is expressed both in ideas and actions. Personal religious beliefs are the (often unspoken) convictions that give structure and meaning to individual lives. Convictions resemble opinions, but they are integral to a person's core sense of being. If opinions are like little "Post-It" notes that express what a person believes at a given moment in time, convictions are more like tattoos that are etched onto one's soul. Convictions define what people hope and trust is true about themselves and the world; they are the assumptions relied upon when life gets rough. Convictions can change, but the process is often difficult and sometimes painful.

Personal religious practices include all of a person's actions to the degree that those actions touch on the things that give meaning and purpose to life. This might well include certain actions that are self-evidently religious, such as pausing during the day for moments of meditation or prayer, but it can also include many behaviors that seem simply moral or even quite ordinary—how a person greets people on the street, treats a spouse, reports taxes, acts while on vacation, or devotes time to helping others. To the degree that any of these actions reflect a basic orientation to life or shape a person's perception of what is or is not really important, they are part of personal religious practice. Does having personal convictions mean that an individual is religious? Is meditating or doing good deeds necessarily a spiritual practice? Some individuals are uncomfortable describing their personal ideas and beliefs as religious. They think of themselves as secular or spiritual, and using the word "religion" to describe their values, convictions, and ways of life seems like misrepresentation. That is a perfectly valid position, and there is no reason to force anyone to use the word "religion" as a self-description. Yet, when the focus is on the individual and the personal, there is no easy way to differentiate religious impulses and actions from nonreligious ones. Whether they are labeled spiritual or religious or secular or simply personal, they all point toward things that really matter to that individual, toward things that move beyond the superficial and provide meaning and purpose to life.

During the era of religious privatization in higher education, the ideas and practices of personal religion were largely boxed out of the formal learning process. The goal of education was to cultivate the intellect and to master required information and skills. Personal religion, along with other personal concerns, was either ignored completely or delegated to the office of student life. But most educators today recognize that supposedly impersonal information and personal formation often intertwine. What people learn and how they learn it—*and* what people don't learn because it is intentionally not included or the context prevents it—can have a significant influence on the kinds of human beings they become. Education is not neutral. Even dull and routine classes nudge personal development in one way or another. A key question that every college and university must then consider is this: *In what ways are personal convictions related to the teaching and learning process?* Of course, it is not only the ideas communicated in coursework that have an effect on students. The whole college experience—from the application and orientation processes to life in the dorms and experiences with the local community to study abroad and eventually to alumni involvement—shape a student's character and sense of vocation. The essential educational question is this: *How might colleges and universities point students toward lives of meaning and purpose?*

The six questions articulated in this chapter point toward six sites where religion and higher learning naturally overlap (see Figure 4.2). The following chapters examine each of these sites in detail, exploring how some colleges and universities might wrestle with these issues. The essays are not manifestos, but are intended as prompts for constructive reflection that will enable colleges and universities to see religion more clearly and to pay attention to religion in ways that are educationally enriching.

	HISTORIC RELIGION	PUBLIC RELIGION	PERSONAL RELIGION
IDEAS	*Religious Literacy*	*Framing Knowledge*	*Convictions*
PRACTICES	*Interfaith Etiquette*	*Civic Engagement*	*Character and Vocation*

FIGURE 4.2 Religion in Higher Education: Six Sites of Engagement

PART TWO

Six Sites of Engagement

5

Religious Literacy

What should an educated person know about the world's
religions?

AMERICA IS ONE of the most highly religious nations in the world, and perhaps paradoxically, Americans are also, as a whole, remarkably illiterate about religion. A recent survey undertaken by the Pew Forum posed thirty-two relatively simple questions about the world's historic religions to a cross section of Americans, and the result was a failing grade. These were "softball" questions, such as whether Mother Teresa was Catholic, or the Dalai Lama was Buddhist, or the Quran was a Muslim holy book. On average, respondents could answer only half of the questions correctly. Most knew that Mother Teresa was Catholic (82 percent), but fewer than half (47 percent) were aware that the Dalai Lama was Buddhist, and only 54 percent could connect the Quran with Islam. A mere quarter knew that most Indonesians are Muslim (Indonesia is, in fact, the largest Muslim nation in the world), but, thankfully, 85 percent knew that atheists do not believe in God. The people who did best on the quiz overall were nonreligious (atheists and agnostics). Religious people knew little about their own religious traditions and less about the religious traditions of others.[1] In a world where the vast majority professes some kind of religious allegiance and where religious tensions are contributing factors to global violence, such ignorance about religion is dangerous.

One bit of good news is that, in general, people who were more religiously committed to their faith communities did better on the Pew quiz than those who were less committed. Educators may also breathe a sigh of relief upon learning that people who had more years of formal education generally scored higher. Individuals with no formal education beyond high school averaged 40 percent correct, those with some college credits scored 55 percent, and college graduates had 64 percent correct answers. Before college professors and administrators start patting each other on the back, however, it might be worth recalling that in most college classes a score of 64 percent on a quiz yields a grade of "D"—an outcome that is usually not celebrated.

Religious Literacy and Illiteracy

Religious literacy, like any form of literacy, is a matter of levels and degrees. Let's look at language literacy as an example. Many university masters and doctoral level programs, especially those in the humanities, require some familiarity with one or more foreign languages, but the language competency that is expected is relatively minimal. The goal is to achieve "research literacy," the ability to read books and articles related to an academic field of study. Anyone who has attained this level of language competence and then ventured into a community where that language is actually spoken will confirm that research literacy does not equate with an ability to carry on an everyday conversation, and it is laughably inadequate when it comes to writing respectable poetry or prose in the newly acquired language. But, although language literacy falls across a spectrum, any language facility, even minimal research literacy, can still be helpful. The same is true of religious literacy: A little is better than none, but just a little may fall far short of what is required for understanding and acting intelligently in a religiously pluriform world.

Most Americans, and especially most young people, seem to be starting college on a lower rung of the religious literacy ladder than their predecessors of a generation or two ago. Up until the 1980s, most students who entered American colleges were at least moderately literate about their own religious traditions. Christians knew something about Christianity, Jews knew about Judaism, and people who came from other religious communities were relatively fluent with regard to their own communities' ideas, ideals, and ritual practices. Professors could assume an aggregate level of basic religious knowledge spread across the students in the classroom, though obviously it varied from person to person. This is no longer the case. Teaching about religion in a college or university class today must usually start from scratch; it is a mistake to assume that anyone knows anything.[2] Thus, a reference to a verse in the Bible might need to be prefaced with something like "This passage is found in the Gospel of Matthew, which is one of the writings in the Bible. The Bible is the Christian holy book, and it is divided into two parts called the Old Testament (or Hebrew scriptures) and the New Testament. Matthew is in the New Testament, and it is one of four 'gospels,' which are the writings that focus mainly on Jesus, who is the founder of the Christian religion." As this information is being relayed, some students will be rapidly scribbling down (or keyboarding) notes, because it is all new to them.

Educationally, America's current religious illiteracy is both good and bad. In the past, students knew more, but most of that knowledge was about their own religion. They knew very little about any other religious traditions, so they had a tendency to view other religions through the theological and moral categories provided by their own faith. Getting them to see another religion in its own light and on its own terms could be difficult. Like beginning language students, they had to have everything translated into their native tongue. In this earlier era, professors had to concern themselves with deconstructing what students knew (or thought they knew) about their own and other religions, so they could then learn better and more scholarly ways of understanding the subject matter. That kind of deconstruction is rarely required in religious studies classrooms today, and in some sense this is a positive development. Another difference is that most contemporary college students already know people who are members of religious groups other than their own. These people may well be their friends, and they may even have visited each other's churches, mosques, synagogues, and temples. Their shared pool of religious knowledge is thin—they are religiously illiterate about most facts pertaining to religion—but most students who enter an introductory religious studies class today arrive relatively free of prejudice and ready to learn. Obviously, there are exceptions, but the majority of students fit this profile.

Religious illiteracy is not limited to the young; deficits in religious knowledge are evident across all age groups. In a recent graduation speech at Wheaton College in Massachusetts, for example, the television journalist Ann Curry mistakenly referred to the well-known American evangelical leader Billy Graham as one of the school's graduates.[3] Billy Graham is indeed a graduate of Wheaton College, just not the one in Massachusetts. He attended the proudly evangelical Wheaton College in Illinois. Her journalistic gaffe, which her peers enjoyed reporting, is understandable because the schools do have the same name, but other instances of ignorance are more troubling. For example, during the summer of 2010 when public debate about a proposal to build a new mosque and Islamic cultural center in lower Manhattan near "Ground Zero" was at fever pitch, New York Governor David Paterson tried to calm the waters by explaining: "This group who has put this mosque together, they are known as the Sufi Muslims. This is not like the Shiites.... They're almost like a hybrid, almost westernized. They are not really what I would classify in the sort of mainland Muslim practice." His comments were supposed to put the public at ease and instruct New Yorkers in the difference between "good" and "bad" versions of Islam. Instead, as one scholar summed it up: "In a few short sentences, the governor managed to offend Sufis, Shi'a Muslims, as well as westernized Muslims, non-westernized Muslims, and 'mainland Muslims' (whoever they are)."[4]

American foreign policy also suffers the consequences of religious illiteracy. After completing her tenure as secretary of state in the Clinton administration, Madeleine Albright confessed that religion played virtually no part in her thinking while in office, not even in her attempts to broker a peace agreement in the

Middle East. She was aware that some people in the region considered religion to be an issue, but she thought of their concerns as simply "echoes of earlier, less enlightened times." Any future peace, she thought, had to be a matter of purely pragmatic secular negotiation and agreement. Only later did she realize the importance of religion in the art of statecraft. It is essential to "know your customers," she writes, and during "a time when religious passions are embroiling the globe" this includes "taking religious tenets and motivations fully into account."[5] That may not be possible if the level of religious literacy among American diplomats and military personnel is as dismal as that of the general population—and it may be. Even after years of involvement in the Middle East and Central Asia, after years of responding to conflicts that are saturated with religion, diplomats are still prone to think of religion only or mostly in terms of religious freedom. Religious freedom is a vital interest, but some of the most ardent defenders of religious freedom seem to have little, if any, knowledge about the religions they hope to make or keep free.[6] Religious practice has always been a significant component of human life, and ignorance has always had a cost, but the ramifications of religious illiteracy today can have dire consequences in our ever more tightly interconnected world.

Three Levels of Literacy: Facts, Familiarity, and Assessment

If religious literacy is a worthy goal, then educators will need to be specific about the subject matter of religion and precise in defining literacy. We take a first step in that direction by identifying three different levels of literacy related to religion, each with its own distinct goals and measurable outcomes: facts, familiarity, and assessment (see Figure 5.1.)

Religious literacy level 1:
Assessment

Religious literacy level 2:
Familiarity

Religious literacy level 3:
Facts

FIGURE 5.1 Three Levels of Religious Literacy

Factual literacy is analogous to acquiring basic vocabulary in a new language. It involves learning important *facts* about the world's different religions. What is and is not a religious fact can and will be debated by scholars, and every religious fact, however seemingly objective, will include some interpretation. However, broadly speaking, facts are basic information of the sort found in a standard dictionary, encyclopedia, or introductory textbook. The second level of literacy is *familiarity*, which is something like learning "conversational" French or German: an ability to have face-to-face interaction with people from different religious traditions. It moves beyond merely textbook facts and requires becoming familiar with the ways in which religious communities actually operate in the world. A third level of religious literacy requires even more: an ability to *assess* the relative merits of alternative religious ways of life and thought. This is not the kind of assessment where success is ascertained by rote answers on objective tests, but rather by a capacity to take part in meaningful conversations about how religious (and nonreligious) ways of life and thought influence individuals and societies, open up or close down the possibility for human flourishing, and promote alternative understandings of basic human concerns like freedom, fairness, moral duty, and truth. People make judgments about religion all the time, but those judgments are often unreflective. Literacy at the level of assessment means developing the ability to be a self-conscious, self-critical, constructive participant in conversations about the relative merits and demerits of the world's religious traditions.

These three levels of religious literacy—factual knowledge, familiarity, and assessment—can be viewed hierarchically, with each serving as the necessary foundation for the next. In a hierarchical arrangement, the mastery of level one (facts) would be a prerequisite for moving on to level two (familiarity), and becoming thoroughly familiar with another religion would be a prerequisite for any attempt at level three (assessment). But what happens in the real world or even in the classroom may not follow this hierarchical process. Sometimes, instinctive and unreflective judgments about religion are expressed in class, and those judgments may call for an immediate response. At such times, talking about assessment can become the doorway through which students enter into the search for facts and familiarity. In other cases—when, for example, students gain experience with a religious community as part of a service-learning course—it might be that familiarity precedes facts and assessment. Wherever the journey toward religious literacy begins, ultimately all three levels of literacy will require attention.

Religious Literacy 1: The "Facts"

The term "religious literacy" is associated with the work of Stephen Prothero, professor of religion at Boston University. His 2007 publication *Religious Literacy: What Every American Needs to Know—and Doesn't* raised the issue with sufficient punch and good humor to catch attention, and his message is simple: "If religion is important, we ought to know something about it, particularly in a democracy, in which political power is vested in voters." The problem, he continues, is that the average American voter "knows embarrassingly little about Christianity and other world religions."[7]

Prothero's proposed solution is straightforward: People should learn more facts about religion, and by facts he means the doctrines and stories of the world's religions—what religious people believe and how they see the world. Religious literacy is "the ability to understand and use the religious terms, symbols, images, beliefs, practices, scriptures, heroes, themes, and stories" that crop up in public life. Prothero is especially concerned about religious illiteracy in America, so his solution stresses what he thinks Americans need to know. Thus, he generally gives more attention to Christianity (the dominant religion in America) and less attention to other world religions, a weighting that is reflected in the "dictionary of religious literacy" that forms the second half of his book. About one hundred of its items are devoted to Christianity and the Bible; the rest of the world's religions are covered in a mere seventy entries.[8]

Almost every scholar of religion we met had a strong opinion about which people, places, ideas, and events are missing from Prothero's list and whether Christianity deserves as much attention as Prothero gives it. Many professors were also critical of Prothero's restricted focus on beliefs and teachings and his relative inattentiveness to the history, demographics, regional geography, social structures, cultural affectivities, and material cultures of the world's religions. Such criticism is probably to be expected in response to any list of "most important facts" about religion. Indeed, this is the central problem with any fact-based approach to religious literacy: Scholars will never fully agree on what should and should not be included in a list of essential facts. But that very problem is also the strength of the fact-based approach to religious literacy: It forces people to think about what really is crucial for students to know about the world's religions.

Different institutions make decisions about course content in different ways. At some institutions, the choices are left in the hands of individual instructors; this is generally the case at private institutions and elite colleges and universities. At public universities and especially at community colleges, the choice about what to teach (about the subject matter to include in courses dealing with religion) is often a group decision. A number of community college professors told us that the only way for them to "stay out of trouble" when teaching about religion was to make a department-wide decision about which textbook to use, get it pre-approved by the administration, and then stick closely to the book's content in their lectures and classroom discussions. Any deviation from that pattern, any personal selection of course content, opened them up to accusations of bias or of teaching religion itself. In some educational settings, defining religious literacy in terms of well-established facts and nothing more is a matter of professional survival.

However, many supposed facts about religion are more slippery than they first seem. Religious literacy defined as facts is not as straightforward as learning vocabulary in a new language. For example, hardly anything seems more religiously factual than the Ten Commandments, but a closer look reveals that the

Bible enumerates those ten "oughts" in two different ways. Even if this ambiguity did not exist, the basic question regarding the educational worth of memorizing the Ten Commandments would still remain. Do the Ten Commandments communicate the actual practices or even the ideals of Jews and Christians? Similarly, a student who memorizes the Eightfold Path of Buddhism or the basics of Hinduism may be greatly surprised to see how these religious principles play themselves out (or do not play themselves out) in real life.

Still, facts are important. Christians, Buddhists, Jews, and Muslims believe different things, revere different scriptures, tell different stories, and see the world from differing perspectives, and knowing some of these factual differences is a necessary step toward better understanding. To help with this task, the American Academy of Religion, the largest organization for professors of religion in the world, recently prepared a guide for teaching about religion in public school classrooms from primary grades through high school. This publication defines "a religiously literate person" as possessing "a basic understanding of the history, central texts (where applicable), beliefs, practices and contemporary manifestations of several of the world's religious traditions and religious expressions...and the ability to discern and explore the religious dimensions of political, social and cultural expressions across time and place."[9] Perhaps it is time to apply these guidelines to higher education as well, and it may also be helpful to identify certain specific "facts" that all college and university students should know—if not at the national level then at least at particular colleges and universities. No one can tell if students are moving toward religious literacy if there is no articulated standard by which to measure it.

Religious Literacy 2: Familiarity

Facts can usually be found in books or other printed material; familiarity requires students to look around the real world and interact with real people. Although religions can be studied as relatively abstract systems of thought and practice, the lived reality of most religion is checkered and uneven, with the actual contours of faith determined as much (or more) by community concerns and existential challenges as they are by philosophical coherence or ideological/theological consistency. Religion as a way of life cannot be comprehended on the basis of textbook knowledge alone, but rather needs to be discovered to some degree "on site." Knowing just the textbook facts about a religion, no matter how completely they are compiled, is like trying to navigate through an unfamiliar city with the largely useless maps provided by most rental car companies. Those maps highlight a few of the main roads and attractions, but they lack practically everything else. Developing religious literacy in the form of familiarity requires getting out of one's cognitive car, putting away the map, and walking around the neighborhood.

Sometimes, that metaphorical walk around the neighborhood becomes a literal one. In an interview, one professor of religion said that the core of his introductory course was a requirement for students to visit various religious sites in the urban community where the school was located. "Many students," he said, "are initially hesitant. They have what I call an 'edifice complex,' fear of visiting someone else's building, fear of stepping into someone else's space. But that is the only way to really begin to know a religion." The fears of those students are, of course, understandable. Stepping into someone else's space is risky. It means entering a zone where the rules are unknown, where offenses and mistakes might happen in spite of good intentions. But sometimes there is no other way to learn.

Religious literacy parsed in terms of familiarity is a cross-cultural endeavor and the aim, as in all cross-cultural learning experiences, is to make the seemingly strange into something comprehensible and the confusing into something understandable. The focus is on getting to know a religion as it is actually lived, according to its own rhythms of time, space, language, behavior, and relationships, trying to understand how that religion "works" for the people involved in it. The goal is to become sufficiently familiar with a religion that one can interpret its activities more or less correctly, converse intelligently with its adherents, and explain it sympathetically—on its own terms and according to its own inner logic—to those who have not experienced it. For example, Warren A. Nord, who founded the Program in the Humanities and Values at the University of North Carolina and directed it for twenty-five years, argues that understanding religion means "taking [that]religion seriously," being open to the possibility that its categories "provide credible ways of making sense of the world."[10]

Some scholars would even go further, suggesting that genuine understanding requires a degree of respect for, or even personal attraction to, the religion being studied. While it may be difficult to adequately understand another religion if it is assumed from the outset that it is despicable, it is surely asking too much of students (and scholars as well) to require them to find another religion positively attractive. Becoming familiar does not mean joining the family, and in some instances people have to attempt to understand religions they really do find revolting. The capacity to do so may be one of the most important skills the world needs today: an ability to understand the religious views of others even when one vehemently disagrees with those views. How else will interreligious tensions be managed or eased? Rather than demanding respect, perhaps it is sufficient to aim for understanding. One female scholar of religion told us that the religion she studies is "something I absolutely hate. Respect [is] not an option." This person is a convinced feminist, and she is an expert in a religion that is sometimes violently patriarchal. It would be absurd to demand that she "respect" this particular religious community, but she understands how it operates and is exploring the realistic possibilities (and impossibilities) of coexistence and change.

Teaching toward this kind of familiarity is not an easy task. Anyone can memorize facts about religion; familiarity often requires some kind of personal adjustment. For religious believers, ex-religious believers, and nonreligious believers alike, gaining familiarity can require the bracketing of their own ideas and ideals. Amanda Porterfield, who teaches religion at Florida State University, says that each semester a few of her students "come to class eager to defend the truth claims of their own religion and to explain why beliefs other than their own are false or even wicked." A colleague told her that the remedy was to require those students "to check their religious beliefs at the door." Porterfield laughed at the idea that religion could be treated as if it "was a hat or coat someone could simply take off and come back for later," but she sympathizes with the sentiment.[11] Studying religions fairly does require some distance from one's own ideas about what religion is or ought to be. Barry Hankins, professor of religion and American culture at Baylor University, explains: "The trick is for [religious] insiders to think critically about their own tradition, while the trick for [religious and secular] outsiders is to try to develop a feeling of affinity for the group he or she is studying."[12]

This same insider/outsider dynamic affects professors too, as they decide how much of their own views and values to bracket within their teaching. Christians comprise America's overwhelming religious majority, and many professors from Christian backgrounds told us they tried to distance themselves from their own religiosity when they were teaching, and especially when they were teaching about other religions. One professor said, "I have to hide my Baptist identity or I can't teach other traditions without being suspect... [so] when I teach Buddhism I teach as if I am a Buddhist and when I teach Hinduism I teach as if I am a Hindu." His job, as he perceived it, was to describe all religions as fairly and neutrally as possible, setting aside his own predispositions and explaining the views of whatever religion was being studied in the best light possible. On numerous occasions, Christian professors, mostly white males, told us that their classroom renderings of various religions were so compelling that their students became convinced they were followers of those religions. Other scholars—mostly women and people of color—questioned whether anyone could be quite so neutral or convincing when teaching about another religion.

Professors affiliated with non-Christian religions have additional challenges, especially when they are teaching courses dealing with their own traditions. A number of them told us that students who enroll in their courses often do so expecting to learn from an "insider." A Hindu professor of Hindu studies described how she revels in this role: "I dress in a sari when I teach so they know who I am from the minute I walk in the door, and sometimes I speak like a Hindu goddess to get my points across." She said students loved it, but she acknowledged that there was some danger in her approach: "Students tend to accept anything I say about Hinduism as if it is absolutely true. So I work at having them develop critical capacities about Hinduism." She wants her students to recognize and appreciate the many different ways that Hinduism can present itself, not just the one she embodies. Teaching toward religious literacy at the level of familiarity is never a rote process. It involves a complex dialectic of engagement and disengagement, of heightened self-awareness held in tension with a willingness (at least sometimes) to let go of one's identity and step into someone else's world. It means suspending judgment, but at the same time it requires critical thinking.

Religious Literacy 3: Assessment

The point of religious literacy as familiarity is to avoid judgment; the point of religious literacy as assessment is to render the judgments that are sometimes required. Robert Orsi, former professor of American religions at Harvard and current professor of Catholic studies at Northwestern University in Illinois, has spent a lifetime trying to understand religions on their own terms. His book *The Madonna of 115th Street* (1988) is a classic, up-close-and-personal, ethnographic study of religion, a touching, compelling, and sympathetic look inside an immigrant Italian Catholic community in New York City. Despite his skill as an ethnographer, Orsi has recently written that it "seems to be virtually impossible to study religion without attempting to distinguish between its good and bad expressions."[13] People cannot bracket *all* their convictions *all* the time. Their beliefs creep in. Somewhere, sometimes, often unconsciously slithering their way into the words or actions of professors, judgments are made. And at times, both professors and students enthusiastically embrace their own judgments about religion.

The events of September 11, 2001, led many people to conclude that making judgments about good and bad forms of religion is an imperative. Taking up that challenge, Charles Kimball, a Baptist minister who was then teaching religion at Wake Forest University, wrote a book called *When Religion Becomes Evil* (2002), which describes five indicators or warning signs that a religion is turning evil: making absolute truth claims, encouraging blind obedience, identifying one specific period of time as a critical moment when religious believers have to act, promoting the idea that a "good" end justifies extreme means, and declaring holy war. Reviews of the book were overwhelmingly positive. A blurb on the back cover by Diana Eck, the distinguished academician who directs Harvard's Pluralism Project, called it "a bold, powerful, truth-telling analysis of the ways in which religion can become destructive." *Publishers Weekly* named it the best religion book of the year, saying that "Kimball's clear and steady voice provides helpful guidance for those trying to understand why evil is perpetuated in the name of religion."[14]

Obviously, the book hit a nerve. People want to know how to distinguish good religion from bad, and the book provided a starting point for overdue discussions.

But its list of five items may be a little too simple. More problematically, the warning signs function appropriately only some of the time. "Blind" obedience is bad, but surely there are times when religious (or secular) people need to take a stand for what they believe is genuinely right and true (e.g., the American Civil Rights Movement). How is blind obedience to be distinguished from steadfast courage in the face of opposition? Are there not critical moments when action is required, times when failing to act results in irreparable tragedy (e.g., the failure of German Christians to speak out against the Holocaust)? Are people like the patriots of the American Revolution to be declared religiously evil because they waged war in defense of their deep values? The book's title itself raises concern. It does not refer to why religions sometimes go wrong or why religious people sometimes do bad things, it purports to describe when religion becomes *evil*. "Evil" is a powerful word, a dangerous imprecation against those to whom it is applied. Bad or wrong actions can be *corrected*, but evil typically needs to be *destroyed*. To label someone or something as evil is to demonize it, putting it in a category of otherness where the rules of normal life do not apply, where the end often does justify almost any means, and where responses like torture might become acceptable. Surely this is an unfortunate title for a book that aims at making the world more religiously peaceful.

Assessments at this level of good and evil are not likely the kind of assessments that most professors want to encourage in their classrooms. Academic inquiry usually involves some degree of nuance and some awareness of irony. Thus, in the process of assessing one or another form of religion, students and scholars alike may suddenly discover that they themselves have become the observed. Scrutinizing the life of "the other" places one's own life under scrutiny. That experience can be both clarifying and disorienting—clarifying because the particularity of one's own values is revealed, disorienting because the firm moral or intellectual ground on which one takes a stand can suddenly feel much less stable. In such a situation, the task of assessment becomes rather more complicated, transformed into a process of conversation and discernment that involves risk, responsibility, and decision-making that is rarely if ever reached with absolute certainty. To some degree, this is precisely the aim of college and university education: to help students understand, as former Princeton president Harold T. Shapiro explains, "that most decisions, in public or private life, are bathed in ambiguity and uncertainty," and yet such decisions must still be made.[15]

Assessment is sometimes necessary and often unavoidable, but it is a process that requires humility, not arrogance. Religious literacy as assessment is not easy to teach and, for the most part, it will only rarely be the main objective of any course or classroom discussion. But if it is lacking entirely, if the issue of assessment never comes into focus at all, then the teaching of religion is doomed to remain mostly a superficial enterprise. The real powers and dangers of religion lie beneath the surface. Good education may require educators to ask hard questions at some points—questions that can lead to vehement disagreements about the world's historic religions and their varied influences in the world.

Student Outcomes and Institutional Settings

It is important to keep in mind that teaching toward religious literacy is teaching about religion as it empirically exists in the world. This is a relatively objective undertaking. It is about religion as a focus of study and not about religion as a source or expression of one's own personal convictions (a matter discussed in chapter nine). Of course, studying religion as it exists in the world is a matter of studying human beings. It is people who say, do, think, and feel religion, and, as in any other area of inquiry that focuses on human beings (e.g., history, sociology, psychology, literature, the arts, and anthropology as well as law, medicine, and business), subjectivity is necessarily interjected into the process. People are subjective beings, and that applies both to the people being examined and the people doing the examining. Taking that subjectivity into account is necessary if the study of religion is to be fair, realistic, and empirical.

The good news is that studying religion—at the levels of facts, familiarity, and assessment—has the same potential for objectivity as any other subject in the humanities or social sciences. Religions are not infinitely plastic; they have describable characteristics that persist through time. What counts as literacy about religion should therefore theoretically be the same, regardless of the context in which religion is being taught. Knowing the facts about historic religions, acquiring an empathetic understanding of the lived realities of those religions, and developing the capacity to critically assess religion will (or should be) the same, whether the educational process is situated at a public, private, or church-related institution of higher education. Similarly, the level of religious literacy that is attained (or should be attained) is independent of whether the student is focused on his or her own religious tradition or the religious beliefs, practices, and traditions of others. Literacy is literacy. It is a matter of knowing religion as it empirically exists, and measures of religious literacy apply the same way everywhere, just as measuring literacy in a language is the same everywhere for everyone. The desired objective is always the same: the ability to observe, understand, and intelligently discuss different expressions of religion as they actually exist in the world.

We should recognize that commonality does not translate into easy decisions about content. As with any academic subject involving human behavior, the possibilities are legion. American educators in the eighteenth and nineteenth centuries, and even well into the twentieth century, were quite willing to limit religious content in their classrooms almost entirely to the Judeo-Christian tradition and the biblical text, but that is not an option in the religiously pluriform world of today. A case can be made for first acquiring knowledge about the Western Judeo-Christian tradition because of its historic role in American culture, but religious literacy for contemporary university students must include the whole spectrum of world religions.

Many colleges and universities are already taking steps to increase religious literacy. Religion is gaining popularity as a subject of study, and programs in religious studies have experienced a growth spurt in recent years. Between 1995 and 2005, the overall number of college and university courses focusing on religion rose by 22 percent, and the number of religious studies majors increased by 40 percent. There are currently about 50,000 students majoring in religion nationwide. Courses on Christianity and the Bible still constitute a majority of all religion courses, but they are declining in number, while the number of courses dealing with other religions is on the rise. During the five-year period from 2000 to 2005, there was a doubling in the number of course offerings on Islam and Hinduism. The matrix of institutions choosing to offer classes about religion is also expanding. In the past, private and church-related colleges and universities had a near-monopoly on religion courses, but an increasing number of public universities now offer coursework in religious studies, including roughly 40 percent of all community colleges.[16]

The American Academy of Religion (AAR) is currently developing guidelines for the religious studies major that are intended to distinguish it from other disciplines, such as history, philosophy, sociology, and theology. The AAR claims that there is a "growing consensus about the characteristics of the religious studies major," which is, by its very nature, intercultural and comparative, multidisciplinary, critical, integrative, creative, and constructive.[17] The AAR also recognizes that there is "continuing debate about the appropriate content of the religious studies major," in part because it is a relatively new and evolving academic discipline.[18] Successful development of these guidelines is crucial, because some of those who major in religious studies are likely to be key players in shaping the way that religion is presented to future generations of undergraduates.

Although interest in religious studies is increasing, it is also true that only a very small percentage of students will choose it as their college major. To raise the level of religious literacy among all undergraduates will require other changes. This might mean modifying general education classes so they pay more attention to religion, or it might mean adding the study of religion to a multitude of other academic programs and disciplinary majors, ranging from art to business to history to psychology. Every college and university is limited in the amount of time, money, and scholarly expertise it can devote to the study of religion. No institution can teach everything, and attaining "complete" religious literacy is impossible, but religion is a topic that educators must address.

American higher education is housed in a menagerie of institutions, each with its own identity and uniquely diverse student body, and with particular goals related to religious literacy. Each educational institution will have to decide for itself how much attention should be given to facts, familiarity, and assessment in its own working definition of religious literacy. Many public institutions will be interested in the development of religious literacy mainly for the purpose of promoting multicultural understanding and civic tranquility. Private liberal arts schools may be more prone to situate religious literacy within the humanities, as part of studying what it means to be human. Some church-related colleges and universities may give attention to religious literacy primarily as a resource for student self-reflection and the development of personal convictions. But whatever emphases, methodologies, and expected competencies are adopted, there will likely be a broad convergence with regard to the underlying rationale: In the contemporary world, religion is simply too visible and influential to ignore.

6

Interfaith Etiquette

*What are appropriate ways to interact with those of
other faiths?*

WHEN STUDENTS OF differing religions interact on a college or university
campus, the outcomes are not always predictable. William Willimon, former
chaplain at Duke University, remembers a nervous call from the parents of a
Southern Baptist boy whose romance with a Muslim girl appeared to be getting
serious. "Talk to him," they pleaded. So Willimon called their son into his office
and asked about the relationship. Thomas, the student involved, said he was
indeed in love with a young Muslim woman and the two planned to wed soon
after graduation. The conversation continued:

WILLIMON: "Tell me what brought you together."
THOMAS: "We had so very much in common."
WILLIMON: "Thomas, you're from South Carolina...and Baptist. She's a
     Muslim...from Ohio. What in the world could you possibly have in
     common?"
THOMAS: "Well, you know me—I don't drink on weekends and I don't
     believe in casual sex. And I'm not really into the success-at-any-cost thing.
     She was the only girl I met who has the same values as mine."[1]

Not all collegiate interfaith encounters are so congenial. For example, the Irvine
campus of the University of California has been dealing for several years with tension between its Jewish students and their off-campus supporters and its Muslim
students and their off-campus supporters. The tension peaked in February
2010 when the Israeli ambassador was speaking on campus and was repeatedly

interrupted by members of the Muslim Student Union (MSU). Muslim students said they were simply exercising their right to free speech and expressing dismay over the treatment of Palestinians in Israel, but to Jewish students, those interruptions seemed disrespectful, pre-planned, and anti-Semitic, and were, in essence, a form of hate speech. The university suspended the MSU for a time, but resentments still smolder.

These two stories—a private matter at Duke and a public one at UC Irvine—illustrate the range of interfaith relationships that exist on college and university campuses today. The vast majority of interfaith interactions on campuses fall somewhere in between these extremes—students are neither falling in love nor screaming curses at each other—but regardless of whether interactions are dramatic or mundane, they call for more attention to be paid to interfaith etiquette. Etiquette in this context does not refer simply to specific expectations at occasional social events like the wedding of a friend of a different faith. Instead, we use the term broadly to describe an ongoing self-awareness and awareness of others that puts people at ease rather than on edge. Good etiquette does not come naturally; it requires learning from others what offends and what is welcoming.

Religious Diversity: The National Numbers and Experiences

Interfaith relationships on campuses are taking place within a wider national context in which the American religious profile is changing rapidly (see Figure 6.1). In 1900, America was still an overwhelmingly Protestant place: Protestants outnumbered the next largest religious group (Catholics) by more than five to one. Only 2 percent of the population belonged to "other religions," and only 1 percent identified themselves as secular or nonreligious. Seven decades later, in 1970, the numbers had noticeably shifted. More than 90 percent of the population remained Christian (66 percent Protestant, 23 percent Catholic, and 2 percent other Christians, mostly Mormon and Orthodox), but members of "other religions" (almost all of them Jews) had doubled to 4 percent, and the percentage of nonreligious Americans had risen from 1 percent to 5 percent. Since then, the changes have accelerated. Today, only 78 percent of the American population is Christian (51 percent Protestant, 24 percent Catholic, and 3 percent other Christians) and 5 percent belong to "other religions." Among these other religions, Judaism remains the largest group, but Islam, Hinduism, and Buddhism—which were mere blips on the demographic screen in 1970—have grown significantly. The most dramatic change by far, however, is that the nonreligious (or religiously unaffiliated) sector now constitutes 16 percent of the total population.

The experience of religious diversity in America is not, however, a matter of the numbers alone. Changing perceptions also need to be taken into account. Thus, some Christians feel as if they are currently under siege by secular and

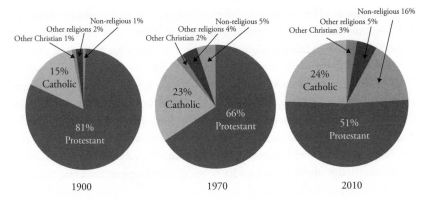

FIGURE 6.1 Changing Demographics of Religion in the USA[2]

non-Christian forces, even though Christianity remains the religion of more than three-quarters of the population. This perception is especially evident within the evangelical world.[3] Non-evangelicals may scoff at those worries given the tremendous political and cultural influence accrued by evangelical Christians in recent years,[4] but evangelicals might counter that the burgeoning number of nonreligious Americans is proof positive that the country is straying from its "Christian roots."

American Jews speak from a very different position. No one doubts that the overall strength of Judaism within the American religious economy has diminished to some degree in recent years. Jews have been present in America almost as long as Christians, and in 1970, they represented more than 3 percent of the American population. Today they account for less than 2 percent, with the decline mostly attributable to religious intermarriage (marrying non-Jews) and assimilation (becoming "just American" and no longer identifying as Jewish). Many Jews now say they feel "bewildered and uncertain" about the future of Judaism in America.[5] Some scholars predict a continuing split in the community with a majority "moving toward religious minimalism and a minority gravitating toward greater participation and deepened concern with religion."[6]

Muslims also feel uneasy about the future, but for different reasons. The American Muslim community has grown tremendously since 1965 when a change in immigration law made it much easier for people to emigrate from Asia. There are currently about 2.5 million Muslims in America (though some estimates are much higher), and about two-thirds of them are recent immigrants.[7] The story of Muslims in America would have been one of unambiguous success, but the terrorist attacks of 9/11 undercut that narrative. Today, many American Muslims feel like they are walking a tightrope, trying to convince other Americans that they are not terrorists, but also aware of continuing public distrust.[8]

Buddhists and Hindus are generally less visible in American society than Jews and Muslims, but they are feeling increasingly at home in the nation. There are about 3 million Buddhists in America, and it has become a mainstream movement.[9] Only one-third of American Buddhists are ethnically Asian; most are Western converts.[10] Hinduism has also grown significantly during the last three decades,[11] but unlike Buddhists, almost all American Hindus are immigrants. Those who come to America often have advanced degrees in science, engineering, technology or computing, and as a group they are doing well economically. But Hindus in America still sometimes feel like religious strangers in a land where public knowledge about India and its religious traditions seems to be obtained mostly from Apu on *The Simpsons*.

Impressions about America's religious diversity, and even the raw numbers themselves, vary greatly from location to location. In New York City, for example, roughly one-third of the population is Jewish[12] and about 10 percent of the public school students are Muslim.[13] Los Angeles has a sizeable Jewish population as well (the second largest in the country), but it is also home to thousands of Buddhists and Hindus and members of almost every other religion on earth. As for Christianity, 78 percent may seem like a huge overestimate to those living in either New England or the Pacific Northwest, where levels of religious devotion and practice are considerably lower than in the nation as a whole, but that number might seem much too low to those living in the Deep South where the regional religious profile remains nearly as Christian and Protestant as the nation was in 1900.[14]

Perhaps the most significant new development in American religion is the expansion of the nonreligious population, a group sometimes referred to collectively as the "nones." The big jump in the number of nones came in the last decade of the twentieth century, when 8 percent in 1990 increased to 14 percent in 2001. Currently, about 16 percent of the population calls themselves nonreligious,[15] but being nonreligious or religiously unaffiliated should not be equated with total disinterest in God or things spiritual. Only 5 percent of Americans say they do not believe in God or a "higher power," and only about one in one hundred is a convinced atheist.[16] The increase in the percentage of nones may be due in no small measure to a shift in American self-consciousness that allows a distinction to be drawn between being "religious" and being "spiritual." However interpreted, the growing size of the nonreligious population clearly signals that Americans' ties to organized religion are loosening and becoming more fluid.

But while American religion may have become more flexible, it has always been in flux. From the Great Awakening of the eighteenth century through bursts of religious creativity in the nineteenth century to the new religious movements of the twentieth century, there have always been Americans who shifted allegiance from one religious group to another, looking for a better religion to follow.

To some degree, this churning is related to Protestantism's influence within American culture, because Protestantism places great emphasis on individual choice and volition. But the volatility of the American religious marketplace is, if anything, increasing, even as the proportion of Protestants in the population shrinks. A recently released national survey shows that almost half the population (44 percent) has changed religious affiliation at least once, and many people have done so numerous times. It is no surprise that Protestants switch allegiances the most, but there is also significant movement back and forth across the line between being religious and being nonreligious: Eighty percent of those who are now nonreligious were raised in some religious tradition, and almost half of the Americans who were raised nonreligious now self-identify as religious. In all this shifting, the Catholic Church has been the single biggest loser. A third of those who were born Catholic have left the church, with roughly half becoming Protestants and the other half becoming unaffiliated. Almost all of this religious switching, regardless of which religions are involved, takes place before the age of twenty-four.[17]

Religion on Campus

Colleges and universities are experiencing the same shifts that are taking place in the larger society, but with greater intensity. As might be expected, the religious profile of entering college students is very similar to that of their parents and the nation as a whole: Seventy-five percent are Christians, 8 percent are members of non-Christian religions, and the rest (17 percent) are religiously unaffiliated.[18] During the college years, this profile slowly changes, and about 15 percent of previously religious students become religiously unaffiliated.[19] In some circles, there is an assumption that this decline is due to the pernicious influence of nonreligious faculty. It is true that college and university professors as a group are less religious than the national population[20] (see Figure 6.2), but blaming faculty for the decline makes little sense given that the falloff in religious affiliation among young adults who do *not* attend college is even greater (20 percent).[21] Whether in college or not, young adults seem to be losing their ties with organized religion, and more than a quarter of all eighteen-to-twenty-three-year-olds now describe themselves as nonreligious (see Figure 6.3). Nonetheless, it is important to note that the great majority of entering college and university students are religious—three-quarters of them report having attended religious services in the previous year (compared to only 40 percent who say they have drunk a beer)[22]—and most remain religious when they leave.

Although the majority of young people remain religiously affiliated whether they attend college or not, young people today tend to wear their religious (and nonreligious) identities lightly. About 40 percent describe themselves as "secure"

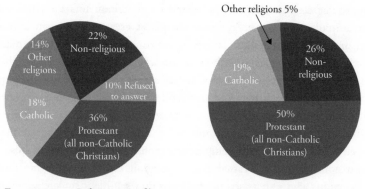

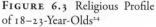

FIGURE 6.2 Religious Profile of College/University Faculty[23]

FIGURE 6.3 Religious Profile of 18–23-Year-Olds[24]

in their faith, while about 20 percent say they are "seeking," 15 percent are "conflicted," and 10 percent are "doubting." Only about 15 percent say they have no interest in religion at all.[25] Nearly half (44 percent) say that religion in some form or another is "very or extremely important" in their daily lives, most (79 percent) have "a lot of respect for organized religion," and most (80 percent) also have "positive feelings" about the religious traditions in which they were raised. These numbers show that the vast majority of students are positively disposed toward religion, but at the same time many of them (42 percent) say that "mainstream religion" is "irrelevant to the needs and concerns of most people my age."[26]

Perhaps the most significant recent change in student perspectives has been with regard to religious exclusivity, the belief that one, and only one, religion is true. Exclusivity is now rejected by a majority (57 percent) of young people. The majority view—that there is truth in many religions—is shared even by 45 percent of evangelical young people and 32 percent of Mormons, two groups that are reputed to insist on the singular truthfulness of their own religions. Young adults are split down the middle (49 percent and 48 percent) about whether it is "okay for religious people to try to convert others." Jews are the most likely to oppose conversion efforts (79 percent), followed by nonreligious students (66 percent) and Catholics (62 percent). Not surprisingly, evangelical Protestants express the greatest support for such efforts, with two-thirds of them approving.[27]

Religious diversity is becoming more pronounced at almost every college and university, but the degree and composition of that diversity varies from school to school based on location, mission, educational programs, student recruitment pool, and pure happenstance. George Mason University in Fairfax, Virginia, represents the kind of student body now found on many public university campuses: Fifteen percent of entering students are adherents of non-Christian religions, and a broad variety of religions are represented in the mix.[28] At private schools, the representation of religious groups on campus varies dramatically from institution to institution. Many church-related colleges and universities are, for example, more Christian in their religious profiles than the nation as a whole. But there are exceptions like Muhlenberg College in Pennsylvania, associated with the Evangelical Lutheran Church in America, where 30 percent of the student body is Jewish (similar to the percentage of Jewish students at places like Tufts, Pratt, George Washington, Harvard, and the University of Pennsylvania).[29] Muslim students also tend to cluster in some institutions rather than others, mostly at schools located in the Northeast and Midwest.[30] Given the varied religious profiles of the nation's colleges and universities, issues of religious diversity will present themselves differently on different campuses, but in one way or another, all institutions of higher learning need to address interfaith issues, because everyone now lives in an interfaith world.

The Etiquette of Face-to-Face Interfaith Relations

College students as a whole are not known for their manners, and yet most of them are skilled social animals. They know how to make friends, how to find their place in the social hierarchy, how to avoid conflict (most of the time), and how to live with roommates not necessarily of their own choosing. And to some degree, they know how to handle diversity, especially when they can see it. But religious diversity presents a unique problem: For the most part, it is invisible. Unless you ask, it might never come up, but offense can still be given. According to a recent survey, 51 percent of Jewish college and university students say they have come in contact with some form of anti-Semitism in the previous three-year period, undoubtedly much of it unthinking. Partly because they have experienced prejudice, most Jewish students want to make sure that they themselves do not discriminate against others. Thus, when asked what they wanted most from the Jewish student organization Hillel, Jewish students did not say they wanted a place where Jews could be by themselves: Eighty percent said they wanted "a welcoming atmosphere for everyone, Jewish or non-Jewish."[31]

Many other students would agree. They do not want religion to be something that separates people, and many of them see no reason why religion should ever be a source of tension or disagreement because, in their minds, there is really nothing much to disagree about. As one student explained: "I think everything has the same principles, you know, obviously we differ in some opinions, that's why there are separate religions. But to have fights and quarrels over religion, you know, [is wrong, since] everyone ultimately wants the same thing in life. I think ultimately the same basic beliefs are active in all these religions."[32] With this kind of all-religions-are-ultimately-the-same assumption, religious diversity is easy to accommodate because it is redefined to be not really an issue at all.

This is a conveniently effective philosophy of interfaith relations, except for one small problem: It isn't true. The world's religions are not all alike.[33]

One student, a member of an American minority religion, told us that many professors have the same head-in-the-sand attitude: "My professors just don't know much of anything about my religion, and they don't seem to want to know more. It's like they would rather make believe we are all the same." Then she added: "But we're not."

Religious differences are real, and because of that, offense can sometimes be given and discomfort can arise even when people are trying to be friendly. For example, evangelical students often feel as if they are being welcoming and hospitable when they invite other students to their meetings, but that is not necessarily how their invitations are experienced. One Jewish student at a public university in the South recalled his discomfort when Christian dorm mates knocked on his door and asked, "Inter-varsity [an evangelical student organization] is tonight, won't you come join us?" He said, "It wasn't anything negative they did, it was just the feeling that there were more of them than me. You know that they don't understand [that] I'm finding myself every week teaching somebody something about Judaism....In a way, you know, that's great—I can teach them, but in a way it's like another part of me is tired."[34] Muslim students report a similarly wearying need to defend or explain themselves. Two researchers from California, Na'ilah Suad Nasir and Jasiyah Al-Amin, said that most of the Muslim students they "talked to had not been actively denigrated, but they felt taxed by the need constantly to manage others' impressions of them," a process so consuming that it sometimes had a negative impact on course work and grades.[35]

Many colleges and universities now have lists of rules that define appropriate interfaith behavior on campus. At Penn State University, the religious "code of ethics" asks students to work with the institution "to create a safe climate where all can practice their religion or spirituality," to eliminate "prejudice, hatred, and violence," and to "promote religious harmony." For most students, this rhetoric may sound overblown, but they generally agree that the campus should be a safe space for everyone, and they have no desire to be violent, disharmonious, or religiously bigoted. There may be an occasional unpleasant episode of prejudice and ignorance, but most students have been taught to be tolerant and have internalized that virtue. The Penn State code of ethics gets interesting when it informs students that "a successful community results only through trust, mutual respect, and the struggle that sharing sometimes requires, as individuals are invited beyond the familiar and across boundaries." This is a call "to recognize differences," and it is precisely the recognition of difference that triggers the need to think self-consciously about interfaith etiquette.[36]

A story from Chapman University in Orange County, California, illustrates the point. In 2004, it closed its old Protestant chapel and opened a new interfaith center that was designed to be a place of worship for people of all faiths. The director of the center, Ronald L. Farmer, sees this as a positive step, a way for Chapman (associated with the Disciples of Christ denomination) to be more welcoming of students from all religions. The problem he has encountered is that most students automatically assume that the center is supposed to be a place where all the world's different religions are blended together. Farmer finds himself constantly needing to explain: "No, no, no—each religion is different."[37] "Interfaith" is not meant to be a new religion that combines and supersedes all others, but rather a place where people from different religions can talk, learn, work together, and sometimes argue about what they share in common and what they do not.

The problem for many college and university students, once they get past the fact that not all religions are alike, is that they simply don't know enough about their own faith traditions to explain them to others. Often, interfaith encounters force students to think more deeply about their own religious traditions even as they learn more about the religions of others. The counselor, Catholic spiritual writer, and teacher (at both Harvard and Yale) Henri Nouwen wrote that "no real dialogue is possible between somebody and a nobody. We enter into conversation with the other only when our own life choices, attitudes, and viewpoints offer the boundaries that challenge strangers to become aware of their own position and to explore it critically." In his view, showing true hospitality to the other requires people to be (or become) "an unambiguous presence, not hiding ourselves behind neutrality but showing our ideas, opinions and life style."[38] But the kind of heart-to-heart conversations lauded by Nouwen are not easy, and many people, including students and educators, feel as if they simply do not have the time or the emotional energy for such conversations.

In this regard, evangelical Christians are both a blessing and a bane for interfaith relations on many campuses. They are a bane, as chaplain after chaplain told us, because many evangelical students have no interest whatsoever in interfaith activities. They do not want to *dialogue* with members of other religions; they want to convert them. But they are also a blessing because they recognize religious differences, they are usually quite articulate about the teachings of their own faith, and they will take the time to engage others. Paul Griffiths, former professor of Catholic Studies at the University of Illinois in Chicago and now at Duke, says the same thing is true about many of his Muslim students. Although they are sometimes assertive to the point of being polemical, his Muslim students have forced him to refine his own thinking and have deepened class discussions, making them feel real and not just theoretical. His conclusion: It is good to have intellectually feisty Muslims (and intellectually feisty members of other religious groups) on campus. After years characterized by the shallow niceness of privatized religion, many campuses have become, in his view, "altogether too frightened of vigorous disagreement about matters of unsurpassable importance."[39] Rather than minimizing differences and encouraging students to keep quiet about their beliefs, some colleges and universities may want to encourage students to explore their own religious traditions more seriously. The educational goal is not to make students more religiously devout, but rather to set the stage for more vigorous and intelligent debate.

If debate is the only or primary mode of interaction, however, that too can be problematic. Suresh Canagarajah, a scholar of applied linguistics and migration studies, explains the concern: "If two people get together and say, 'Let's sit down and debate whose faith is superior,' I think this will lead to a pointless, if not dysfunctional exercise." Instead of debate, Canagarajah says that what is needed is transactional conversation: "If one says: 'I am going through a dark period in my life, and I would like to get your advice,' this is a transactional goal and can lead to a dialogical theological engagement. By the same token, if someone is talking to another only with the intention of converting that person (without relating to the real human needs the other person has), there is nothing shared or transactional about this encounter."[40] Debate is an important and necessary component of college or university learning, but debate by itself is a limited mode of interfaith conversation and often serves only to reinforce existing opinions. Transactional encounters, by contrast, change people and create space for actual friendships to emerge. (The national organization that is most visibly promoting transactional interfaith conversations on college and university campuses today is the Interfaith Youth Core founded by Eboo Patel. This organization connects interfaith etiquette with civic engagement and is discussed in chapter 8.)

Transactional interfaith encounters can be encouraged on college and university campuses in any number of ways, ranging from informal dorm discussions to carefully planned joint service projects. An especially interesting recent example of transactional interfaith engagement occurred at Vassar College. The "Sukkah City project" was a campuswide competition to see who could build the best and most interesting Sukkah (a temporary structure for religious gatherings during the Jewish holiday of Sukkot). Part of what made the project both difficult and appealing is that the rules for constructing a proper Sukkah are fairly extensive. It was not an ordinary student art competition, yet the art majors (many of them not Jewish) took it on with gusto and soon involved many of their friends as well. In the campus newspaper, a student reported that it was "amazing to me personally to see people working so hard on this project who were not Jewish. . . . If there's one thing that this experience taught me, it's that working together as a community is one of the greatest feelings you can possibly experience, perhaps it is even akin to the idea of religious fulfillment."[41] Transactional religious encounters are not required to be serious and sober discussions of difference; sometimes they can just be fun.

Institutional Etiquette: Structures and Ethos

In 2009, more than 20 million students were enrolled in America's roughly 4,500 colleges and universities. The largest campus by far is the online giant University of Phoenix, where 380,000 were enrolled, dwarfing the enrollment of 68,000 students at Arizona State University, the largest bricks-and-mortar campus. But most institutions of higher learning are not huge. Only 13 percent of colleges and universities enroll more than 10,000 students while 39 percent of them enroll fewer than 1,000 students.[42] Roughly 60 percent of all four-year colleges and universities are predominantly residential, and these residential schools educate slightly more than half of all college students currently enrolled in four-year institutions.[43] About one-fourth of the nation's four-year undergraduate institutions are public, one-third of them are religiously affiliated, and around 40 percent are private but nonreligious.[44]

Every college and university, large or small, public or private, religiously affiliated or not, has to make decisions about how to deal with religion. Even online schools have choices to make about matters like religious holidays and religion in the curriculum, but at residential colleges and universities, decisions about what place and role religion should have on campus are especially important. Any number of arrangements are theoretically possible, but we think that virtually all residential schools embody one of six alternative approaches that we label: (1) the free market model; (2) the House of Representatives model; (3) the Senate model; (4) the "state church" model; (5) the one-party rule model; and (6) the homogeneous model.

The Free Market Model: In this model, the structure of religion on campus is determined by the direct action of students. If a predetermined number of students from any religious group requests recognition, they will get it. The free market model treats student religious associations exactly like all other student organizations. In some cases, recognized groups qualify for financial support from the institution. Certain legal rules also apply, most notably antidiscrimination legislation, which sometimes causes tension when conservative religious groups want to restrict membership or leadership on the basis of certain behaviors or beliefs.[45] Some free market campuses provide religious groups with offices and meeting space on campus, but others do not, which often leads to what one faculty member described to us as "the pearl necklace of religious houses ringing the perimeter" of her own public university campus. The main outcome of adopting this model is that historic religion will be visibly present at the institution only to the degree that students themselves organize and demand recognition. Because it dovetails so nicely with the notion of church–state separation, the free market serves as the default approach for most publicly funded colleges and universities.

The House of Representatives Model: Some colleges and universities are more proactive and do not want to wait for students to organize themselves. Instead, the institution itself assumes responsibility for making sure that all religious groups are recognized and accommodated. This approach can take two different forms; one of them is the House of Representatives model in which each religious group, large or small, is given recognition and resources commensurate with its size. Perhaps the easiest place to see this model in action is at the U.S. Air Force Academy (USAFA) in Colorado Springs, where it is built into the campus architecture. The USAFA Chapel is one of the nation's most impressive and recognizable religious buildings. It has a large sanctuary on its upper level for Protestants, who constitute the largest religious group at the Academy. On the lower level, there is a Catholic worship area, perhaps a third as large as the Protestant area, along with smaller meeting rooms for Jews, Buddhists, and Muslims. In the spring of 2011, an outdoor site for pagan worship was established on the hillside above the Chapel.

Policy at USAFA illustrates both the strengths and weakness of this model. The strength is that every religious group on campus has a place to call its own—a place that the institution itself has provided. The weakness is that the larger religious groups can become overbearing because of their more visible power and influence. Several years ago, the Academy came under intense public criticism for allowing evangelical Protestants to promote their faith (and sometimes to denigrate other religions) with little or no check on their behavior. Between 2001 and 2005, fifty-five separate complaints of religious discrimination were filed against the school, and in 2005, the national organization Americans United for Separation of Church and State released a report claiming that the evangelical climate of the campus not only allowed harassment of non-Christians, but was also driving highly qualified potential candidates away from the school.[46] Eventually, the USAFA leadership recognized the seriousness of the situation and took steps to address the problem. When we visited the campus in 2010, everyone we met (including some of those who had filed complaints) agreed that significant progress had been made. The USAFA experience is a warning to schools with this model: Controls need to be in place to ensure that proportional support for religion does not become differential privilege for larger religious groups.

The Senate Model: The Senate model avoids the dangers in proportionality by treating all religious groups exactly the same. All religions present on campus are given the same support and recognition regardless of the size of the group. Groups like Baha'i and Zoroastrianism (the Rhode Islands of American religion) are given the same attention and opportunities as evangelical Protestants (the Texas of American religion). Wellesley College in Massachusetts has been at the forefront in adopting a Senate-style approach, and the Wellesley chaplain has employed the Senate metaphor to describe the school's recent history. He says the transition to a Senate model was not easy: "Initially it was necessary for me to spend a great deal of time working with the Christian community to help them understand that, in the work of religious pluralism, they are one religious community and that the fragmentation of Christianity into denominations was not an excuse for multiple representation." Before the transition, Wellesley's Interfaith Council had fourteen Christian representatives, one Muslim, and one Jew. After the transition, fifteen different religious groups (Baha'i, Buddhist, Christian, Hindu, Jain, Jewish, Muslim, Native African, Native American, Shinto, Sikh, Taoist, Unitarian Universalist, Wiccan, and Zoroastrian) were allowed to have two representatives each.[47]

The Senate model of religious representation guarantees that no one group will dominate the others and that no one group will receive more institutional resources than it is due, but the exaggerated flatness of this model creates other problems. Defining what is and is not a separate religion is a fraught process. For example, Sikhs and Jains are given separate representation at Wellesley, but in India, the global homeland of most Sikhs and Jains, these two religious communities are grouped with Hindus in the legal code. As for Christianity, many people—especially non-Americans—consider Protestantism and Catholicism to be two entirely different religions, but Wellesley does not. On the other hand, Wellesley allots two representatives to Unitarian Universalism, even though this group is sometimes almost indistinguishable from liberal Protestantism in New England. Decisions about the composition of a Senate that represents the diverse religions on campus are inevitably subjective.

The "State Church" Model: This model has also been called the "established church" model.[48] In this model, one university chaplain wears two very different hats, simultaneously overseeing the religious life of the entire campus and also serving as the parish minister of a local on-campus congregation. This is the arrangement that exists at Duke, Harvard, and Princeton. At all of them, the congregations that still meet on their campuses are now ecumenical (or interdenominational), and they seek to welcome everyone and all religious faiths in their worship. However, their chapels remain visibly Christian, and a theologian would likely be able to guess their denominational histories—Congregational at Harvard, Presbyterian at Princeton, and Methodist at Duke. To some people, this state church model seems woefully out of touch with modern sensibilities, a throwback to medieval Europe when one church dictated religious life for everyone. However, the state churches that exist today in places like Scandinavia are not at all coercive, and they are expected to serve the religious needs of the entire society. An "established church" at a university functions in much the same way.

The advantage of the state church model in comparison to the preceding three models lies in its provision of ready-made mechanisms for addressing the spiritual needs of the entire campus community. Colleges and universities are not just learning factories. Symbolically and literally, campuses are communities where people know each other, care for each other, and sometimes experience joys and sorrows together. Especially when tragedies strike, there is a great need for campus-wide commemoration and consolation. No one can forget the photo images of candlelight vigils at Virginia Tech after the tragic shooting that took place there, and anyone who was on an American campus on September 11, 2001, can recall ways that groups came together on their own or were brought together intentionally because everyone needed a place to share their pain, grief, fear, sadness, and confusion.

Campus gatherings during times of crisis seem at some level to be spiritual and religious, and times of celebration can also take on a spiritual or religious aura. At the College of William and Mary, a public university in Williamsburg, Virginia, for example, seniors congregate in the courtyard of the historic Wren complex on the eve of graduation for a ceremony that culminates with hundreds of candles held aloft as the graduating class sings the alma mater. Many other colleges and universities have similar rituals, and all of them represent a kind of de facto, but unarticulated, state church approach to uniting the campus as a community. The state church model makes explicit what is implicit at many other schools: that a sense of community and an appreciation of diversity need not be at odds. A state church approach acknowledges the particularity of the institution and intentionally welcomes religious diversity on campus, but it also provides a structure that allows the spiritual needs of the campus community as a whole to be named and addressed. Of course, there is a downside to adopting the state church model. By definition, it seeks to embody the lowest common denominator of spiritual expression. No matter what choices are made, some constituents will perceive tasteless mush while others will feel that they are being force-fed a stranger's diet.

The One-Party Rule Model: In contrast to the state church model, one-party rule gives special power and pride of place to one specific religion. A single historic religion dominates the campus, although people and programs from a variety of other religious traditions will also be recruited and welcomed. This model is standard at most church-related colleges and universities and covers a spectrum of institutions, ranging from schools like the University of Notre Dame (founded by a Catholic religious order, the Congregation of Holy Cross) where the faculty and student body are quite diverse to places like Brigham Young University (BYU) where the Church of Jesus Christ of Latter-day Saints (the Mormon church) has an overwhelming near-monopoly presence on campus. Non-Mormons account for only 2 percent of the student population at BYU, but a sizeable portion of them are Muslim students attracted by the school's policies prohibiting alcohol and its conservative views on gender and sexuality. Most one-party campuses require all students to take coursework related to the dominant religion. For example, Notre Dame requires two theology courses (taught mostly from a Catholic perspective) and two philosophy courses (which, at Notre Dame, often deal with religious topics). BYU similarly requires three courses in "doctrinal foundation" related to

Mormonism, including one on the Book of Mormon. (For a time, BYU offered non-Mormons a special version of this course, but it was discontinued when the professor who taught the class retired.) Some one-party schools also require students, whether they are members of the dominant religion or not, to attend a certain number of chapel services.

Any entering student who was expecting a flat playing field where all religions are treated equally would be in for a rude awakening upon arriving at a school with one-party rule, but these institutions usually advertise their religious identities quite clearly. New arrivals know what is in store, and outcomes are usually harmonious. Typically, these institutions are committed to ensuring that minority religious groups are shown respect and treated fairly, and they often make significant religious accommodations. BYU, for example, has set aside a separate prayer room for Muslim students. Despite the clear dominance of a single religion, one-party rule schools can be places where people from many different religious traditions are made to feel welcome, if only as honored guests.

The Homogeneous Model: The sixth model is one that seems, at first glance, antithetical to the whole notion of religious diversity. At institutions with a homogeneous model, all faculty members (and, at most of these schools, all students) are required to agree with the school's religious stance. Wheaton College in Illinois fits this description, and departures from orthodoxy are taken seriously by the institution. In 2006, Wheaton fired a philosophy professor because he had converted to Catholicism. (He had previously been Episcopalian.) Despite his conversion, this particular professor said he could still in good conscience sign the college's statement of faith. Leaders at the school asked for his resignation nonetheless because they deemed Catholicism as a religious system to be incompatible with the institution's staunchly Protestant and evangelical faith.[49] But as homogeneous as a place like Wheaton can seem from one perspective, it can seem quite diverse from another. Samuel Schuman, former chancellor of the University of Minnesota, visited the Wheaton campus as research for his book *Seeing the Light* (2010), and students told him how faculty "came from all these different perspectives."[50] And in some sense, they do: Baptist, Episcopal, Pentecostal, and Presbyterian professors work and teach side by side. They are all evangelical, but under that homogeneous umbrella, there are variations in their religious allegiances.

Homogeneous institutions are unapologetic about their lack of religious diversity, and their proponents say it is that very homogeneity that makes them educationally effective. In settings where multiple religions are present, each religion feels compelled to present itself in the best possible light. No one wants to air dirty religious laundry in public. But in religiously homogeneous settings, where everyone is part of the family, religious views can be critically examined. At religiously homogeneous schools, the intellectual underpinnings of a tradition are the subject of vigorous debate and constant refinement, a task for which homogeneous religious schools are precisely suited and one that cannot be easily undertaken by churches, whose focus is usually on worship, nurture, or outreach and not on theological reflection. Homogeneous institutions may be prone to navel-gazing, but some of them have also very intentionally developed curricula and off-campus programs for preparing students to live with others peaceably in a religiously heterogeneous world.

On the surface, the first three structural models—free market, Senate, and House of Representatives—seem more naturally amenable to religious diversity. They seem self-evidently fairer to everyone involved. But, in many cases, these same institutions treat religion as a potential problem that needs to be controlled, instead of seeing it as something that has the potential to enhance learning on campus. The religious needs of students are addressed because they must be, but the goal is typically to manage religion, not to engage it educationally. And careful attention to interfaith etiquette can also be lacking. On such campuses, members of different religious communities have to find their own way and negotiate their differences in much the same way that religion operates in American society as a whole, in an ad hoc manner. Groups might quarrel, cooperate, compete, or just ignore each other, and none of it is of much concern to the institution as long as it doesn't boil over into campus disruption.

However, some colleges and universities that have adopted these first three models have moved beyond this kind of merely bureaucratic oversight; they actively support religion on campus, helping students develop both their faith and interfaith skills. Penn State's exemplary program, combining ethics and religion, has already been mentioned in this regard (see chapter 1). Another example is provided by the University of North Dakota, which has incorporated spirituality into its campuswide wellness program. The university's wellness center website explains: "Whether it is involving yourself in religious activities, meditation, or engulfing yourself with art and music, spiritual wellness is an integral component of wellness. Research has consistently indicated that spirituality cannot only help people recover from serious illness, but it can also help people live longer and enjoy life more."[51] In this case, spirituality is not merely being managed, it is being recommended.

As for the other three models—state church, one-party rule, and homogeneous—there seems to be an inherent bias toward one religion, and thus a demeaning or dismissive posture toward other religions. That may be an accurate observation when applied to some campuses, but structure is not necessarily destiny. Attitudes and ethos also matter. The state church model, for example, can be bent in a more embracing or a more exclusive direction, and members of religious minority communities will likely be able to tell almost immediately which way any particular institution is oriented. But sometimes structural adjustments are needed. At Yale, for example, it was recently decided that the old Protestant state–church model could no longer be stretched wide enough to provide the kind of multifaith welcome the university wanted to offer students.[52] To that end, the role of the "university chaplain" was redefined as a position that focuses on interfaith dynamics, and it is no longer assumed that the university chaplain will be a Protestant. But Yale has also retained a position for a Protestant chaplain, who now reports to the university chaplain and continues to lead the ecumenical worship service at the University Church every Sunday. To some degree, then, the state church model remains intact at Yale even though it has been significantly modified.

Regardless of which one of the six structures is in place, interfaith etiquette on any campus relies on the school's ability and willingness to serve as a good host. The act of hosting recognizes difference (there is, after all, a guest and a host), and it also acknowledges the importance of place. The host welcomes the guest into that place, and a good host is often more attuned to the special needs of guests than to the needs of the household itself. When schools recognize their own particularity, and especially their own religious (or nonreligious) particularity, this hosting function may become more straightforward and more gracious. Awareness of particularity may be especially necessary at those schools where it is assumed that all vestiges of religious bias were eliminated long ago. This point was made clear to us in conversation with a Jewish scholar who had attended one of the most elite and liberally minded private colleges in the Northeast. She described how she had felt overwhelmed by the Protestant demeanor of the place. The school had never been affiliated with any church, but the whole tenor of the institution was Protestant in a New England-secular kind of way. Although she had fond feelings for the school, she was still irritated by the institution's seemingly willful blindness to its own particularity, a particularity that had made her feel like a religious outsider even while the self-congratulating rhetoric of the school endlessly repeated that it was a place where there were no religious insiders or outsiders.

Interfaith Etiquette for the Real World

College and university concerns related to interfaith etiquette largely focus on campus dynamics, but the issue of religious diversity does not end at the campus boundary. Along with everyone else, institutions of higher learning have become more aware of religious practices in the "real world." The religious dimension of public life was often ignored by colleges and universities during the twentieth century, but that is no longer a plausible option for educators. The vast majority of the world's people are religious, and as the globe shrinks, all of these religious people are in much closer contact, and there are more instances of interfaith tension and violence. This is the real world that graduates will inhabit, and many colleges and universities want to prepare students not only to understand that world but also to be agents of interfaith peacemaking in that world. Ultimately, it is the religious communities themselves that have to learn how to get along, but colleges and universities can play a significant role both by contributing to the education of future religious leaders and by providing the world's religious communities with places for dialogue and partners who can help them sort through interfaith issues.

The University of Southern California (USC) is one school that has enthusiastically embraced this interfaith role. Located in south-central Los Angeles, USC reflects the messy vibrancy of life that is Los Angeles itself, and the faculty with whom we spoke described the school as an entrepreneurial place where vision and talent are rewarded. That attitude is in keeping with the school's official motto, which was adopted in 1908: *palmam qui meruit ferat.* "Let those who bear the palm [the Greco-Roman symbol of victory] earn it." USC is a place of action, not just ivory tower theorizing, and it excels in fostering learning at the untidy edges where academia and real life meet.

Like many other academically acclaimed universities, USC has a vibrant Office of Religious Life that oversees a wide range of student programs designed to foster spiritual wholeness, moral reasoning, personal responsibility, a sense of community, and reflection on religious commitment within the context of religious pluralism. The staff of the Office of Religious Life clearly communicates a pluralistic, interfaith commitment. Rather than being led by a pleasantly liberal Protestant minister, which is still the norm at most elite universities, the dean of religious life at USC is Varun Soni, an affable young Hindu lawyer, the first Hindu to hold this kind of position at any college or university in the country. His predecessor, Rabbi Susan Laemmle, was the first Jew to hold the lead chaplaincy position at a major American university. USC's commitment to religious pluralism in its staffing provides its students, and notably its Christian students, with an opportunity to work alongside leaders who are religiously different from themselves.

USC's commitment to interfaith education, however, reaches far beyond the campus and engages directly with historic religious communities. The Casden Institute for the Study of the Jewish Role in American Life (founded in 1998) "supports research that aims to spur dialogue and achieve greater understanding not only about what it means to be Jewish in America but what it means to be American in a pluralistic society."[53] Since 2005, USC has also been home to the Institute for Advanced Catholic Studies, which is "rooted firmly in Catholic tradition and thought, and dedicated to ecumenism and interreligious dialogue," with a mission of helping "move the [Catholic] Church thoughtfully into the 21st Century."[54] More recently still (in 2008), USC launched the Center for Muslim-Jewish Engagement, which has the goal of promoting grassroots and academic partnerships between the two religions, and the American Muslim Civic Leadership Institute (AMCLI), which seeks to promote democracy by developing "human capital and leadership potential among American Muslims."[55] The AMCLI is housed within the Center for Religion and Civic Culture, which was organized in 1996 to oversee dozens of research projects and community partnerships designed both to strengthen religious communities and to help them interact more constructively with each other and with society as a whole.[56]

USC is not alone in providing university leadership related to interfaith etiquette in the real world. Harvard's Pluralism Project makes available a wealth of resources for understanding other religions and encouraging interfaith cooperation.[57] The Kroc Institute for International Peace Studies at the University of Notre Dame is another significant center, helping religious and nonreligious leaders alike learn how to negotiate differences and facilitate more peaceable social and political relations. Yale University has begun a Faith and Globalization Initiative, launched in 2008 in cooperation with former British Prime Minister Tony Blair. Finally, at least one school, Soka University in Orange County, California (a school that describes itself as "founded on the Buddhist principles of peace, human rights and the sanctity of life"[58]), has opted to function as one large experiment in interfaith, intercultural education. By design, half its students are citizens of the United States and half are international students.

The outcomes of intercultural, interfaith education can be significant even when the articulated goals are modest. Kwame Anthony Appiah, a philosopher who teaches at Princeton University and who has written extensively on the topic of cosmopolitanism, says that intercultural "conversation does not have to lead to consensus about anything, especially not values; it's enough that it helps people get used to one another."[59] That is also a reasonable goal for interfaith etiquette. The goal is not to have everyone agree on anything, and it is also not to remove all sense of difference. But if people can "get used to one another," then they may be able to live amicably together despite their differences and disagreements. To ignore religious difference is to potentially allow socially destructive, interreligious hatred and misunderstanding to fester.

The future of the world depends on people of differing faiths developing the capacity to cooperate and work with each other, and American higher education can have a significant part in building that capacity. Many campuses now function something like experimental communities where students of differing faiths are learning how to relate to each other as friends and colleagues and not just as religious "others." Nowhere else do members of differing religious traditions mingle as freely, talk with each other as honestly, or engage with each other more easily. Encouraging good interfaith etiquette on campus may be a modest goal for a college or university, but it holds the potential to change the world.

7

Framing Knowledge

*What assumptions and rationalities—secular or religious—
shape the way we think?*

THE MODERN UNIVERSITY is founded on the principle of *sapere aude* ("dare to know"). This phrase was made famous by Immanuel Kant in his essay "What is Enlightenment?" (1783), which argued against a reliance on long-dead authorities and religious dictates in making decisions about what is and is not true. According to Kant, it was time for humanity to emerge from its self-imposed childhood, and for individuals to think and reason for themselves.[1] In 1896, Andrew Dickson White, the cofounder and long-time president of Cornell University, picked up this same theme in his lengthy book *A History of the Warfare of Science with Theology*.[2] His argument was not against religion per se, as he considered himself to be a religious individual; it was against "theology." For White, theology meant dogma, and dogma meant religion telling scholars what to think, how to do their work, and what conclusions to draw. That kind of religion, he said, had no place in the academy.

White's concerns were recently rehashed in public when President Obama appointed Francis Collins to be director of the National Institutes of Health (NIH).[3] Collins had supervised the groundbreaking Human Genome Project, so his academic credentials were unquestioned, but he is also an outspoken evangelical Christian who has written about the ways in which science and his faith are related.[4] There was concern about whether his religious views might influence and distort his work as head of the NIH, and some critics asserted that a deeply religious person could not be a reasonable, fair-minded broker of scientific investigation and discovery. In their way of thinking, science is rational and religion is not, so the appointment of anyone as religiously devout as Collins is a self-evident mistake. Such a stance is, however, not compatible with Kant's dictum of daring to know. If dogmatic religion (religion that is unwilling to reconsider its views regardless of contrary evidence) is antithetical to the work of the academy, so too is a secularist posture that would refuse to examine ideas simply because they originated from a person who is religious. When secular ways of thought take on this demeanor, they themselves become as intransigently dogmatic as any kind of religion, setting up precisely the kinds of intellectual roadblocks that Kant sought to dismantle.

The job of colleges and universities is to articulate, examine, and judge whether any particular idea (regardless of its affinity to religion) is worthy of being called knowledge. Higher education does not have an absolute monopoly on the task of framing knowledge, but more than any other topic discussed in this book, framing knowledge is the distinctive responsibility of colleges and universities. There are other institutions besides colleges and universities—churches, synagogues, mosques, and temples—that have more direct concerns with historic religion, and individuals themselves are ultimately responsible for their own personal religion. The *practices* of public religion also fall largely outside the purview of the academy, situated in politics and social action. But the adjudication of public ideas is the responsibility of the academy. It is in the university that society's ideas are tested and assessed. Thus the title of this chapter begins with a gerund, a verbal construction, to signal its difference from the other chapters in the second section of this book which are titled with simple nouns. Framing knowledge is not just a "site of engagement," it describes the university's defining activity.

The use of the term "framing" in relation to knowledge is meant to communicate several different connotations. In the simplest sense of the word, to frame something is to build or construct. Carpenters frame houses and scholars frame knowledge— they build it from the ground up through careful observation, planning, reflection, experimentation, and logic. The word framing can also, however, be used in a different sense, meaning to set in context. People frame arguments not merely by making a logical case for what they believe, but also by situating their arguments within various larger schools of thought and social developments. Framing knowledge in this sense of the term does not focus directly on facts and data, but on how facts and data are interpreted—and there are inevitably alternative interpretations or framings of knowledge for any given set of inputs. Finally, framing can also mean to position evidence falsely so that an erroneous conclusion is reached or an innocent person seems guilty of a crime, as in the plaint of the accused in a murder mystery who cries, "I didn't do it, I was framed." Everyone agrees that framing as falsifying evidence has no place in the academy, but almost every scholar also knows how easy it is to fall into this trap. When analyzing the ideas of people with whom we disagree, it is hard not to frame those ideas in the worst light possible, while we simultaneously frame our own thinking in the best light.

The Complex Framing of Knowledge

How knowledge is framed—both how it is formed and how it is surrounded with interpretation, contestation, and sometimes misrepresentation—has become a complex phenomenon in the contemporary academy. Not that long ago, at the dawn of the twentieth century, things looked easier. Positivism was then the reigning philosophy, and it was widely assumed that the construction of knowledge was something like building a house. The point was to collect as many solid building blocks of truth (facts) as possible and then to fashion them together into a house of knowledge. What mattered in this task was dispassionate skill, not the passions of faith, fervor, or personal reward. According to the early twentieth-century German sociologist Max Weber, scholarship required an academic form of asceticism. Like monks, scholars were to subject themselves to the "discipline" of their particular fields of study and to obey the methodological rules of their academic order. Everything was to be "governed by the logic of the academic disciplines, never from purposes external to them, much less from inclination or pursuit of pleasure."[5] In Weber's mode of framing knowledge, each discipline had its own highly refined and subject-specific way to discover facts and methodically connect those facts together.

There is no disputing the success of this discipline-focused system of research and knowledge production. Humanity now knows vastly more about the world than it did a century ago, or even a decade ago, and much of it is the result of painstaking, striving-to-be-as-objective-as-possible research into very narrow and tightly defined areas of inquiry. Specialization works, but the limitations of this approach have also become increasingly visible. As persons trained to see the world through the lenses of one, and only one, discipline, many scholars become functional reductionists. To a hammer, the whole world may look like a nail, or so the saying goes, and to many scholars, the whole world can sometimes begin to look like the discipline or sub-discipline they study. To a biologist, the world functions biologically. To an economist, the world is defined by the interplay of economic concerns. To a literary critic, the world is a jumble of overlapping plots and narratives. To a political scientist, the world is about politics and power relationships. With specialization, there are fewer experts with the ability or the academic willingness to conceptualize knowledge in terms beyond their own disciplines.

A second concern is that the Weberian, positivist view of knowledge misunderstood how pliable "facts" can be. Rather than being impermeable little nuggets of truth, facts in many disciplines are much softer and more pliable than people had originally expected. No longer anticipating that they will immediately ascertain the world as it really is, scholars study the world through the particular lenses, both physiological and ideological, that they happen to have available to them. The first inklings of this new point of view were articulated in the early twentieth century by people like Karl Mannheim when positivism was still the dominant posture.[6] By the 1960s, however, the tide was beginning to turn, and the publication of Thomas Kuhn's *The Structure of Scientific Revolutions* can be taken as symbolic of this shift.[7] Kuhn argued that science progresses not just incrementally on the basis of new facts and logic, but sometimes dramatically on the basis of a changed perspective or a new paradigm. In other words, facts and logic do not explain everything that we count as knowledge. Fashion, whim, and passion also play roles, as does academic lassitude or what the philosopher Richard Rorty once described as "what your contemporaries let you get away with."[8]

Feminists, multiculturalists, and postmodern scholars have been driving this point home for nearly half a century now. All forms of knowledge, they say, are tinged with human subjectivity and situatedness, and sometimes public "knowledge" is also deformed by class interests, personal privilege, and sheer prejudice. The simplest words employed to describe reality are sometimes dripping with bias. Feminists pointed out, for example, that the study of "man" is hardly a fair or neutral way of describing the examination of human history and to say that someone is a "seminal" thinker codes into scholarship a host of beliefs about male activity versus female passivity. Because all knowledge is tinted (or tainted) in this way, many scholars, and feminists in particular, now begin their academic presentations with some explanation of the researchers' own background, assumptions, and intentions, so that these factors can be taken into account in assessing their work. This does not mean that personal predilections now determine everything in the academy—that is certainly not true—but it does mean that, in addition to assessing the validity of arguments and the reliability of data, it often makes sense to ascertain where a scholar is coming from and what experiences and commitments may have shaped the way that person sees reality and interprets it.

This is part of what was going on when scholars questioned the appointment of Francis Collins to lead the NIH, but the other dynamic at work was power. People wondered how Collins would use his power as head of the NIH to shape the production of knowledge. Exploring the ways in which power and knowledge intertwine was the central focus of concern for the French theorist Michel Foucault. His conclusion was that "power and knowledge directly imply one another...there is no power relation without the correlative constitution of a field of knowledge, nor any knowledge that does not presuppose and constitute at the same time power relations."[9] These kinds of connections between power and knowledge are obvious to anyone today whose research project requires financial support. In particular, external funding now drives much of the research agenda in the sciences. Recently, there have been widely publicized skirmishes over environmental research, especially related to climate change, and some scientists have even been sued over their reported findings.[10] In educational areas far removed from the sciences, external funding can also shape teaching and research outcomes. Recently, for example, Guilford College, a small liberal arts school in North Carolina with historic roots in the social-justice traditions of the Society of Friends (Quakers), agreed to require its business majors to read the pro-capitalist, virtue-of-selfishness writings of Ayn Rand in exchange for a donation of $500,000 spread over ten years.[11]

To contemporary scholars, it now seems obvious that framing knowledge is a complex and fraught process. There are some relatively stable bits of data (facts) about which everyone agrees, and some theories are supported by so much evidence as to seem functionally indisputable, but much of what counts as knowledge today can be seen as "true" only after a particular interpretive approach or frame of knowledge has been adopted. Knowing requires making choices, and the pursuit of knowledge has become a matter of what the philosopher Ludwig Wittgenstein once described as "passionately seizing hold of *this* interpretation" of reality rather than another.[12] Wittgenstein's quote is especially interesting in the context of this chapter, however, because it was originally used in reference to religion, not knowledge, but today it applies equally to knowledge. Gone are the days of Weberian asceticism; scholarship has become a matter of passion as well as intellect. Scholars seize hold of one particular understanding of one part of the world, and they often defend their perspectives with religion-like ardor and argument. They fight and scrap with those with whom they disagree, sometimes haggling over minor points of interpretation. In the extreme, they denounce each other as academic imposters or heretics.

There is no doubt that religion too is a passionate affair—almost all forms of religion involve some leap of faith beyond what may be tightly, logically deduced from "the facts"—but religion is rarely pure passion. It is also a matter of observation, reflection, assessment, and, yes, rationality. Like anyone else who has a point of view, religious believers think, they evaluate options, they make choices about what they consider to be better and worse interpretations of reality, they debate with themselves and others, and sometimes they change their views based on new evidence and improved arguments.[13] Religious believers can be, at times, bullheaded and dogmatic, but this is true of nonreligious individuals and scholars as well, who sometimes cling tenaciously to their perspectives long after the preponderant body of evidence and logic points in a different direction. Religiously influenced scholarship is no different than scholarship that is influenced by any other passion or perspective—and in today's world, academicians recognize that every form of scholarship or knowledge is influenced or framed in some way.

Two Styles of Intellectual Engagement: Monist and Pluralist

Regardless of the specific contents of their views, contemporary intellectuals (religious and nonreligious alike) participate in the creation and evaluation of knowledge in one of two distinct styles: either as monists or as pluralists. Monists, as the name implies, view the world primarily through a single lens. To use another metaphor, their perceptions and interpretations of reality are strained through one particular sieve of foundational principles, methodological commitments, modes of rationality, and habits of thought. This is the default way that thinking proceeds for people in general and for most professors as well. Typically, scholars are nurtured into the monistic thinking of their different academic disciplines during graduate school, and they continue to view the world through those lenses for the rest of their careers. Monists do not necessarily claim that their particular take on reality is the one and only way to properly understand the world, but they are not looking for alternatives. They know where they live intellectually, and they are convinced that their monistic frames of reference provide helpful and accurate information about the world, along with intellectual questions sufficient for a lifetime. Pluralists, by contrast, eschew singularity, convinced that reality is far too complex to be captured adequately by any one philosophical or methodological point of view. Pluralists have no permanent intellectual address. They are cognitive backpackers, always looking for new ways of seeing the world and forever questioning the sufficiency of current orthodoxies. For monists, the dynamic of the academy is best described as one of competition between alternative, comprehensive paradigms; for pluralists, the academic enterprise is a much more fluid, never-ending, always-in-revision exploration of the world that values many kinds of data along with alternative modes of comprehension and explanation.

The single lens through which a monist views the world can be highly complex and subject to ongoing debates over accuracy, comprehensiveness, and coherence, but monists are constitutionally committed to mapping reality by means of a single intellectual grid. For a monist, the study of the world should not eventuate in an awkwardly stitched-together patchwork of oddly shaped stuff—something pluralists could live with easily—but rather in a smoothly woven fabric in which everything comports naturally with everything else. Some monists become so thoroughly convinced of the rightness of their own particular vision of the world that they dismiss all others as intellectually deficient, if not morally corrupt. When religious monists do this sort of thing, they are often labeled dogmatists; when scientific monists adopt this kind of stance, it is called "scientism," since they are claiming "that science is the only valid way toward knowledge, and that it can be used to interpret all other forms of knowledge."[14]

Academic pluralists often seem a bit irritated when they encounter the monist's dogged intellectual commitment to one particular interpretation of the world. Some of the intellectual pluralists with whom we spoke told us quite bluntly that they thought monism no longer had any valid place in the academy because it is simply wrong. Reality, they assert, is so obviously complex that only an intellectual dolt would be attracted to monism. Not so, says the literary critic Wayne Booth, who argues that monists have a vitally important role to play in the academy. He explains that a person is "lucky if, somewhere along the line, [he or she] finds a really able monist, one who knows what he knows and why, who is not afraid to teach what he knows, and who knows how to show its radical difference from the benighted ideas of all other critics."[15] Intellectual monists are eager to point out any sloppiness of evidence and to ruthlessly expose any slips of logic, forcing their opponents (both pluralists and monists of other stripes) to defend their views with much more care and precision than otherwise might be the case. Such encounters, according to Booth, are a boon to the academy because they prompt advances in thinking.

Monisms as Competing Worldviews

In recent years, perhaps the most self-aware monists in the academy have been evangelical Christians, scholars who ascribe to a particular brand of conservative Protestantism.[16] They revel in the term "worldview," a single compound word that is used to describe the sum total of a person's pre-formed attitudes, beliefs, affections, and habits of mind. They assume that everyone possesses a worldview in this sense of the term and that scholarship will be honest and open only when worldviews are made explicit, both to oneself and to others.[17]

Intellectuals who are not evangelicals are less likely to use the compound word, and refer instead to "world view," written as two separate words and signifying a personal perspective. For example, a recent New Yorker article describing the hometown involvements of the family of Roger Ailes, the powerful chairman of Fox News, noted that some people in the neighborhood "did not share the Aileses' world view."[18] The compound version, "worldview," is exemplified in the writing of Charles Colson, the former aide to President Richard Nixon who later became a conservative Christian activist, when he explained: "The [American] culture war is not just about abortion, homosexual rights, or the decline of public education. These are only the skirmishes. The real war is a cosmic struggle between worldviews—between the Christian worldview and the various secular and spiritual worldviews arrayed against it."[19]

Many evangelical scholars would be uncomfortable with Colson's bombastic rhetoric, yet they would still employ the notion of "worldview" in their academic work. The distinguished philosopher Nicholas Wolterstorff, who taught for many years at church-related Calvin College and later at both Yale and the Free University of Amsterdam, argues that every scholar has a worldview that contains "control beliefs" influencing what kinds of facts and interpretations of the world that person is willing to entertain.[20] Acknowledging such worldviews or control beliefs in public is thus construed to be not merely an act of self-revelation, but a necessary part of the sharing and dissemination of scholarship, a form of methodological transparency that allows others to take the effects of worldview filters into account when analyzing scholarly work. The inability or unwillingness to identify one's operative worldview can be considered, from this vantage point, as a kind of intellectual dishonesty, a corrupted "framing" of knowledge that impedes the search for truth.

What happens when a university assumes a monist or worldview approach to the framing of knowledge? The person who has most systematically described these implications is the philosopher Alasdair MacIntyre, once a thoroughgoing secularist who converted to Catholicism in the early 1980s and then completed his long and distinguished career at the University of Notre Dame. His life history, including his self-conscious switch from a secular to a religious worldview, underscored his position that colleges and universities should be places where students can experiment with various different worldviews as part of their educational journeys. Such experimentation, he said, would not only result in an effective learning experience, but would also provide practice for dealing with the clashes of values and ideas that are part of everyday experience in the real world. MacIntyre suggests that universities ought to see themselves as "places where conceptions of and standards of rationality are elaborated, put to work in the detailed practices of enquiry, and themselves rationally evaluated, so that...the larger society [can] learn how to conduct its own debates, practical or theoretical, in a rationally defensible way." He says this can happen only when the university becomes "a place where rival and antagonistic views of rational justification [i.e., differing worldviews]...are afforded the opportunity both to develop their own enquiries, in practice and in the articulation of the theory of that practice, and to conduct their intellectual and moral warfare" with each other.[21]

MacIntyre is convinced that educators must, in a sense, be double agents. On the one hand, they rightly see themselves as partisans in the conflict between worldviews, articulating their own views, criticizing the perspectives of others, defending their beliefs and assertions when attacked, and trying constantly to test, refine, and enlarge the agendas of research spawned by their own specific worldviews and disciplinary perspectives. But he also believes that educators as educators (not just as scholars upholding particular viewpoints) simultaneously need to be genuinely nonpartisan, seeking to sustain the university as an arena of fair and honest intellectual debate, carefully nurturing students into competence as participants in that debate, regardless of whether those students agree with the views of their teachers or not.

MacIntyre sees these two roles as complementary. Precisely because of monism's focus and self-confidence, the clash between worldviews can lead everyone to craft better, more intelligent arguments. It is an intellectual gift to have someone with whom to argue, to have the opportunity to debate with a peer who has firm views and who does not meekly accept whatever is proposed. That capacity—to hear a perspective that arises from an alternate worldview and receive it as an intellectual gift rather than as a competitor's battle cry—is, as McIntyre wrote, something that has to be nurtured. But the ability to engage widely divergent monists in rational academic conversation is likely to become even more necessary as American society—and the world at large—grows more diverse even as our interconnections grow tighter. Diana Eck, the director of the Pluralism Project at Harvard University, says that it no longer makes sense, for example, to simplistically describe people as either secular or religious: "Even humanists, even secularists, even atheists have to rethink their worldviews in the context of a more complex religious reality. With multitheistic Hindus and nontheistic Buddhists in the picture, atheists may have to be more specific about what kind of 'god' they do not believe in."[22]

The great strength of a monistic worldview approach to learning and knowledge lies in monism's recognition that every scholar is intellectually grounded in some particular understanding of the world and in its assertion that academic integrity requires resisting those ways of framing knowledge that a person sees as intellectually wrongheaded. Simultaneously, however, scholars must also be willing to speak openly and honestly with each other across their worldview differences as fellow travelers in the search for better knowledge of the world. Summarizing this stance, the Islamic scholar Tariq Ramadan offers the following advice to Muslim scholars and, by extension, to other scholars as well: "Hold to one's convictions; express one's principles and hopes; make clear comments and criticisms; keep to one, open way of speaking (with Muslims and with one's fellow-citizens)... [offer] the brotherhood of one's soul and humanity to all people of conscience... inviting them to travel with one, training oneself to keep on resisting and learning how to be a friend, *faithfully*."[23]

To be a monist or worldview thinker does not equate with being a wooden dogmatist, locked forever into a single unchanging and unchangeable understanding of reality. Scholars with integrity, including even the most convinced monists, seek to enlarge and improve their own visions of the world. The nineteenth-century Catholic scholar John Henry Cardinal Newman was a convinced Catholic monist who believed that ultimately all truth was compatible with Catholic faith—that Catholic doctrine provided the one best way to frame all knowledge. Yet, he was also aware that his own intellectual capacity was limited and that his own particular view of reality was likely to be mistaken at times, something that could be said of everyone. His conclusion: "In a higher world it is otherwise, but here below to live is to change, and to be perfect is to have changed often."[24]

The University and Pluralism

Although many professors, perhaps most, are monists of one stripe or another, some scholars approach scholarship in a much more eclectic fashion, looking not for coherence of system or for confirmation of any one particular vision of the world, but for the unexpected, the contradictory, and the baffling. These scholars are pluralists. They see the world as "one great blooming, buzzing confusion," to use the famous phrase of the late nineteenth/early twentieth-century psychologist William James. For pluralists, the world is a place of wonder and paradox that can never be shoehorned into any one worldview. Rather than defending any particular vision of reality, pluralists are intrepid collectors of new information and points of view. They are willing collaborators in the search for new knowledge, keen to avoid the territorial protectiveness of singular theories or datasets. Wayne Booth describes pluralists as typically engaging other scholars by saying something like this: "Presumably, what you have said can lead us further. Let's begin by being sure I have understood you, then let's see where it leads, what it enables us to do, and what, if anything, it prevents our doing."[25]

To be a pluralist is by definition to be open-minded, but not so open-minded that anything goes. Pluralists in the academy do not automatically accept everything they hear or read as worthy of consideration. They are critical thinkers, and, like monists, they make decisions about what ought to be taken seriously and what is nothing more than intellectual fluff or fantasy. Making these distinctions is more complicated for pluralists than it is for monists, however, because pluralists must take a much wider range of factors into consideration. Monists tend to focus on coherence and system; pluralists are willing to look at other factors as well—particularity, uniqueness, difference, practicality, functionality, and paradox. Further complicating matters is that many pluralists refuse to draw a hard-and-fast distinction between so-called objective knowledge and the more subjective dimensions of human knowing. Ethics, values, affectivity, and even religion may need to be taken into account.

Pluralism's epistemological inclusiveness makes it more difficult to evaluate the different ways that knowledge is framed. At the very least, it calls for something beyond narrowly construed rationality as the basis for making those judgments. The philosopher Robert C. Solomon, who teaches at the University of Texas, explains why claims of rationality are problematic: "Philosophers ever since Socrates have made philosophical reflection the hallmark of rationality, even a condition for a life worth living. Needless to say, this eliminates from candidacy a great many cultures in which self-reflection and self-criticism have not been encouraged or developed. In such cultures, myth and metaphor remain far more interesting than unimaginative, literal description.... Philosophers often exercise great ingenuity to establish what they in fact all began by acknowledging, that rationality is the virtue best exemplified by [themselves]."[26] When it comes to comparing, contrasting, and judging the many different kinds of insight that contribute to the construction of knowledge, Solomon would prefer, and pluralistic thinking requires, a more multilayered system than the narrow sense of rationality employed by most philosophers.

Most pluralists believe that a more free-wheeling style of scholarly interaction holds the potential to improve both scholarship and public debate. Austin Dacey, who is associated with the secular humanist Center for Inquiry in New York City, says, "[S]ecular liberals must lift the gag orders on ethics, values, and religion in public debate." He adds that the "moral and religious claims" of believers and unbelievers "should be held to the same standards as other serious public proposals: honesty, consistency, rationality, evidential support, feasibility, legality, morality, and revisability."[27] Dacey argues that the academy would do well to adopt something like the "open source movement" of the computing industry as the default mode of operation. Instead of approaching a problem with a "single centralized intelligence," the open source method "mobilize[s] many different intelligences to attack different parts of the problem or the same problem in different ways."[28] In his view, scholarship should operate like genuinely democratic political movements, with all voices being welcomed and then judged equally on the basis of reason, evidence, insight, practicality, and the potential to generate new research agendas.

The feminist scholar Elizabeth Minnich is a pluralist of a different stripe, and she is suspicious of some of Dacey's suggestions. In particular, she notes that intellectual standards like consistency, feasibility, and legality have all been used in the past to keep women silent. She also points out that sometimes simply bearing witness to one's own idiosyncratic experience is sufficiently eloquent to upset the structures of power that determine the contours of knowledge, whether or not that witness is fully rational or consistent. Minnich writes: "I do not share the fear that recognizing the personal, the privatized, the politically nondominant in the quest for knowledge leads us ineluctably to the slippery slope of relativism. What it does, or can do, is open up space for the renewal of thinking that is compatible with diversities, plurality, particularities, change—and relationality."[29] Minnich is also much more wary than Dacey about the benefits of inviting religious perspectives into the pluralistic conversation. Too often, she says, religion has been a source of oppression rather than liberation. By making "the error of conflating partial truths with Truth itself," religion sets itself up to be the arbiter of what is good, true, and just. She wonders whether religious believers, especially religious traditionalists, can truly entertain the notion that truth might emerge from many sources and that "Truth" in its fullness will never be known.[30]

Religion in the Academy, Monist and Pluralist

People often assume that religious intellectuals incline toward monism—which is Minnich's perception—and, of course, this is sometimes the case. For example, many Christians believe that there is a single, right way of understanding the world, a propensity shaped by centuries of drawing ecclesiastical distinctions between orthodoxy (right belief) and heresy (wrong or mistaken belief). Within Islam, the notion of *tawhid* (oneness) has produced a similar effect. Muslims affirm that there is only one God, that God is singular in essence, and that God's oneness implies that truth itself is ultimately one and undivided. It follows that there should be one, and only one, right way of understanding the world. This is hardly a recipe for pluralism, and historically most Christians and Muslims have inclined toward monism.

In contrast to most strands of Christian and Muslim thought, however, the thinking of many Hindus and Jews naturally bends toward pluralism. For Hindus, this inclination derives from polytheism, which claims that there are many gods and spiritual forces in the world and that all of this sometimes contradictory complexity needs to be taken into account when reflecting on reality. Hindus do not necessarily expect the world to make logical sense, because reality itself may not be logical. Wendy Doniger, one of the foremost scholars of Hinduism in the world, writes that Hindu "mythology celebrates the idea that the universe is boundlessly various, that everything occurs simultaneously, that all possibilities may exist without excluding each other...[that] untrammeled variety and contradiction are ethically and metaphysically necessary."[31]

The pluralism in Jewish thought is embedded in a different source: centuries of midrashic practice, scholarly arguments revolving around the meaning of texts. Judaism is a tradition of questioning and debate, of ongoing tension between revelation and human reasoning, of unchanging laws that require ever-changing applications, and of sensitivity to varying contexts that require perpetual rethinking of what has been taught and handed down. It is a tradition in which clever and wise disagreement is embraced as something positive, not as a threat to faith but rather as a way to stay religiously and intellectually alive, fully engaged in the moral and intellectual creativity that is life itself. Lee Shulman, former president of the Carnegie Foundation for the Advancement of Teaching, refers to this Jewish way of engaging reality and religion as the "midrashic imperative." Using the image of a web that both allows spiders to move and simultaneously catch insects in its sticky strings, Shulman says that human webs of knowledge and meaning necessarily both liberate and limit; they are both generative and constraining. The webs of knowledge, belief, and meaning that people construct allow them to see and do certain things, but they simultaneously make it more difficult to perceive and respond to other dimensions of reality, and there is no way to separate these two dimensions. Because that is the case, Shulman suggests that such webs need to be woven with care and in ways that are open to revision and change, or else they run the risk of becoming harmful to both oneself and others. Shulman concludes: "The conception of scholarship and teaching that I see emanating from this [Jewish] religious tradition is one of debate and dialogue, of ceaseless questioning and a quest for ever more inventive interpretations, commentaries, simplifications, and complications. It lends itself to pedagogies of engagement and inquiry, the celebration of doubt and deep skepticism about intellectual convergence. And yet it seeks to engage Jews in the obligation to repair the world."[32]

Framing Knowledge: The Role of Religion

The same rules of academic discourse apply equally whether religion is part of the conversation or not. Religious monists are as welcome to participate as religious pluralists, and so are nonreligious monists and pluralists of all stripes. Every scholar is required to marshal evidence in support of any particular position and to accept criticism and critique. Understanding the role of religion in framing knowledge sheds light on the ways in which knowledge of the world intertwines with all divergent assumptions and rationalities. Making space for religion—recognizing the role that religion plays in the ways many people, including many scholars, frame their knowledge of the world—signals that academic conversation is open to consideration of all the many other factors that influence the framing of knowledge. Conversely, if religion is avoided or ignored, it signals that limits are being placed in advance on what will be deemed to be academically respectable.

Some institutions are testing whether religious worldviews, intelligently included in academic conversation, might expand and enhance learning, scholarship, and critical thinking. For example, the religion department at Princeton University now explicitly describes itself as "secular" (methodologically evenhanded with regard to religious or nonreligious sources of ideas and arguments) as opposed to being "secularist" (antireligious).[33] One senior member of the department told us its methods are Socratic. Citing Plato's dialogue *Euthyphro*, he explained Socrates "thought Euthyphro's assumptions were incoherent and foolish. But Socrates understood that it would only be begging the questions if he, Socrates, merely assumed that Euthyphro's assumptions were false. So he engaged Euthyphro in a conversation designed to get both Euthyphro's commitments and his own out on the table where they could be critically examined." Princeton operates in a similar fashion, he said, because "we recognize that there will be a lot of disagreement about what ought to be counted as just, wise, courageous, and responsible. The best way to proceed is to make explicit our commitments about those and related topics and expose those commitments to rigorous questioning from all angles—and to get our students doing the same."[34] Another department member said the goal is to create an open, intellectually stimulating environment where students can argue their points of view in class, with the caveat that everything expressed is subject to analysis and critique. One result of this pedagogical practice is that evangelical Protestant students who used to avoid the department's courses are now among the most likely to enroll, because they welcome the opportunity to present their views and have them debated by their classmates.

What Princeton sees as a religiously neutral stance is perceived by others in the academy as "religion-friendly," and it may have contributed to the university's recent designation by the conservative, pro-religion magazine *First Things* as the third best school in America—just behind the vigorously evangelical Wheaton College (Illinois) and the staunchly Catholic Thomas Aquinas College. [35]

To welcome the viewpoints of pluralists and monists of every religious and nonreligious stripe into intellectual debate is a daunting task, but the social, political, moral, and spiritual challenges facing humankind may require the attempt. No one has argued this more forcefully than the Canadian philosopher and political thinker Charles Taylor, a pluralistic Catholic who is deeply troubled by the divide between religious and secular thinkers and their frequent inability to work together or even seriously talk with each other. One of his recent intellectual forays is a massive tome entitled *The Secular Age*, which traces the long history of cooperation and battle between the ways of religion (especially Christianity) and the ways of secular thought, life, reason, and affectivity in Western culture. His conclusion is that, at present, both religious and secular thinkers have reasoned their way into insurmountable quandaries, into puzzles and contradictions that cannot be solved by either religious or secular thinking on its own. A dialogue is needed, a new kind of cooperation, or synergy, bringing together religious and quasi-religious and nonreligious thinkers. Taylor pleads:

> Instead of reaching immediately for the weapons of polemic, we might better listen for a voice which we could never have assumed ourselves, whose tone might have been forever unknown to us if we hadn't strained to understand it. We will find that we have to extend this courtesy even to people who would never have extended it to us.... This, of course, leaves us with an immense set of messy, hermeneutical issues: how the different approaches relate to each other; how they relate together to questions of over-arching truth. We will never be without these issues; the belief that they can finally be set aside by some secure instance of authority, whether the Bible or the Pope, is a dangerous and damaging illusion. [36]

All human beings share the same fragile world, and better understanding of that world is to the advantage of us all. The production of knowledge is not merely a matter of academic concern, but rather is a matter of concern for humanity as a whole. Knowledge has practical consequences. Perhaps it will be possible in the years ahead for scholars to eschew simplistic dichotomies between religious and nonreligious ways of understanding the world, and to create an academy where all voices—monist and pluralist, religious and secular—can be heard, tested, criticized, revised, sometimes rejected, and sometimes combined into new and better ways of making sense of the world. The work of framing knowledge often follows a complex and sometimes convoluted route from worse ways of understanding reality to better ones, and there are many points along the way where the process can go awry. In this journey, the only sensible option for scholars is to express themselves as clearly as possible, to listen to others with care and respect, and to pay attention to all the ways that knowledge is framed, regardless of provenance or pedigree.

8

Civic Engagement

*What values and practices—religious or secular—shape civic
engagement?*

AT A LUNCHEON with a group of Ivy League professors, a sociologist shared his
view of the classroom. His job, he said, was to teach students objectively about
the world as it really is, nothing more and nothing less, and he then added, "My
assumption is that if I do that well the only reasonable response of my students
will be to go out and advocate for justice in every way they can." Did he see himself as an activist? "Of course not," he said, "I teach objectively." But despite that
disclaimer, this professor, along with many others we encountered, is an idealist
who wants his teaching somehow to change the world for the good. Most institutions of higher learning share that sentiment, and a quick survey of the mission
statements from public universities and private institutions will reveal, almost
without exception, a portrayal of campuses as places where students learn how
to help local communities, serve those in need, promote the common good, and
make the world in general a better place for everyone.[1]

Motivation for civic engagement in America can arise from many sources, both
secular and historically religious. The sociologist at that Ivy League campus, for
example, is a Roman Catholic with an undergraduate degree from a Jesuit college
known for its emphasis on social justice. He may be relatively unaware about how
his religious background may have shaped his teaching practices, but those connections might seem obvious to others. But historic religion is not the only kind
of religion at play in civic engagement. In America, civic practices are often intertwined with a kind of public religion (or "civil religion") that exists apart from
faith concerns of the nation's historic religious communities. Princeton professor
Jeffrey Stout explains that "we are bound to misrepresent the relation of religion

to politics [and by extension the relationship of religion to civic engagement] if we ignore either the presence of sacred concerns outside of organized religion or the contestation over sacred concerns within particular organized religions."[2] Religion, in the broadest sense of the term, is a major factor that shapes how Americans operate in the public sphere. If higher education hopes to serve as a training ground for participation (and leadership) in American public life, then it will need to take religion into account.

The Divided Soul of Civic Engagement: Change Agents and Community Servants

In 1993, the American Association of Colleges and Universities launched its "Diversity, Democracy, and Liberal Learning" initiative with a statement that noted: "Traditionally, the academy has emphasized the benefits of higher learning—both intellectual and economic—to each individual learner. But diversity and democracy together press educators to address the communal dimensions and consequences of higher learning."[3] One of the reasons that service programs have become so popular—and so ubiquitous—is that they combine concern for individual learning with "communal dimensions and consequences." Civic engagement is deemed to be good for the student and simultaneously (and concretely) beneficial to others. Of course, educational administrators are aware that such programs also visibly demonstrate that a college or university is being civically responsible in the city or neighborhood where it is located. When students perform good deeds, they provide a human face for the school. Partnerships with local businesses, civic and cultural associations, and government agencies are measurable ways of "giving something back" to society.

In spite of their obvious appeal, programs related to civic engagement are being scrutinized along with everything else in education in the current challenging environment. Some educators fear that support is beginning to wane, both at colleges and universities and in the broader public sphere, and they would like that trend to be reversed. For several months in early 2011, different groups of higher education leaders met in Washington, D.C., to craft a plan for re-energizing civic engagement on campuses across the nation. These meetings were jointly organized by the Global Perspective Institute and the Association of American Colleges and Universities, which had been awarded a Department of Education contract to develop a National Action Plan for "strengthening students' civic learning and democratic engagement as a core component of college study."[4]

One step in crafting the plan involved about two-dozen faculty leaders and scholars of community engagement (including one of us) who gathered around a seminar table at the Department of Education and spent a day talking about ways to increase and improve the current level of civic engagement in American education.

Although there were widely diverging observations and opinions, an overarching divide became apparent: There was one camp, the "change agents," who perceived civic engagement largely in terms of political advocacy for social transformation, and another camp, the "community servants," who construed engagement mostly in terms of helping others and serving the needs of their local communities.

The change agents at the meeting expressed alarm that the current generation of college students is becoming disengaged from civic concerns. Overall rates of civic involvement on the part of young adults are lower than in the past, and many young people seem to be more interested in pursuing nonpolitical forms of engagement than in political action. One report states somewhat ominously that although "young people are being trained in the habits of civic participation [they] are not learning the ropes of political activism—and it appears to be taking a toll."[5] Other social activists charge that higher education itself is partly to blame, having "largely sidestepped the political dimensions of civic engagement."[6] This led activist educators to frame the discussion in terms of an impending crisis of democracy. Young adults are not, however, the only Americans who have become less politically active; Americans overall have become less civically engaged. Most of the activists assume that the tide will turn only if and when the next generation—current students—become more politically engaged. Although some participants were heartened by higher rates of student involvement in politics during the 2008 presidential campaign, when many students were energized by the candidacy of Barack Obama, the change agents at the meeting expressed a general sense of longing for the "good old days" when university students were at the forefront of a societal march toward increased rights for the disenfranchised and dispossessed.

The emotional tenor of the community servants in the group was something more akin to discouragement or frustration. They are discouraged because, in an era of tight and tightening education budgets, community service is sometimes perceived as an optional frill, rather than as a core educational concern. Their frustrations are also fueled by the inability of community service advocates themselves to agree on how to move forward. Are programs that stress community-based learning the best vehicles for promoting service opportunities on campus? Should those programs be distinguished from the fairly robust service-learning programs already in place at many institutions, and are those programs to be differentiated from simple "service" itself? Or should institutions try to have it both ways: stressing the practical learning that will accrue to individual students who are involved in community service while also reaping the public relations boon that results? And what about employing older concepts like citizenship, civic duty, and public service, terms that are now frequently associated with holding political office? Given the state of politics today, does that mean these terms are now tarnished beyond repair, or should they be rehabilitated? The community servants at the meeting seemed uncertain about which options had the most promise.

Political Activism as Civil Religious Practice

Civic engagement in the form of political activism is often viewed as a thoroughly secular affair. It is about mobilizing people and energy around a moral cause for a politically reasonable end. Yet, a form of public religion is often embedded in these practices. As explained by the University of California sociologist Robert N. Bellah, public religion or "civil religion" in America consists of a deep commitment to the "American Way of Life," expressed in the nation's ideals of freedom, equality, and justice for all. American civil religion is not the same thing as unreflective patriotism. Bellah says American civil religion "does not remove us from moral ambiguity, from being, in Lincoln's fine phrase, an 'almost chosen people.' But it is a heritage of moral and religious experience from which we still have much to learn as we formulate the decisions that lie ahead."[7] For many citizens, it seems obvious that America is a special place, and they want America to live up to its own ideals. In fact, they want the United States to become an even better place than it currently is. This was the credo of the Civil Rights Movement as it was led by Martin Luther King Jr., one of American civil religion's greatest prophets; this is also the faith of many proponents of political civic engagement on campuses today. And "faith" is the right word here—a deeply held belief about what really matters.

The linkage of civic engagement, higher education, and the American way of life is not new. As the United States regrouped after World War II and reflected on its new role as the leader of the free world, President Truman's Commission on Higher Education issued a six-volume "Truman Report" (1947) recommending the establishment of community colleges. The commission was preparing for a huge influx of students into postsecondary education because of the G.I. Bill, and they did not want this new cohort of community college students to receive an inferior education. The report cautioned schools in advance to blend occupational training together with "that human wholeness and civic conscience which the cooperative activities of citizenship require."[8] The National Science Foundation that was created around the same time (1950) also envisioned easy and natural connections weaving together science, citizenship, the common good, and national advancement. The same rhetoric about making America and the world a better place was part of the argument for establishing the National Endowment for the Humanities in 1965: "Democracy demands wisdom.... To know the best that has been thought and said in former times can make us wiser than we otherwise might be, and in this respect the humanities are not merely our, but the world's best hope."[9] The use of words like conscience, human wholeness, the common good, wisdom, and hope when talking about these endeavors signals something more than mere pragmatism or politics as usual. A sense of sacred national calling is implicit in all of these mid-century initiatives.

The blunt faith in America that informed American culture after World War II has taken a beating in the years since. The political upheavals of the 1960s, Watergate, the anti-federal legacy of President Ronald Reagan, and a host of other developments have raised a wide range of questions about the trustworthiness of government and the moral behavior of the nation. But the optimistic sentiments of the 1950s never entirely disappeared, and especially since 9/11, the language of civic responsibility and national calling has made a comeback in chastened form. This is evident in the book *Educating Citizens: Preparing America's Undergraduates for Lives of Moral and Civic Responsibility* (2003), which was produced by the Carnegie Foundation for the Advancement of Teaching. It argues that colleges and universities have a duty to foster the attitudes, values, and virtues that define and support the American experiment at its best: honesty, trustworthiness, concern about how one's actions affect others, social conscience, compassion, a commitment to the welfare of those outside one's immediate sphere, an appreciation of the richness of diversity, and a willingness to treat everyone equally. The hope expressed by this book is to produce something far more robust than either community service or simple political activism. The volume calls on colleges and universities to "educate for substantive values, ideals, and standards...to examine the values they stand for and make conscious and deliberate choices about what they convey to students."[10] For the authors of *Educating Citizens* and for many other educators, the goal of "civic learning" is for students to internalize the values that will help America be the place it is supposed to be, and that is a profoundly religious sentiment.[11]

The religious dimension of politically oriented civic engagement is not always acknowledged, but Martha Nussbaum, the well-known educator and outspoken humanist from the University of Chicago, has recently made this connection clear. She argues that the "overlapping consensus" about the proper moral shape of society that exists in America—a position she describes, following John Stewart Mill, as the "religion of humanity"—is so far beyond question that it should be accepted as the nation's unquestioned sacred ideal and should be taught in all public schools. She further argues that this education ought to include the formation of affect as well as the mind: "My program...is going to need real artists to carry it out, not just well-intentioned public servants," because only art (or "public poetry" as she calls it) can evoke the necessary "emotions supportive of the[se] political norms."[12] For Nussbaum, this natural "religion of humanity" should not merely define public policy; it should be internalized as the personal faith of every American.

Nussbaum is aware that supporting one and only one public religious vision of society over all others—even if it is the "religion of humanity"—will require a significant amount of persuasion, and perhaps even mild coercion. She says that dissonant views of public life and values will have to be politely, but firmly, discouraged. She explains that "religious and other views of the good that do not support toleration and equal respect will not be suppressed or denied the right to speak," but people who hold those alternative views should be made to see that their views are inappropriate and out of touch with the mainstream. "Religions may stick to their intolerant guns," she writes, "but if they do, and if citizens affirm the political principles [of the religion of humanity] ... such religions are likely to gain fewer adherents over time, since people dislike living with such emotional and cognitive tensions."[13]

A vision of political change and societal improvement that relies on a single story—whether it is Nussbaum's narrative of the "religion of humanity" or anything else—makes many Americans become very nervous. They would argue that it is not one story that has made America great, but a plurality of sometimes conflicting stories that are all bound up together. On this subject, Robert Bellah has, once again, been a path-breaker. His multi-authored book *Habits of the Heart* (1985) identifies four different stories that have shaped and continue to shape public life and civic engagement in the nation: the biblical story, the republican story, the utilitarian story, and the story of expressive individualism. Each of these stories formulates America's civil religious values in a different way.[14] The biblical story focuses on America as a righteous empire destined to be a model of virtue for the whole world. The republican story depicts America as a land of brothers and sisters who fend for themselves but who also care for each other. The utilitarian story is a narrative of ingenuity and success describing the American capacity to come up with solutions whenever problems or challenges arise. Finally, the story of expressive individualism celebrates the unique gifts and characteristics of each person, a tale of individual flourishing and authenticity.

Political Activism and Historic Religion

Since *Habits of the Heart* was published in the mid-1980s, America has become a more diverse nation in almost every way, but especially religiously. The four stories that Bellah and his co-authors describe may no longer encompass all the many ways that Americans are motivated toward involvement in politics, social change, and community service. New stories may need to be added to the repertoire, and some of them might originate in historic religions. As part of an effort to build constructive institutional connections with the local community, Gail O. Mellow, president of LaGuardia Community College in Queens, New York, recently sent faculty and staff volunteers into the surrounding neighborhoods to visit churches, mosques, synagogues, and temples. Their goal was to collect the many different religious stories told by people in the community that have the potential to make Queens a better place "where all people are respected and can safely practice their religion and express their personal beliefs."[15]

Whatever else civic activism may entail in contemporary America, it will require cognizance of the incredibly varied religious terrain where these matters now play themselves out. The world's historic religions have a multiplicity of views about what constitutes the common good, including different opinions about whether members of their communities ought to be involved in politics at all. Some historic religious groups are ardent supporters of active participation in the give and take of politics, some would prefer to simply dictate moral rules to the rest of society, and some consider politics to be almost antithetical to religion. Even within a single historic religion, there are widely varying practices, as illustrated by the differences between two groups of Protestant Christians, the Amish and the Religious Right. The Amish, many of them in rural Pennsylvania and Ohio, reject all things modern, including modern democratic politics. They have derived their lifestyle from a "two kingdom" theology: They are responsible only for the kingdom of God as it is embodied in their own community, and they have no part in the politics of the kingdom of this world, not even voting in elections.

Meanwhile, Protestant churches aligned with the Religious Right and its powerful lobbies in Washington, D.C., see politics and religion as intertwined, and their goal is for the public laws of the nation to be as closely aligned as possible with their vision of the eternal rules of God. Supporters of the Religious Right often feel they are embroiled in a culture war over the moral and religious values of American society as a whole. The book *Culture Wars* (1992), written by the University of Virginia sociologist James Davison Hunter, provided much of the social analysis that informs the Religious Right's view of politics and religion.[16] But over the years, Hunter's perspective has changed, and his recent book *To Change the World* (2010) argues that organized political activism is usually ineffective at changing the prevailing moral norms of a society. Rather than making the world a better place, explicitly religious political activism often produces rancor, division, and suspicion. He now urges conservative Christians to set aside their efforts to gain political power and to instead adopt a posture of "faithful presence" within society. He writes bluntly that it is time for the Religious Right (and Christians in general) "to be silent for a season and learn to enact their faith in public through acts of *shalom* rather than... through law, policy, and political mobilization." The goal of faithful presence is to generate "relationships and institutions that are fundamentally covenantal in character, the ends of which are the fostering of meaning, purpose, truth, beauty, belonging, and fairness—not just for Christians but for everyone."[17]

There are many scholars in addition to Hunter who now assume that the diversity of contemporary America makes it impossible for any one particular group to win over the entire society to its views. Gaining sufficient political power to force a single view on others would be a hollow victory, even if it could be accomplished. Instead of seeking victory in a culture war, educators are suggesting that "for democracy to function successfully in the future, students must be prepared to understand their own identities, communicate with people who are different from themselves, and build bridges across cultural differences."[18]

It is unclear whether America's elected officials or media pundits have gotten that message, and quite obviously, not all cultural warriors have put down their arms. But it is and always has been the role of colleges and universities to think ahead of the rest of the culture, not just follow it. In the arena of contemporary political civic activism, this may translate into helping students to peaceably yet effectively present their views and values in a religiously complex public world, learning to appreciate that the mutual modeling of alternative proposals ("faithful presence") may sometimes promote change more effectively than making louder arguments or building more powerful political coalitions.

The group that is currently most visible at the intersection of religious pluralism and civic engagement is the Interfaith Youth Core (IFYC), founded by Eboo Patel and working out of a funky one-floor office in the Greek Town section of Chicago. Patel was raised in the Chicago suburbs in an Indian Ismaili Muslim family, and he has described attending a high school where there was more religious diversity around the lunchroom table than at most official interfaith gatherings. He was also raised in a family where concern for the common good was simply part of life. In 1998, he founded the IFYC around the central vision of creating "a world in which young people from diverse religious and philosophical perspectives interact peacefully to create understanding and collaboration, thereby strengthening civil society and stabilizing global politics."[19] Patel and his organization assume that contemporary religion will always be pluriform, and they are not interested in forced consensus. Their aim is "proactive cooperation that affirms the identity of the constituent communities while emphasizing the well-being of each.... [T]he common good is best served when each community has a chance to make its unique contribution."[20]

The IFYC mobilizes students, faculty, and staff at colleges and universities all over the country around the twin goals of interfaith friendship and civic engagement. By working side by side on joint projects and discovering how much they share in common, students from different religious traditions discover new possibilities for interfaith friendship and cooperation. Described this way, civic engagement can appear to have been transformed into an instrumental strategy for building positive interfaith relations. But the IFYC considers the enhancement of interfaith relations itself to be a contribution to the common good, diminishing the likelihood of religious violence. Patel explains, "If we get that [model of interfaith relations] right in America, the rest of the world may pay attention, and the model we build in Boston might have repercussions in Belfast, Bombay, and Baghdad."[21]

Civic Engagement as Community Service

In contrast to civic engagement as political activism, civic engagement as community service shifts attention away from thinking about the creation of a better future and focuses instead on meeting the needs of individuals and groups in the present. That focus on the here and now is a primary reason why students are increasingly attracted to community service rather than political involvement. Service takes place in the present, it has a measurable impact, and it is rewarding. Having been shaped by a world of instant experience, enabled by new technologies, many students prefer to direct their energy toward acts of service that have an immediate impact, rather than getting involved in the long slog and uncertain outcomes of the political process.

Statistics reveal a significant shift away from political involvement and toward nonpolitical forms of civic engagement over the last four generations. In a 2002 poll about civic involvement, 31 percent of the civically engaged individuals from the World War II generation described their work as political, while only 9 percent said their engagement was nonpolitical. In the baby-boomer generation, 19 percent indicated that they were politically focused, and the same number said their civic engagement was mainly nonpolitical. As for gen-xers, born between 1965 and 1976, only 13 percent said they were politically engaged, and 21 percent were involved in nonpolitical service. The trend line of political involvement for the current generation of students seems to be heading yet further downward. Each successive generation has become less politically active, and American culture as a whole seems to have become less optimistic about politics and more attuned to service. When asked about what motivates them to be involved, most civically engaged Americans today, regardless of age, say their goal is simply "to help others"; only one in four indicates that their actions result from political convictions or from a commitment to social activism.[22]

The shift is apparent on campuses across the country. It is relatively easy to organize students in response to basic human needs: raising funds for health research or a children's hospital, providing hands-on assistance to victims of hurricane Katrina, or even participating in mildly political activity, such as lobbying for the end of sex trafficking or child labor in some distant part of the world. But organizing students for overt, old-fashioned political action is difficult at best. Paul Loeb, a frequent campus speaker on topics related to civic engagement, says that students today, compared to those in the past, "are involved in the community in more bounded ways. They will volunteer at a soup kitchen, but won't advocate around hunger issues."[23] Loeb describes students' lack of interest in political action as rooted in "the burden of cynicism," the inability to believe that one's actions really can change the world. That may be a partial explanation, but their choices might also be construed as a kind of spiritual responsiveness.

For the current generation of students, social responsibility may not be heard as a call for new government policies or political action, but rather as an invitation for face-to-face relationships. It is not the abstract issue of "poverty" that grabs their attention, but instead the homeless families and individuals in their own neighborhoods or in some specific community in another part of the world that they have seen in a video or visited while studying abroad.

Students may be "bounded" in their individual responses, but their service projects are almost infinite in their variety. Each campus, or sometimes various subunits of a college or university, develops its own culture of service. Usually, the participation of individual students is voluntary, but not always. At Tulane University in New Orleans, all students are required to complete a service-learning course during their first two years and then a second service-learning requirement during their last two years. This second requirement can be fulfilled in a number of ways, some of them quite creative. One option is to take a communications course that films women from local cultural groups as they prepare for Mardi Gras Day, thus "helping preserve the centuries-old tradition of the Indian queens."[24]

Flexibility in the definition of service allows students to connect meaningfully with the local community and to take information and skills learned in classes and apply them to worthy purposes. But sometimes the notion of civic engagement can become so elastic—perhaps helpfully or perhaps not—that the distinction between voluntary, not-for-profit *service* and contractual, for-profit *services* is lost. For example, under the rubric of "business and civic engagement," the Bloch School of Management at the University of Missouri defines its mission as "serv[ing] and partner[ing] with the greater Kansas City business, non-profit and civic community as a thought leader, business builder, career builder and civic catalyst."[25] A university in suburban Philadelphia recently advertised for a new administrative position, assistant dean of civic engagement, to advance "the mission of student engagement and service learning" in part through successful communication of "brand awareness."[26] This merging of service with school "brand" has become so commonplace that a cadre of respected scholars recently warned that civic engagement is in danger of being reduced to little more than the "public relations function of making known what the campus is doing for the community."[27] Their concern may be overblown, but without doubt there is a temptation for service-oriented programs of civic engagement to be deployed by colleges and universities in instrumental ways that benefit the school as much as or more than the community itself.

Community Service and Historic Religions

The term "community service" is often a cipher, a vague term referencing all the different ways that people are doing good deeds in the world around them. A look beneath the allusion's surface reveals something noteworthy: Community service often has direct connections with historic religion. A recent groundbreaking study by Robert D. Putnam (from Harvard) and David Campbell (from Notre Dame), published as *American Grace: How Religion Divides and Unites Us*, concludes: "The evidence we review suggests that religiously observant Americans are more civic and in some respects simply 'nicer'" than their less religiously involved fellow citizens. Religiously observant people, they say, "are more than twice as likely to volunteer to help the needy, compared to demographically matched Americans who rarely, if ever, attend church." Religiously observant people also tend overall to be more generous, more altruistic, more empathic, more likely to "belong to community organizations," more likely to "take part in local civic and political life," and more likely to "press for local social or political reform" than those who are less religious. In short, the more religious a person is, the more likely it is that he or she will embody the lifelong traits of civic engagement that so many colleges and universities are trying to promote.[28]

When Putnam and Campbell looked for the "secret ingredient" that makes religious people more civic-minded than others, they found no statistical correlation between individual behavior and the moral or religious teachings of any particular religious group. "Nothing that we can discover about the content of religious faith adds anything to our understanding or prediction of…good neighborliness." They found instead that social connections are the key. It is religious friends who make the difference—and not just friends, but "supercharged" friends from one's church or synagogue or mosque or temple. These kinds of friendships are "morally freighted in a way that most secular ties are not," so pleas for help or involvement from these friends are difficult, if not impossible, to ignore.[29]

Putnam and Campbell found no statistical connection between a particular religious tenet and community involvement, but many individuals construe their own acts of kindness, duty, and mercy as having been motivated by religion. Virtually every historic religion contains some injunction akin to the Golden Rule ("do unto others what you would have them do unto you"), and many religions explicitly direct their members to do as much as possible to heal the woes of the world, as exemplified by the concept of *tikkun olam* in Judaism. Studies by the Princeton sociologist Robert Wuthnow conclude: "In nearly all of the comparisons, people who are more actively religious or traditionally religious are more likely to be engaged in charitable or service volunteering than those who are less actively or traditionally religious." Among Christians, "the largest difference is between those who read the Bible regularly and those who do not," and there is also a large difference between those who pray or meditate regularly and those who do not.[30] Being reminded of one's moral duties to one's neighbors on a regular basis either through reading, prayer, or listening to sermons appears to have an impact on whether and how much people volunteer. Although being reminded to behave well might have the same effect on those who are nonreligious, such reminders are not built into the ordinary routines of their lives.

Another more mundane factor is at work as well: Religious organizations provide members with ready-to-go volunteering options. Religious organizations serve as liaisons, connecting individuals with organizations in need of their special skills, easing the way for members to become involved in good works. Just as importantly, many religious communities train their members so they will be more effective when they are called into service. Whenever a disaster strikes a community, lots of SUVs ("spontaneous untrained volunteers") show up who want to help, but there is usually a shortage of people with skills and equipment—and that is precisely what religious organizations can often supply. When dozens of tornadoes recently struck northeastern Alabama, for example, a group of Southern Baptists showed up a day ahead of the Red Cross and set up an enormous mobile kitchen to begin feeding those who had lost their homes. Even earlier, the Baptists had sent in chainsaw teams to clear the roads so emergency vehicles and their own mobile kitchen could get to the affected areas. The Red Cross acknowledges that "churches can often get deeper into a community faster than secular rescue teams," but there is a catch. At times, the volunteer service provided by religious organizations and religiously motivated individuals is accompanied by expressions of religious devotion or even suggestions of conversion. Many Americans see this as questionable, if not problematic; they think that religion should be kept invisible when services are provided. Others reply that volunteers cannot be expected to mask their religiosity when it is part of what motivates them toward service.[31]

The practices and priorities of professors do not always align with those of "all Americans" (who were the subject of the research conducted by Campbell and Putnam and by Wuthnow), but in matters of religion and public service, they do. A survey completed by more than 37,000 full-time faculty members who teach undergraduates found that faculty who rate high on "spirituality" are twice as likely as those who rate low to also have high scores in "civic-minded practice" and "civic-minded values."[32] Not much data on the subject has been collected from college and university students, but the available information points in the same direction: Personal religion (or spirituality) correlates with civic engagement. There are some discouraging elements in the student data. In contrast to the 20 percent of the national population that is involved in charitable service, the number is only 12 percent for students entering college, and that number falls to 9 percent by the end of the junior year. The one exception to this downward trend is students at self-described "evangelical" colleges and universities, who show a small increase in community service during their college years, moving up from 13 percent to 14 percent.[33]

A similar connection between religion and student volunteering is evident in data collected in 2008 by Campus Compact, a coalition of more than 1,100 colleges and universities committed to community service.[34] According to its survey, students at faith-based colleges had an engagement rate of 61 percent compared to a national student participation rate of 31 percent. The higher rate of participation may be due in part to the fact that most of the religiously affiliated schools are residential campuses, but this alone does not account for all the difference. Perhaps counter-intuitively, Campus Compact also found that the level of community service measured in terms of average hours of service per student per week was lower at church-related schools (2.9 hours per week) than the national average (3.7 hours). It is unclear why this is the case, but it may be that the opportunities to serve simply cannot keep up with student demand at religiously affiliated schools; there are more volunteers than needed and the hours have to be spread around. Perhaps the most interesting finding in the Campus Compact study, however, is that the students at historically black colleges and universities are by far the most involved. The student participation rate at these schools is 61 percent, which matches that of faith-based institutions, but their average individual contribution is an astonishing 13.9 hours per week. It appears that the historically black colleges and universities have somehow managed to create a kind of "perfect storm" on campus when it comes to producing high rates of civic engagement.[35] Here too, however, religion may be a factor. African Americans as a group are significantly more religious than the American population as a whole, which means that religion may well be a hidden motivator prompting such amazing levels of community involvement.[36]

Religion is not only a factor on the "provider" side of community service. The recipients of aid or service also shape the encounter. Chris Stedman, who now works in the office of the humanist chaplain at Harvard University, tells a poignant story from his undergraduate days at Augsburg College in Minnesota when he worked with a student organization called "Campus Kitchen." Its mission was to deliver food to various needy communities in the Minneapolis area, and his route took him to the Brian Coyle Community Center (BCCC) in an area of the city that was primarily Somali and Muslim. One evening, he had a conversation with a young woman from the community who explained to him how hard life could be, and how she derived strength and comfort from her belief in Allah. Suddenly, the conversation seemed way too personal and way too religious for him. He froze. Stedman says, "She wasn't proselytizing…[she] hadn't condemned me, she hadn't even blinked," but suddenly he realized how superficially he was connected with the people he thought of himself as "serving." He didn't really want to know about their lives; he didn't want to know about their personal religious faith; he just wanted to do good in his own way and on his own terms. Later, he reflected: "By refusing to engage the religious lives of those at BCCC, I wasn't living up to my aspirations of empowering individuals and seeing them as deserving of dignity and respect."[37] Even when religion is not a motivation for community service, religion can erupt into the experience in a host of unexpected, but often highly educational, ways.

The Conflict of Loyalties: Defining the "Civic" in Civic Engagement

The term "civic" comes from the Latin word *civicus*, meaning citizen. In the ancient world, citizens were members of a *civitas*, an autonomous city-state or local community, and it was assumed that citizens belonged to one and only one *civitas*. There was no ambiguity about where loyalty belonged. The world in which students live today is very different. It is a place where everything is interconnected and where proper prioritization can be hard to manage. The object of the "civic" in civic engagement is no longer a given, and who is included in the "common" in "common good" is no longer self-evident. Today, loyalties are negotiated and defined in ways that could not have been imagined in ancient Greece or Rome, or even in recent American history.

Several years ago, one of our children was in the midst of her college search, and the president of one prestigious institution we visited told a group of prospective science students: "The goal of your future work as scientists is to keep America strong and ahead of the rest of the world." For this university president, the common good was simply whatever was best for America. Our daughter, however, had spent her childhood in a neighborhood comprised mostly of plain-spoken but culturally inclusive Mennonites, known for their service to those in need worldwide. She was shocked that an educated person could voice such "unworthy" sentiments. "Isn't the goal of education to help everyone," she asked, "not just those in the United States?" Even today, the rhetoric of "keeping America first" still pervades higher education, sometimes in places where it is not expected—for instance, in the Lumina Foundation, an organization founded in 2000 for the laudable purpose of helping students from the lowest quartile of the American economic spectrum to graduate from college. There is no reason to expect the concept of American strength to be part of Lumina's mission, but one of their board members explains that it is: "Our nation can only retain its position of power if all of its citizens are prepared to keep it strong. [The Lumina Foundation] is dedicated to increasing the number of adults with a credential that will prepare them to make that reality happen."[38]

Whether or not their aim is to "keep America first," most Americans are aware that college and university graduates today enter a world with far more complicated international dynamics than could have been imagined by prior generations. Martha Kanter, current U.S. undersecretary of education, recently said that "international education cannot be seen as an add-on. It's not an extra in higher education or K-12."[39] Internationalism is now a necessity. Many students today see themselves as citizens of the world. Yes, America matters, but so do the values, well-being, economic status, and cultural riches of all the other nations and people on the planet. Community service or political action designed to make America a better and stronger place has a role in their thinking, but not an exclusive role. And even for those whose focus remains on the United States, they know that in our global era, no nation exists on its own. What happens in one country has the potential to affect everyone else.[40]

But even internationalism does not provide a sufficiently broad notion of civic responsibility to satisfy some students. These students see themselves as having responsibilities related to all life on the planet, not just human life. For them, it is the whole planet in all its "ecozoic" diversity—including all forms of life and all the many ways those forms of life are interconnected and interdependent on each other—that is the object of their devotion, reverence, protection, and loyalty when they sort through the life options before them and the moral choices they face. Just as no nation any longer exists apart from international financial markets, they assert that no single species, including *homo sapiens*, exists apart from the natural world. Some might even argue that sustenance of the planet as a whole might, at times, call for sacrificing some human benefits or even human lives. Such attitudes have recently been labeled "dark green religion," and that is an apt description.[41] What is at stake is more than mere politics; it conveys that, for some people, environmentalism is an ultimate value. In today's world, a comprehensive discussion of civic engagement must take the whole spectrum of loyalties into account, starting with loyalties to family, friends, and local community and then expanding to include nation, world, and all living things (see Figure 8.1). Prioritizing these various loyalties is fundamentally a religious choice, a decision about which social responsibilities have the most claim on an individual's life. The religiosity involved in such a choice is not that of traditional (historic)

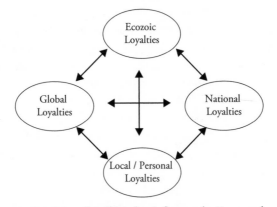

FIGURE 8.1 Loyalties that Influence the Focus and Content of Civic Engagement

religion, but rather it is public religion—the values and practices that guide and inform public life.

Questions about the proper focus for civic devotion are not new. People have always experienced tension between their loyalty to family, friends, and local community and their loyalty to other larger causes. In American history, this was especially evident during the conflagration of the Civil War. Although choices have always had to be made about where devotion should be directed, the new overlays of internationalism and ecozoic consciousness have dramatically complicated the task. Deciding which of these different "civics" has the largest claim on one's life and learning how to balance competing claims is a challenge.[42] Understanding the role of religion in these choices is complicated, especially when historic religion itself becomes an additional focus of loyalty. For some individuals, there are times when fealty to a historic religious tradition exists in tension with allegiances to community, nation, the globe, or all living things. In such cases, historic religion can become another competing "civic loyalty" that must be weighed in comparison to other objects of devotion.

Civic engagement is not simply about getting involved or changing the system or doing good; it involves making important decisions about how, when, and why one becomes civically engaged. And those decisions revolve around more than merely personal ideals and preferred ways of life. Civic engagement embodies socially negotiated, often contested conclusions about what really matters to local communities, nations, and the world. Helping people, defending values, and protecting threatened species and ecosystems are all religious declarations of a sort, ways of making one's own ultimate concerns visible for others to see and of entering into the ongoing and never-ending debate about social values and practices. Giving sustained and intelligent attention to the religious dimensions of civic engagement is one way that colleges and universities can encourage students to become more self-conscious, self-directed, and self-critical participants in public life.

9

Convictions

In what ways are personal convictions related to the teaching and learning process?

A FACULTY MEMBER from a major Midwestern research university told us about a student in her astronomy class who arrived during office hours one day, wondering if they might talk about something a bit personal. The student recounted how she had been a convinced atheist when she began the astronomy course, but what she had learned about the complexity and beauty of the universe had made her uncertain. Its intricacies were turning her into some kind of reverent agnostic, and she wanted to talk about it. Experiences like this one are not uncommon. For many students, the undergraduate years are a time of faith lost or modified or sometimes regained, with faith in this case meaning the ideas, ideals, hopes, and desires that define the core of how a person sees and feels and commits to others and the world.

Thinking about personal faith, beliefs, and convictions is different from the analysis that is typical of scholarly discourse within the academy. In the academic debates of the public sphere, what matters is evidence and argument. These factors matter too in the private domain of convictions and commitments, but other considerations are at least as important. As the seventeenth-century mathematician and mystic Blaise Pascal once said, "The heart has reasons that reason cannot know."[1] The academic and the personal are interconnected, not independent, arenas. The reasoning of the heart can be swayed by reasons of the head (and vice versa). But the connections between these two different ways of thinking, assessing, and coming to conclusions are rarely straightforward. Academic reasoning and personal reflection intersect at a slant, making it hard to predict the outcomes of their intermingling.

Convictions are the bedrock beliefs that shape how people think and live, the beliefs that they figuratively, and sometimes literally, bet their lives on. Like all ideas and beliefs, convictions are neither good nor bad in the abstract. Strongly held convictions produce prophets and poets who seem to see the world more clearly than the rest of us and who have the courage and ability to "speak truth to power," but strongly held convictions also yield dangerous fanaticism and destructive fantasies, the catalysts for suicide bombers and for parents who refuse medical care for their children because they believe God will heal them. Weak convictions lead to different problems: people who have "no mind of their own," sheep incapable of principled choices who are led to the slaughter by the first charismatic leader to arrive on the scene.

The convictions that students bring with them to college will shape what and how they learn, and conversely the material in college and university courses can unsettle previous convictions, as it did with the atheist-turned-agnostic astronomy student. Disinterested logic and academic analysis are major components in the learning process, but personal convictions often drive thinking and decision-making. This is true even for the most rational of all college and university professors. Understanding the role of convictions is a necessary component of the examined life. Becoming aware of one's own convictions and the convictions of others and learning how to converse intelligently about them goes to the heart of why colleges and universities exist.

Theories of Development

There are many different theories about how human beings learn and how we develop our differing sets of convictions. Theories of development often describe a series of cognitive, social, or moral stages that individuals progress through sequentially.[2] The theory that has been most influential in higher education is one laid out by William G. Perry in *Forms of Intellectual and Ethical Development in the College Years* (1970).[3] Perry postulates that college students generally progress through three stages. When entering college, most students are dualists; they see the world in simple binaries (good/bad, us/them, right/wrong). The second stage is one of moral and cognitive relativism, when students become aware of multiplicity. In the third stage, students transcend the confusion of pure relativism and take steps toward mature self-awareness and nuanced commitment. Like most stage theories of human development, Perry's assumes that moving from one stage to the next requires a personal crisis, a moment when it becomes apparent that one's existing beliefs or convictions are no longer adequate. It is the crumbling of prior belief structures that gives individuals the gumption to undertake the hard work of rethinking and reconfiguring the convictions that guide their lives.

Many professors, or at least many of those who have been around for a while, assume that Perry's stage scheme is a generally accurate portrayal of what students should (and will) experience during the college years. That is, professors have assumed that students enter their university years encumbered by a host of pre-critical attitudes and pre-formed views of the world that need to be dismantled in order to clear the way for new learning and critical thinking. For some professors, this task alone comprises the necessary and sufficient job description for teaching at the university level. The professor's role is to open students' minds by intro-ducing ideas that conflict with the inadequate ones they currently possess, and it is then the responsibility of students themselves to rebuild a new convictional framework that moves beyond mere relativism.

It is questionable whether such a strategy continues to make sense today, given that many students now enter college already firmly established in Perry's second stage. They already understand multiplicity, arriving on campus as comfortable relativists who are fully aware that the world is a complicated place populated by different groups of people who see the world from different perspectives. They still may be pre-critical in their thinking and may have a host of unexamined beliefs, but the deconstruction of naïve dogmatism no longer seems to be the pre-dominant need. Instead, many current students know they are afloat, and they are looking for a firm place to stand. This is not so much a search for cognitive grounding as for something worthy of trust. What should one hope for? What values should one rely on for guidance? Where can one find a life compass for thinking and living? Or should people just let themselves drift along in whatever cultural currents happen to catch them?

Although students do have a host of "big questions" in front of them, those questions are not necessarily the same big questions that educators would like them to discuss. Professors are often attracted to the kinds of deep human ques-tions that emerge from reading the great published works of the past and present, and they are disappointed when students react as if those grand musings have little or nothing to do with their own life questions and concerns. And even when professors do try to link course material to the existential concerns of students, students are still sometimes reluctant to engage. A student at one college explained to us that some professors try to introduce topics that are just "too personal for class. No one is going to reveal that much of themselves in class." Discussing big questions and student convictions in a college or university course is not nec-essarily easy, even when both students and professors favor its occurrence. One option is for colleges and universities to just stop trying, to ratchet back expecta-tions regarding student learning. In his book *The First Year Out,* sociologist Tim Clydesdale argues that first-year college students are typically in no position to reflect deeply (or even shallowly) on who they are and what they believe. Most college and university students, he says, have their hands full simply dealing with the details of "daily life management," and they keep "their core identities in an 'identity lockbox'" that is largely immune to change. During the sophomore and junior years, there may be a brief window of opportunity when deeper questions can be raised, but by the time they are seniors, the only thing on their minds is getting out and getting a job. The result, according to Clydesdale, is that the thinking of most students remains "remarkably conventional" and "the vast majority... are quite uninterested in seeking new self-understandings."[4]

Rather than trying to force students to examine their convictions, explore a range of different possibilities, and develop more refined views of the world, Clydesdale says it probably makes more sense for colleges and universities to adjust their unrealistic ideals to align more closely with the modest, circumscribed goals of their students. Although a few students—drawn disproportionately from those who are either highly religious or highly antireligious—are looking for a self-critical, intellectually liberating, socially broadening education, those kinds of students are rarities even at the most prestigious institutions of learning. According to Clydesdale, the statistics show that there is only one institutional subset where life-changing higher learning often takes place: at evangelically oriented Christian colleges like the one he himself attended. He hypothesizes that the high concentration of very religious students at these schools is the secret of their transformational educational success.[5]

Clydesdale's realism will be attractive to some: Let religious colleges and universities require students to engage whatever big questions they prefer, but let the rest of the academy do its work without getting bogged down in time-consuming and ultimately futile attempts to force students to reflect on their personal convictions. But is this really an option for higher education? The developmental psychologist Sharon Parks would answer "No." She argues that "higher and professional education is distinctively vested with the responsibility of teaching critical and systemic thought and initiating young lives into a responsible apprehension first of the realities and questions of a vast and mysterious universe and second of our participation within it."[6] She insists that this is not a matter merely for the intelligentsia, pointing out that asking and attempting to answer such questions is a requirement for leaders in practical fields like law, medicine, politics, and education, and that the need for higher order thinking extends far beyond the professions. If society is to be healthy, then individuals in a multitude of roles, including stay-at-home parents and those with positions in all sectors of the business world, must also think about the universal questions of humanity. If colleges and universities (except for those with an explicitly religious perspective) fail to offer this opportunity to students, then who will? For people like Parks, what seems unrealistic (and unacceptable) is for a college or university to shy away from providing students with this kind of soul-stretching, self-reflective education.

Professorial Convictions

Professors are often portrayed, and often portray themselves, as people who think and live rationally. Rather than being driven by various personal beliefs or convictions, their work is dictated by the disciplines and methodologies of their various fields of study (as discussed in chapter seven). Their goal is to study and teach that material, not to share their life journeys or values with their students. But while their training may not encourage (and may even actively discourage) them from talking about their own beliefs, professors, like all other human beings, possess personal convictions and in the right circumstances they can bubble to the surface.

We learned this early in the research for this book when we asked a colleague to arrange a discussion group composed of faculty drawn from a variety of different disciplines and institutions (public and private, church-related and not) in southern California. The twenty or so participants were selected partly because their work seemed to have the potential for connections with religion, but the group represented multiple disciplines (from computer science and engineering to art, literature, and business) and multiple religious perspectives (from conservative members of major historic traditions to atheists). The event coordinator opened the meeting by asking the participants to briefly introduce themselves, perhaps by sharing something about their own life journeys, whether those were religious or not. The response was overwhelming. People began to talk, and they couldn't stop. The two of us had anticipated an analytic discussion, but instead the participants spent nearly an entire day simply recounting their own stories— stories of faith lost and faith regained, stories of religious disillusionment, stories of frustration with institutions, stories of human compassion, stories of connecting with students, stories of searching for and sometimes finding meaning in life. Their obvious hunger to talk about their own spiritual journeys was, simply put, astonishing.

During a later campus visit, we were told a story about a similar gathering, but with a very different outcome. The location was a prestigious East Coast research university, and the office of religious life had invited professors who were "faculty of faith" to gather for a discussion about the connections between their academic work and their religious convictions. More than sixty faculty members showed up, all of them looking a bit surprised to find so many others who were also "secretly" religious. The discussion leader talked for a moment about similarities in the training regimens of scientists and monks, and then the floor was opened for discussion. The conversation was robust and personal, until someone said, "But I'm an expert in science, not a faith expert," and in an instant the positive dynamic dissipated. Scholars are warned against venturing beyond their areas of expertise, and that is most decidedly something to keep in mind when meeting with colleagues at a prestigious research university.

Professors know firsthand just how much work it is to master a subject, and they are respectful of expertise. After spending a major chunk of their lives becoming credentialed in one narrow subject, most professors have high regard for expert opinions, and the most academically successful scholars usually speak in public only about those fields of study in which they have academic standing. The moral philosopher Susan Neiman has deftly described the unfortunate result: "This sounds like the stance that Irish poet W. B. Yeats described long ago: 'The best lack all conviction/while the worst are full of passionate intensity.'...The noninterference pact that leads philosophers to refrain from talking about history, and historians from talking about morality, pretty much insures that few people with professional competence will jump into the fray—except in discussions too qualified to interest anyone but other specialists."[7] Professors often operate out of something like a code of silence regarding any subject outside their own narrow field of expertise, but that does not make those other concerns go away, nor does it eliminate the influence of convictions in their lives and work. Like everyone else, professors have convictions and, examined or not, those convictions influence how they see the world, teach their classes, and interact with students.

Formation and Information in the Classroom

Information and formation are intermingled in every classroom. Information is the subject content of the course; formation has to do with the impact (whether strengthening, undermining, changing, or complicating) that the course in its entirety has on the personal convictions and behaviors of students. For most instructors, the course is the information it contains, and successful completion of a course is measured by the acquisition of a predetermined quantity of knowledge and the mastering of a particular academic skill set. One of our now long-retired graduate school professors personified this understanding of teaching when he began each class by saying "I'm pitching and you're catching." He pitched balls of knowledge for students to catch, and most of us did just that: We tried to take it all in as best we could. His classroom style was stridently unidirectional, with no questions asked and the professor in charge, but even this statistics course was a formative experience. An understanding of advanced statistics left some students much less willing to be swayed by the passionate stories of individuals; it was now the numbers that mattered. Others left the class feeling personally incompetent and, in self-defense, harboring a deep-seated distrust of statistics.

The material included in a course and the way it is communicated to students (through lecture, assignment, discussion, or service-learning project) is never formationally neutral. Information changes people, and the choices professors make about what information to include and what to ignore can greatly alter the experiences and convictions of students. The "simple" act of choosing texts can be formative in powerful ways. Anouar Majid, chairman of the English department at the University of New England, describes how a devout Muslim friend, a highly educated engineer, had his conception of the United States (and to some degree his own faith) completely revolutionized by a careful reading of the Declaration of Independence. Majid asks, "How would he have reacted had he read Jonathan Edwards and the texts of other early American writers about the varied religious movements in American history, all struggling to establish the ideal society on earth? That classic American struggle, pitting pure faith against worldly success, is something Muslims could learn from, particularly educated youth looking for answers to their own cultural frustrations and identity crises."[8]

A college or university course is always more than its mere content, but content itself can carry a formative punch. We spoke with one psychology professor, for example, who told us that adding more information about "positive psychology" (the study of the attitudes and behavior of psychologically healthy individuals as opposed to people suffering from psychological problems) had changed the tenor of his courses. His current students are more apt to talk about ways of improving their own lives. He said they were still taking in lots of information, but they were processing it differently, not just mentally cataloguing it to regurgitate on an exam, but using it to make connections to their own hopes, dreams, and personal beliefs.

Critical Unsettling and Transcendent Unsettling

Students expect higher education to change them. One student who was making a decision about where to go to college tried to explain to her parents why she wanted to attend a school other than the one they preferred: "If I went to that college, it would fit the person I have been. I am choosing this college because it fits the person I am becoming."[9] Another student gave us a similar explanation for the way she selects her elective courses: "I choose classes on how they will affect me, how they tie in with what I need to deal with as a person." These students think that higher education is not just about learning "more stuff." It also concerns learning about yourself and how to become "more you" in the best possible way.

A story about Mahatma Gandhi illustrates the point. An irate opponent once accused him of having no integrity, because he said something that contradicted what he had said the week before. Unperturbed, Gandhi replied that his opponent was indeed correct about the discrepancy, but it was because "I have learned something since last week."[10] Gandhi's quick reply to his opponent communicates his awareness that learning has the power to change people, but it (perhaps wisely) ignores another aspect of the learning process. When the process of learning challenges personal conviction, it can be disturbing. It takes hard work to learn an academic subject or professional discipline, but the emotional ante goes up whenever learning overflows into questions of conscience or conviction. In the language of developmental stage theory, convictional development is often triggered by a cognitive-emotional crisis: The values and convictions that formerly gave grounding and direction to life no longer seem viable. Although a crisis may not be required, people often need some degree of unsettling or affective uneasiness before they will re-evaluate their own convictions.

A poignant example is provided by Mark C. Taylor, a postmodern theologian who is currently chair of the department of religion at Columbia University, but who spent most of his career at Williams College in rural Massachusetts. One day his class was discussing the existentialist writers Sartre and Camus—two major figures in the history of philosophy, who say that human life is fundamentally meaningless—when a student named Jake asked, "Isn't Camus the guy who killed himself in a car wreck?" Taylor said yes, adding that suicide was "not the only response to the human dilemma as existentialists see it. Rather...the absence of a given meaning for our lives gives us the opportunity to create our own meanings." The student was asking a personal question, however, not an academic one. His convictions were in play, and he wasn't satisfied with that response. So he persisted: "If Sartre is right, how can we hope? And if we cannot hope, why go on?" Once again, Taylor gave an academic response. He writes: "Rather than telling them what I really thought, I proceeded to explain how the writers we were reading would have responded to that question. Scholars, after all, are not supposed to think for themselves but are trained to analyze and report what others have already thought." But Taylor says that, when his eyes met the student's eyes, "I knew that he knew that I knew I had failed his test." Taylor did not want to communicate his own personal sense of "suffering and uncertainty" to his student, but Jake, and probably most of the other students in the room, knew what he really thought, just like children know what their parents really think.[11]

Taylor is a gifted teacher, and he also obviously understands how disconcerting it can be to question long-held beliefs. He also knows that some convictions are harder for human beings to bear than others. In particular, he did not want to force his own convictions, his own sense of stark realism, onto his students. His self-judgment that he "had failed" his student may, however, be overly harsh. Taylor responded as any good teacher would: He gave his students the information and insight they needed to make up their own minds about what to believe. He did not push his own conclusion on his students, but—and this is crucial—he obviously let enough of himself shine through that his students ascertained his own views. Perhaps it was impossible for him not to do so. When anyone is as deeply convinced as Taylor is about the accuracy of Camus and Sartre's vision of life, it is hard to hide those convictions from others. Nonetheless, Taylor admits that he has tried to become more hopeful in recent years (he is now a grandfather), even though hope remains elusive for him. He writes: "When hope is authentic, it hangs by the thin thread of *perhaps*.... Perhaps there is hope. Perhaps hope is the impossible possibility that helps us go on when everything seems hopeless. Perhaps."[12] Taylor's behavior in the classroom communicated this ambiguity—an ambiguity about hope that was both honest and at the same time hesitant enough to allow students to think for themselves.[13]

Taylor's quandary about how deeply to engage his students is familiar territory for many professors. The kind of unsettling of convictions Taylor describes as having taken place in his classroom is central to the process of liberal education. Criticism of what has been taken for granted is seen as the primary pathway toward both better knowledge about the world and more nuanced and reasonable self-understanding. Most professors are adept at facilitating this kind of questioning. They know how to criticize received wisdom, how to present oppositional views, how to point out contradictions, and how to identify gaps in logic. Scholars not only read texts and analyze events, but they also present alternative interpretations and look for hidden agendas that lie beneath the surface of what people think they know. This in-depth style of inquiry has the potential to challenge students because it raises questions that can reveal the limitations of their existing convictions. Such unsettling may be a prerequisite for personal growth, but there are dangers to this approach and one of them is the threat of despair— from which Taylor wanted to protect his students. Another potential danger is cynicism. The well-educated cynic can analyze every viewpoint and every value and then declare all of them irredeemably flawed. Such an outcome is surely not the desired educational goal, but sometimes cynicism can and does result.

Concerns about cynical outcomes were part of what prompted Wendy Doniger, distinguished professor of Asian religions at the University of Chicago, to give a convocation talk on the topic of "thinking more critically about thinking too critically." Critical thinking is a good and necessary thing when it has to do with "criticism" understood as the informed judgment of quality, and it also has a legitimate function when "criticism" means pointing out weaknesses and errors. But if criticism only operates in these judgmental and negative modes, it leaves students with very little in the way of constructive foundations. Doniger says that "we need to balance what literary critics call a hermeneutic of suspicion—a method of reading that ferrets out submerged agendas—with a hermeneutic of retrieval or even of reconciliation." Turning the spotlight of criticism around 180 degrees, Doniger concludes by calling the critics to account: "The purpose of a great liberal education...is to free us not only from our own prejudices but from our prejudices about other peoples' prejudices, to teach us to see through the walls of both our prisons and theirs.... Above all, it teaches us not just how to criticize but how to praise."[14]

Praise is a very different mode of reflection than criticism. Sometimes we run into people—from the past, in the present, face to face, or characters from short stories, novels, and films—who are so genuinely worthy of respect or admiration that they elicit spontaneous praise. Their attitudes and actions, their convictions and courage, are better than our own. They call us to a higher and better way of being human. No one is perfect, everyone has flaws, but the actions and words of some people set the standard higher for everyone. They inspire us to enlarge our souls. When we are lucky enough to run into such people, that experience can sometimes be just as unsettling, in terms of our own convictions, as any form of criticism. They force us to see our own smallness, or more pointedly to *feel* our smallness, our cramped views of others and ourselves, and the narrowness of our thinking. These are moments of "transcendent unsettling," because they not only challenge our convictions, but also call us toward a better way of being human.

Three Classroom Styles

Parker Palmer, the well-known writer and lecturer on education, says, "Teaching, like any human activity, emerges from one's inwardness, for better or worse. As I teach, I project the condition of my soul onto my students, my subject, and our way of being together."[15] Teaching is surely much more than simply the projection of a professor's "soul" onto students in a classroom, but there is more than a grain of truth in what Palmer says. Teachers bring all of who they are into the classroom with them, and that includes their convictions. Becoming aware of one's own convictions and learning to manage them in the classroom may well be a prerequisite for good teaching.

In general, faculty members assume one of three different strategies for dealing with the issue of their own convictions in the teaching and learning process. Some professors opt for anonymity, trying to hide as much of themselves as possible, other professors try to be transparent, publicly acknowledging their own convictions, and still others engage in advocacy, trying to convince students to adopt the same convictions that they themselves hold. Each of these approaches has its pedagogical strengths and weaknesses.

Anonymity: This first approach seeks, as much as possible, to keep the professor's own convictions hidden from view. Often, professors have had this style drilled into them in graduate school. They have been told: "Scholarship is not about you, it is about the subject being studied. Be objective and keep yourself out of the picture." Those who believe that professorial objectivity is possible may consider this to be the only proper way to teach, but even those with less confidence in objectivity can find reasons for adopting this stance. Perhaps the weightiest consideration relates to the fact that the professor is an authority figure in the classroom, and too much professorial self-revelation can cow students into adopting (or at least feigning to have adopted) the same views as the professor. Some students assume that course grades are dependent on agreeing with the professor on all matters, even when the professor claims otherwise. One student told us quite dramatically: "The classroom is tricky. It is okay to have your own opinion, but that doesn't mean you have to express it. Professors have to grade you—and that's something that will affect you for the rest of your life." By keeping personal convictions out of sight as much as possible, the professor minimizes the pressure to conform and makes space for students to develop their own perspectives and convictions. The problem, of course, is that concealment is never complete. Intentionally or not, the professor's perspectives leach into the classroom by way of the topics chosen, the approaches taken, and the conclusions drawn.

Transparency: This approach provides an alternative to anonymity, a model that encourages (or even requires) teachers to reveal their personal views. The logic is obvious. Because the convictions of professors inevitably shape the learning experience and introduce bias, the only antidote is to name those convictions (or points of view) so that students can factor them into the learning process. Once the professor's transparent self-revelation has brought everything into the open, then students are free to debate, reject, or intelligently appropriate the views of the teacher. Although there is significant merit in such an approach, there can also be problems. Very few professors, for example, can explain their convictions in a purely neutral manner, and even fewer can then genuinely invite students to analyze, criticize, and reject those convictions if they so choose. One wise educator asked, "How does a faculty member generate enough courage to disclose parts of her or his inner life in class and also possess enough humility to welcome students' explorations of alternative perspectives?"[16] The intention of those who adopt the transparency model is to reveal their own convictions in ways that empower others to think for themselves, but that is not always the result. Sometimes transparency can stifle discussion, and sometimes it can become an unacknowledged form of advocacy.

Advocacy: The strength of the advocacy model is its total honesty. A professor following this approach teaches the subject with straightforward passion, with no intention of limiting instruction just to the accepted facts and theories in the field. It's not just ecology or biology; it's saving the planet. It's not about sociological theory; it's about justice. It's not about a book; it's about what constitutes great literature. It isn't about religion; it's about life-changing faith or dangerous superstition. The professor's convictions are projected fully and forcefully into the classroom. There is a place for this kind of teaching in higher education. In fact, the American Association of University Professors says that advocacy is sometimes necessary: "Vigorously to assert a proposition or a viewpoint, however controversial, is to engage in argumentation and discussion—an engagement that lies at the core of academic freedom. Such engagement is necessary if students are to acquire skills of critical independence. The essence of higher education does not lie in the passive transmission of knowledge but in the inculcation of a mature

independence of mind."[17] Yet, most educators also know that unmitigated advocacy has the potential to undercut the hard, often dispassionate work of the academy, which focuses on trying to understand the world on its own terms, without
any agenda. Advocacy that never relents may be more likely to force dissenting
students into compliant silence (without changing their existing beliefs) than to
foster mature independence of mind.

Taken together, the three models of anonymity, transparency, and advocacy represent the full spectrum of pedagogical approaches that professors have
available—there really are no other options. These three approaches are not, however, mutually exclusive, and many professors employ the models strategically,
varying teaching styles in accordance with particular objectives. Teaching is an art,
and it takes creativity and sometimes subterfuge to get the job done. But all three
models implicitly acknowledge that the passions and convictions of the teacher
cannot be ignored. The professor's personal views must be taken into account,
regardless of whether the intention is to minimize or maximize their influence.
A professor who makes believe that his or her convictions have no salience for the
classroom is living a fantasy.

Mentors and Mentoring Communities

The standard responsibilities of college and university professors have been
described as the triumvirate of teaching, research, and institutional service.
Increasingly, however, the notion of mentoring is being added to the mix. A mentor is a model and, in that sense, adding mentoring to the list of faculty responsibilities is simply to acknowledge reality; all faculty members are mentors whether
they want to be or not. The teaching and learning relationship places educators
in the position of being models for students, at least with regard to their fields of
expertise and sometimes with regard to life in general.

But the use of the term "mentor" usually signals something more than this.
The dictionary definition is "wise and trusted counselor," and mentoring in that
sense means that professors are expected to take an active role in molding and
shaping students' lives and inspiring them as people. Today, some even go so far
as to talk of "the professor as spiritual guide."[18] That kind of language puts many
faculty members on edge, because it seems to cross a professional line: A teacher
is a teacher, not a guru or spiritual guide.[19] One faculty member told us: "I was
not trained as a counselor, and I have no desire to be one. I am an expert in my
field and I introduce students to the discipline—something I do very well. But
I am not there to hold hands, listen to student stories, and tell them how to live.
That's not my job." We have no doubt that this particular educator is an excel-
lent teacher, but the same attitude in a less gifted instructor can produce horrible
results. One recent posting by a student on a rating site for professors provides an

extreme example: "If given the option of having Professor X for this class or Satan, I would definitely choose Satan. Satan probably has more of an interest in seeing you succeed in [this class] than X does. He most likely has a better personality as well."[20]

Most professors have a relationship with students that falls somewhere in the middle, not quite a spiritual guru but certainly better than Satan. In recent years, many disciplines have discouraged old-fashioned "sage on the stage" lecturing strategies and encouraged professors instead to adopt a "guide by the side" posture. Professors are expected not only to be effective classroom teachers, but also to direct independent student research projects and serve as academic advisors for individual students and student organizations. With multiple roles and many occasions for informal interaction, the professor has the opportunity to become not only a mentor, but also a friend. In our campus conversations, however, some students describe their uneasiness with that ideal. One student informed us: "We don't want faculty to be our friends. We don't want to pour our lives out to them either. All we want is someone sometimes to talk to who is older than us, and maybe a little wiser—someone who is a little further down the road and who might have a slightly more mature perspective. That's it, just a little adult conversation now and then."

This student's comment seemed to align with the way most students describe the ideal faculty mentor: someone who once in a while is willing to be a real human being with students and not just a stick-to-the-topic teaching machine. Most students are not looking for immense measures of care, guidance, and handholding, but on occasion they would like to take off their student hats and have faculty members take off their professorial hats and then just talk with each other as ordinary people. In such conversations, convictions (of both students and faculty members) will sometimes be evident—these are the ideas and beliefs that define us as persons, so how could they not?—but they will not necessarily be the focus. More likely, convictions will season the conversation like spice in a meal: Spices make a meal richer in flavor, but if they are all you taste, then the seasoning has been overdone.

Taking this culinary image a step further, a well-seasoned dish usually has a variety of spices in it, and students too need a variety of mentors. The goal is not for any one faculty member to be the sole mentor of anyone. Instead, good colleges and universities are mentoring communities,[21] where different kinds of people provide a wide range of models and mentors for students to seek out or serendipitously encounter during their years of study. These influential "others" may not be professors, but rather students who have similar questions and passions—or students who have very dissimilar questions and eye-opening passions. In a wonderful short essay, thirty-something novelist Salvatore Scibona describes how his life was changed by his experience at a small liberal arts college: "It was akin to taking holy orders, but…in place of praying, you read." Remembering how he gathered with his friends to parse the meaning of the opaque texts comprising his school's Great Books program, he confides, "The gravity of the whole thing would have been laughable if it hadn't been so much fun, and if it hadn't been such a gift to find my tribe."[22]

Finding one's tribe—that group of people with whom one can feel totally one-self and at home—is indeed an exhilarating experience, and it has a lot to do with shared convictions. Too much overlap in group convictions can, however, short-circuit the need to ever rethink anything, because everyone just reinforces each other. Higher education at its best allows students to find their tribes without becoming unhealthily tribal. It starts students on a lifelong journey of discovering their convictions and examining those convictions, by themselves and in conversation with others, to see if and how they might need to be reconsidered. That quest is simultaneously spiritual and intellectual. It is a matter of the head, but it is also a matter of the heart, and it can be immensely beneficial for both individuals and society. For individuals, an examination of convictions keeps learning alive and allows growth as persons. For society, it is an antidote to fanaticism, but it still allows passions to flower. If one of the implicit goals of every institution of higher education is to help students become dedicated lifelong learners, the interplay of convictions and knowledge (of formation and information) will be a central concern.

10

Character and Vocation

How might colleges and universities point students toward
lives of meaning and purpose?

STEVE JOBS, THE late CEO of Apple Computers and Pixar Animations, gave the commencement address at Stanford University in 2005. The fourteen-minute talk, like all good commencement speeches, was short and to the point, and this was his advice: "Your time is limited, so don't waste it living someone else's life. Don't be trapped by dogma—which is living with the results of other people's thinking. Don't let the noise of others' opinions drown out your own inner voice. And most important, have the courage to follow your heart and intuition. They somehow already know what you truly want to become." What Jobs was telling his graduating audience that day was simple and straightforward. Meaning and purpose matter. You only get one life, so make it your own. Find out what *you* love—find out what you are called to do, what perhaps you and you alone can do—and do it. He concluded: "Everything else is secondary."[1]

It would be hard to find a more succinct description of personal religious practice, which centers on what a person genuinely trusts in, hopes for, and values above all else. It is the pattern of behavior that constitutes individual identity what gives direction and meaning to life. Sometimes an individual's personal religion is significantly informed by historic religion (by Christianity, Judaism, Hinduism, Islam, or some other tradition), but often personal religion has nothing to do with historic religion. It is what provides identity, grounding, meaning, and purpose to an individual; it is what makes life really worth living; and, to use Jobs's language, it is what makes everything else secondary by comparison.

Educational Idealism and Realism

Though rarely identified as such, the concerns of personal religion have often been used by colleges and universities to describe the function of higher education to young Americans. Going to college is presented formally or informally as a way of finding oneself, preparing oneself for the future, and then pursuing one's dreams. Jobs's commencement speech encapsulated that vision, and it is indisputably inspiring. The concern today, however, is that fewer and fewer students believe the rhetoric, and their doubt is grounded in clear reasoning. They know that they are deeply in debt. They know that everything is not possible. And they know that they need a job. They are not shooting for the stars; they just want to keep their heads above water. One college student, speaking in a way that would resonate with many peers, describes the purpose of life as "just having a good job, being stable, not having to worry about things, bills and all that, without struggling, being able to pay for the bills. And being able to go out once in a while… I think that'll be a good life. To have a home, to travel.… That's probably about it, just to know my wife, too, and then love her."[2]

Meanwhile, colleges and universities are also ratcheting back their expectations, even though institutional rhetoric often remains grandly upbeat. One public university we visited rewrote its mission statement a few years ago to include the magnificent goal of helping students become imaginative thinkers who are capable of making well-founded ethical decisions and "shaping a global community with vision, justice, and clarity." The statement describes the school as poised to become an "intellectual and cultural nexus" not only for the local community, but for the nation and the entire globe. However, the informally, but insistently, communicated word on campus is that the main concern of faculty should be serving the business community by preparing students for available jobs. Colleges and universities, just like the students they teach, are being forced by current political and economic realities to scale back their hopes and dreams. Institutional survival and helping students find work is the first concern; following your "heart and intuition" has become secondary.

And yet, huge numbers of incoming students (about three-quarters of them) still say they are hoping that their college or university experience will help them gain or maintain a sense of meaning and purpose in life.[3] When asked what this means, most students are inarticulate. They are not adept at translating their hopes into words, but they are looking for something. They want the opportunity to reflect realistically on who they are and who they are becoming and to consider whether their hopes and dreams and present practices are sufficient to sustain them through life and to contribute to the maintenance (or construction) of a world where others can also survive and flourish.

The great Jewish theologian Abraham Joshua Heschel once said that "the meaning of life is to build a life as if it were a work of art."[4] Heschel well understood that this is not an easy task and that life will include obstacles that can make this goal seem almost patently absurd. Yet, the goal remains: to find oneself, to be oneself, and to do what one is called to do despite the forces that may be arrayed against you. The question raised in this chapter is how colleges and universities can help students do precisely that.

The Problems of Emerging Adulthood

The process of making a life or discovering one's true self has perhaps become more challenging in recent decades. The years between the ages of eighteen to twenty-four, when many young people attend college or university, are now described by developmental psychologists as being part of a longer period in life they have termed "emerging adulthood." The period stretches out through the twenties, and for many individuals into their thirties, a partly self-chosen and partly imposed parenthesis between adolescence and adulthood. Emerging adults are quasi-independent, but still often reliant on financial support from their parents. They are connected with a whole network of friends, but they are delaying marriage and the commitments it entails.[5] They are on their way to adulthood and self-responsibility, but they have not yet arrived. Some emerging adults are uncertain they ever want to become fully adult. Sociologist Jeffrey Arnett has catalogued conversations with emerging adults who say things like "In some respects I kind of hope I never become an adult. Maybe I associate adultness with being constrained or something." Another emergent adult speculated, "I don't think I'll ever feel I've fully reached adulthood, because I think every day is going to be a quest for me. . . . Once you accept that you're an adult and there's nothing else to learn, then your life becomes stagnant."[6] Adulthood, as it is being modeled for them, is not especially appealing.

Many emergent adults find themselves largely on their own in terms of figuring out who they are and how to live. Traditional sources of guidance like parents and religious communities often seem relatively clueless. Parents did not experience challenges similar to what their children are facing, and they cannot comprehend why life seems so difficult for their grownup offspring. Many parents want only to get their sons and daughters out of the house and living on their own and help them avoid doing any permanent harm to themselves or others before they finally settle into full adulthood. Meanwhile, churches and other religious organizations often simply ignore emerging adults, figuring that many of them will eventually "return to the flock" when they settle down and become "real" adults. In turn, many young adults consider their churches, synagogues, mosques, and temples to be laughably out of touch with the realities of life on the ground, especially for youth and young adults.

Emerging adults—and all Americans—now live in a culture characterized by what the well-known social commentator Alan Wolfe has called "moral freedom."[7]

Faced with a huge range of choices in life (about both immediate actions and long-range life trajectories), individuals find themselves without any coherent moral or spiritual framework to help them assess which options are better and which are worse. Moral freedom, as it is used in this sense, is not an ideology and not the equivalent of passionately embraced ethical relativism. Moral freedom is a description of reality. In America today, individuals have to decide for themselves which moral guidelines or values will define their behavior, and they have to reach those conclusions in a culture where the language of morality is unclear and where new moral questions are constantly arising. Older individuals can fall back to some degree on prior personal experience, but young people are skating on thin ice without much prior experience and often without having (or wanting) anyone who can coach them along the way.

Adding to the stress is that many emerging adults are confronted with what appears to be an infinite number of life options. They have been told over and over again that they can be anything they want to be; the choice is theirs. There are so many potential avenues to follow that having to choose only one can be like ordering from the huge menu at a Cheesecake Factory restaurant with its 200-plus tantalizing items.[8] It can be paralyzing. Most emerging adults are smart enough to know that not all of the alternative pathways in front of them are real options and that trying to follow some of them will lead only to frustration and failure. Yes, they could prepare to audition for *American Idol,* but the likelihood of success is almost zero. Or they could opt to become investment bankers, but, oops, since the economy crashed, that item has been scratched off the menu. College and university students today are realists, and given the current state of the economy, they have to be. Often, though, even the more realistic choices seem to lead to dead ends. A recent report found that only about half the jobs landed by recent college graduates actually require a college degree. Entering the job market today is a humbling experience.[9]

Rather than seeing the future as endlessly open, many young adults have come to view life as a puzzle. They look at the world and their own futures in the same way they looked at the *Where's Waldo?*[10] books they read as kids. The point is to find Waldo, in his chipper red-and- white striped shirt, who is hidden on each page among hundreds of other characters. For emerging adults, the point is to somehow find "The Plan," the one life pathway among all others that comes dressed in a metaphorical Waldo shirt and leads to happiness and fulfillment. Many are simultaneously searching for "The One," the single individual in the world who is destined to be their partner in following "The Plan." Expectations for encountering The One are amazingly widespread. A recent survey found that 88 percent of people in their twenties believe there is one "special person, a soul mate, waiting for you somewhere out there."[11] Fixating on The Plan or on finding The One can be even more debilitating than dealing with the Cheesecake Factory menu. It is hard to be sure when you have identified The Plan correctly, and if you partner up with the wrong One, your life may be ruined forever.

William Damon, professor of education and director of the Center on Adolescence at Stanford, says that all of this ambiguity and worry about the future is leaving a deep mark on the current generation of young people. It is not that they are devoid of hopes and dreams for themselves—they are often full of idealism—but they seem unwilling or unable actively to pursue those hopes and dreams. It is as if the gear shifts of their lives have been locked into neutral. Damon estimates that only about 20 percent of young people have a clear sense of purpose and "have found something meaningful to dedicate themselves to." He identifies another 30 percent as "dabblers," individuals who "have tried out a number of engaging pursuits," but have yet to find a good reason for committing themselves to any of them. Roughly 25 percent are "dreamers" with some "idealistic aspirations," but who have never done anything to follow up on them. And finally, 25 percent are disengaged, directionless, or drifting, with no discernible sense of purpose or meaning in life.[12] If Damon's conclusions are right, only a fraction of young people possess a clear sense of what they want from life, and the rest of them, the large majority, are more or less just floating along.

Christian Smith, professor of sociology at Notre Dame and director of the highly acclaimed National Study of Youth and Religion, concurs. He argues that the current generation of young people is morally adrift and almost totally captive to American consumerism. Emerging adults drink too much, have sex with each other without ever thinking about the personal or social consequences, and are politically disengaged. Smith is careful to nuance his argument, and he provides percentages making it clear that not all emerging adults conform to the worst-case scenario. But the composite picture is not encouraging: According to Smith, most emerging adults are "lost in transition."[13]

The Rhetoric and Realities of Life on Campus

Inquire at any college or university and you will be told that helping students avoid getting lost in the transition from youth to adulthood is a central institutional goal. How that goal is to be accomplished is rather less clear. The typically unstated assumption seems to be that, somehow, the end result of a college education—the sum total of its parts, including all the courses, co-curricular activities, and experiences with professors, fellow students, and others—will be self-knowledge, self-confidence, social and intellectual maturity, and the formulation of some fairly specific plans to be actualized after graduation that will result in both personal flourishing and benefit to humankind. That is the goal; campus realities often differ.

There is a long history of universities yielding disappointment. The origins of the university system go back to the monasteries of the Middle Ages. The students, many of them monks, were supposed to lead more disciplined lives than the rest of the population. This did not always happen, and records show that students in the fourteenth and fifteenth centuries often misbehaved much like they do today. However, the monastic ideals were there for guidance. Today, the college years are perceived in a quite different light: not as a kind of temporary monasticism designed to create disciplined learning and personal development, but rather as a moral holiday, a time for experimentation and fun, with no rule other than avoiding long-term harm to self or others.

There is an analogy in the practices of the horse-and-buggy Amish of Lancaster County, Pennsylvania. Many Americans observe the Amish with nostalgia and a bit of longing, because they seem to embody the virtues of an earlier era when life was simpler and problems few. They are also admired for their self-discipline, for being people who know what it means to live by rules and who have strict cultural codes marking them as different from the "English," the term by which the Amish refer to everyone outside their own community. Amish young people participate in an informal ritual called *rumspringa* during late adolescence, a time for sowing wild oats before they make a decision about whether to become full members of the Amish church. They buy pickup trucks and drive into town, they watch TV, they smoke, dance, and drink, and they find other ways to sample "the world." The purpose of *rumspringa* is to enable Amish youth to make an informed choice about life. If they choose to join the church, they will follow its rules. If they cannot give up the things they sampled, then they should not join the church.

Some people—including many people involved in higher education—think of the college years as a kind of massive *rumspringa* for young adults in American mainstream culture, a time when there are no rules and when anything goes prior to settling into adult responsibilities. It is assumed that, like the Amish, college students can decide later on what kinds of people they will be as adults. However, this analogy ultimately fails because there is no decision point at the end of college that equates with the choice facing Amish youth. For students in mainstream American culture, there is no settled community with proscribed roles and discipline to which they can and will return. They are morally free in college, and they will be morally free after college. There is no break between life in college and life after college, and a student's style of life will not magically metamorphose into something else upon graduation. College is part and parcel of ongoing life.

Viewed as a moral holiday, college can be exhilarating for some, but exhausting and debilitating for others. The scope of that reality was made clear to us when we attended the annual meeting of the Association of College and University Religious Affairs (ACURA) that was held on the campus of Stanford University in the fall of 2008. ACURA is a national organization for chaplains (or those with equivalent roles but different titles, such as "director of religious affairs") at American colleges and universities, and its membership includes chaplains from many well-known schools including, among others, Brown, Carleton, Cornell, the University of Chicago, Dennison, Emory, Furman, Princeton, and the University of Denver. Almost all of these chaplains would describe themselves as socially and religiously progressive, and they are by no means a prudish bunch. But when we listened in on a session devoted to "stories from the field," their list of concerns was topped by alcohol, sex, and depression, with the three often interrelated.

Later, in private conversations, many chaplains expressed dismay about a perceived gap between their institutions' stated educational goals and actual campus practices. One chaplain vented about the atmosphere on his campus: "Living a meaningful and coherent life is way down the list. Prestige and money are the real priorities of the university and students know it. All the warm rhetoric about meaning and purpose and quality of life seems inauthentic—like a parent saying 'do what I say, not what I do.' But students know the operative values." Almost to a person, the chaplains said their dream was to have a part in helping to move realities on their campuses in the direction of their schools' articulated goals, but instead they were spending their time in therapeutic roles: keeping a lid on problems and helping students deal with issues defined as "personal" by their institutions.

Personal Practices and the Development of Character

Students know why the chaplains are concerned. A recent editorial in *The Eagle*, the student newspaper at American University in Washington, D.C., describes the problem bluntly: "The longer I stay in college the more I fear for humanity. Let me out of this place—now! Tuesday night—drink; Friday night—drink; Saturday night—drink. Not that I'm above it. I'm not. I drink, I party, I can throw down too…[but] we are in arrested development. College has become a four-year summer camp, except we have more money to play with and fewer rules to govern us." The student editorial ends with a simple call for moderation, for students to grow up and "embrace the responsibility that each of us has towards our families, our world and ourselves. We can't do it drunk or stoned—it needs to be done sober."[14]

If alcohol causes problems on campus, sex may cause even more of them, especially for women, given that 20 percent of female college students report being forced into sex against their will at least once during their college careers.[15] Many of these cases go unreported, sometimes because everyone involved is too drunk to ask or consent to anything. Few doubt that male culture at some schools can be disrespectful toward women. According to one expert, 20 percent of college men watch pornography, much of it demeaning to women, on a daily basis.[16]

In a recent incident at Yale, a group of male fraternity members gathered outside a women's center holding signs that read "We love Yale sluts" and chanting "No means yes."[17] Federal officials are currently investigating claims that Yale is a "sexually hostile environment" for women, but it is only fair to point out that these same concerns could be raised about many other institutions.

Women's safety demands immediate campus attention, but some observers are expressing concern even about consensual sex. In *Sex and the Soul* (2008), Boston University professor Donna Freitas describes the "hook-up culture" that prevails on most college and university campuses.[18] "Hooking up" is sex with no commitments. Nothing is promised, and no further "relationship" is expected; in fact, no relationship is desired. The whole purpose of hooking up is to have relationally unencumbered sex. Freitas says that many students want something more: They want to be appreciated, they want to be respected, and ultimately they want to be loved. They are looking for "romance"—a kind of "spiritual" intimacy that is linked with friendship—but they are not sure it exists. Harvard Divinity School professor Stephanie Paulsell explains that this kind of intimacy is much more than merely sexual: "If we are lucky, our first kisses and caresses, and all those that follow, will be marked with the same reverence that Emerson talks about in relation to friendship.... When we approach another's body without reverence, the potential for doing harm is great; just as when we pursue a friendship for its advantage to us."[19] To talk about sex in terms of reverence for the body is not likely the typical language used by college students, but it gets some support from conclusions being reached in academic fields like gender studies, neuropsychology, biology, and cultural studies. What people do to and with their bodies shapes who they are as total persons. As one scholar summarizes, "Nothing about human experience remains untouched by human embodiment: from basic perceptual emotional processes that are already at work in infancy, to...the acquisition and creative use of language, to higher cognitive facilities involving judgment and metaphor."[20]

To the degree that student practices related to alcohol and sex or anything else are dehumanizing to themselves or others, they are antithetical to the purpose of higher education. Colleges and universities say they are in the business of personal maturity and the formation of individuals who are self-disciplined, socially responsible, community-minded, and compassionate toward others, but student practices like habitual intoxication and depersonalizing sex are often allowed to go on without comment. It would be absurd for a college or university to say it was committed to helping students be environmentally aware and then make no effort to nudge student practices toward ecological responsibility— no recycling containers on campus, no "greening" of the campus facilities, no academic programs focusing on environmental concerns. And yet, this is akin to the position many institutions assume with regard to facets of student life related to character and vocation and the practices of personal religion in general. Students will have to make choices about these matters for themselves, just like Amish teenagers choosing to join or not join their church. But there is nothing admirable about denying college students the opportunity to consider various options. Orchestrating intelligent conversation about these domains of human practice and providing models for various ways of living seem like reasonable educational aims.

Character and Vocation: Institutional Reconsiderations

Higher education as a whole seems to be slowly meandering in the direction of taking concerns like the development of character (who one is) and the exploration of vocation (what one is "called" to do) seriously once again. As with everything else that was perceived as spiritual or religious—and character and vocation are inherently religious because they concern things that really matter for individuals, however historically religious or irreligious those individuals may be—such issues were sidelined by much of higher education during the later twentieth century as matters that ought to be handled privately, rather than in the public context of a college or university's formal educational program. Instead, the goal of higher learning was to expose students to the full spectrum of human life without morally or religiously stacking the deck one way or another.

That posture of presumed moral neutrality is now being questioned. Elizabeth Kiss (president of Agnes Scott College) and J. Peter Euben (professor of political science at Duke), in particular, have pointed out that no college or university is morally and spiritually naked: "Every association has a moral end, a hierarchy of values, which is cultivated through its everyday norms and practices" and this includes colleges and universities whose "moral ends and purposes [are] expressed not only through institutional statements and curricula, but also, and often more powerfully, through the hidden curriculum of everyday campus life."[21] According to Kiss and Euben, colleges and universities are far from being morally neutral settings for education. Every campus is flush with moral values and agendas, and it would be good for institutions of higher learning to become more conscious of how these values and agendas influence educational outcomes for students.

The Association of American Colleges and Universities (AAC&U) takes a further step, asking schools to think seriously about the ways in which their educational programs and cultures contribute to the formation of students as moral agents. The AAC&U, an association of more than 1,200 institutions, wants to make sure that "the advantages of a liberal education are available to all students regardless of background, enrollment path, academic specialization, or intended career." The central term in this statement of purpose is "liberal education," and the AAC&U has put years of effort into defining the meaning of liberal education in the increasingly job-oriented system of American higher education. Starting in 2005, the AAC&U began to suggest that "educating students for personal and social responsibility" was one of the "core commitments" that any reasonable definition of liberal learning should include. Carol Geary Schneider, president of the organization, thinks that schools ought to encourage students to make conscious commitments "to reach for excellence in the use of their talents, take responsibility for the integrity and quality of their work, and engage in meaningful practices involving both action and reflection that prepare them to fulfill their obligations as responsible citizens."[22] In essence, this is a call to pay more attention to character and vocation.

Institutional concerns regarding character are also evident in recently rewritten honor codes and campus "creeds" at various colleges and universities. Ten or twenty years ago, most such statements would have been limited to academic integrity and would have focused mainly on the problem of plagiarism. Today, many of these codes have been expanded beyond academic integrity to include larger ethical issues. Thus, the "Carolinian Creed" of the University of South Carolina includes, among other items, a requirement to "respect the dignity of all persons," "discourage bigotry," and "demonstrate concern for others, their feelings, and their need for conditions which support their work and development."[23] The University of Southern Oregon asks students to promise to be environmentally "green."[24] And the University of Mississippi not only asks each student to affirm the dignity of all persons, practice integrity in personal and professional life, and act as a good steward of the world's resources, but also to "encourage others to follow my example."[25] However these kinds of statements play themselves out in actual practice, their mere existence indicates that life values and behaviors—the concerns of personal religion—are becoming more visible in higher education.

Although various campuses and educational organizations have been giving more attention to character and vocation in the last decade, the linking of these matters with religion has been especially evident at colleges and universities affiliated with the Program for the Theological Exploration of Vocation (PTEV) that was developed and supported by the Lilly Endowment headquartered in Indianapolis, Indiana. The Endowment was very intentional in using the word "theology" in the title of this program as a signal of direct engagement with religion, albeit religion broadly defined. Between 1999 and 2009, a total of eighty-eight American campuses each received roughly two million dollars to develop programs that nurtured religious and spiritual reflection on practices that might help students gain a sense of vocation in life. All of the participating schools were private, and many of them were church-related. Some, like Baylor, Duke, Notre Dame, Pepperdine, and Wake Forest, were nationally ranked universities, while others were smaller and less well-known institutions. Currently more than 150 schools are involved in the Network for Vocation in Undergraduate Education

(NetVUE), administered by the Council of Independent Colleges (CIC), which seeks to sustain and expand the vocational insights generated by the PTEV project.

The PTEV project never formulated a singular definition of vocation. Each of the participating schools developed its own campus-specific visions, but a definition penned by the writer Frederick Buechner came to have near canonical status at many institutions. Vocation, according to Buechner, is "the place where your deep gladness and the world's deep hunger meet."[26] This definition was attractive largely because it balances self-awareness with concern for the practical needs of the world. Some participants in the project, however, felt that Buechner's definition was a bit too breezy and easy. It is indeed wonderful when one's gladness and the world's deep hunger meet, but sometimes life doesn't work that way. Encountering the hunger of the world can cause sorrow as well as joy, and sometimes it is a deeply unsettling experience. Dorothy C. Bass, a writer who was influential in shaping the PTEV project, notes that thinking about one's own vocation can "bring us to places of risky engagement where the pain of the world and awareness of our own shortcomings will pierce our hearts…[making it] impossible to ignore just how not-whole we and our world actually are."[27] As used in the PTEV project, the term "vocation" was not simply about finding one's dreams and following them; it was also about becoming aware of imperfection and brokenness in oneself and others.

Pacific Lutheran University (PLU) in Tacoma, Washington, illustrates how the PTEV project was meant to work. As its name implies, PLU is a Lutheran institution, but only 25 percent of its students are Lutheran, and many are nonreligious or only tangentially affiliated with some historic religious tradition. The faculty members too represent a wide range of religious and nonreligious perspectives, so their program needed to talk about vocation in ways that everyone and not just Lutherans could affirm. Accordingly, their "Wild Hope" program asks every student in multiple settings spread over all semesters of enrollment: "What will you do with your one wild and precious life?" This question does not mention religion by name, but it is solidly Lutheran nonetheless—in sync with the sentiments of the sixteenth-century religious revolutionary Martin Luther, founder of the Lutheran movement, who turned the world upside-down with his new ideas. But it is not just Lutherans who like asking the question. Everyone we talked to on campus, faculty and students alike and irrespective of their personal religious or nonreligious identities, told us the program was a great success, and they seemed thoroughly convinced that every high-quality college or university ought to ask their students something along the same lines. Inviting students to think about their lives in terms of vocation has enlivened the campus both morally and intellectually.

Other schools developed different emphases reflecting both their institutional missions and the students they serve. Santa Clara University, a Catholic (Jesuit) institution in California, stresses the role of discernment—consciously reflecting on decisions being made, often with input from others—and highlights the importance of social justice. A key element is taking students on "immersion trips" to Central America, a place where the Jesuits have a long history of working with and for the poor.[28] At Guilford College, a Quaker school in Greensboro, North Carolina, the school's vocation program is built around five core Quaker affirmations: the "direct and immediate access to god-truth by the individual, peace, simplicity, equality, and integrity."[29] At Guilford, as at Santa Clara, the goal is to help students think about the trajectories of their lives through a prism of meaning and purpose quite different from the perspectives of mainstream American culture. Some schools take a more generic approach. Hastings College in Nebraska, for example, simply asks students to think about what it might mean to pursue "a passion bigger than yourself,"[30] and Denison University in Ohio encourages students "to reflect upon their career paths and the relationship between their plans and personal values."[31] The PTEV program at Butler University also takes a broad-brush approach, telling students:

> It takes courage to heed a call—to find your true vocation. But there's no doubt that each of us is called to do something with our lives that engages the world beyond our own self-interest. Often, it's hard to figure out just what that vocation or calling may be. Many influences pull us away from what our hearts or souls or guts may be telling us and towards something practical, lucrative, ambitious or prestigious.... So where do you begin? Listen to yourself. Pay attention to the life around you. Think about where you have been and what you have achieved already. Search for insight through your religious or spiritual tradition, if you follow one. Pray about it. Write about it. Paint or draw about it, and see what rises. Ask yourself, what do you love to do? Where do your talents lie? What concerns you most about the world? What worries you or makes you angry? What gives you hope? Talk to your friends, your professors and your mentors about your passions, ideas and gut-feelings. Simply speaking with others can bring clarity and build confidence.[32]

What is significant about all of these initiatives, from the AAC&U's emphasis on personal and social responsibility to the way honor codes are being redefined on various campuses to the PTEV program's emphasis on vocation, is that they reflect a new willingness to raise questions that go beyond narrowly defined academics and point in the direction of personal practices, personal maturity, and personal religion. Far from being anti-intellectual or merely subjective, all of these initiatives are also profoundly knowledge-related. They all connect thinking and doing.

Character and Vocation: The Student Quest

Although institutional programming related to character and vocation can provide students with opportunities to reflect on their current practices and future hopes, it is students themselves who decide who they are and who they want to become. Every college and university graduate will walk down life's pathway in a uniquely personal way, with their different choices often influenced by three competing visions of the good life: (1) the well-planned life, which identifies long-term goals and plans activities around them; (2) the authentic life, a life of passion and self-knowledge lived fully in the present; and (3) the summoned life, one spent being attentive and responsive to the needs of others.[33]

The Well-Planned Life: Many college and university students have been trained to be high achievers, and they are already adept at pursuing the well-planned life. They know how to set goals for themselves and are practiced in accomplishing them. According to Harvard Business School professor Clayton Christensen, such planning is the key to a meaningful life: Meaning grows out of purpose. He explains that living a well-planned life is similar to running a successful company: "If a company's resources allocation process is not managed masterfully, what emerges from it can be very different from what management intended." In much the same way, individuals who don't "keep the purpose of their lives front and center as they [decide] how to spend their time, talents, and energy" will likely end up dissatisfied.[34] Christensen's own life purpose grows out of his religious faith, and religion serves as the source of purpose for many people, but "faith isn't the only thing that gives people direction." Once a person makes a decision about life purpose, then the rest is consistency and follow-through. "Think about the metric by which your life will be judged, and make a resolution to live every day so that in the end, your life will be judged a success."[35] The well-planned life takes discipline and foresight, and it bears a strong resemblance to the classic Protestant work ethic. Rather than following one's passions in the present—passions that can push a person off-track—the key to success and meaning in life is to stay on message and stay the course.

The Authentic Life: Not everyone finds the well-planned life appealing. In fact, some individuals think that living a well-planned life is a recipe for disaster. The highly regarded leadership expert Robert K. Greenleaf once commented: "If we can name it and describe it precisely, the chances are we are seeking the wrong things."[36] What Greenleaf and many others (including Steve Jobs) would say is that authenticity is the better goal, striving to stay in touch with your true self (or higher self) and pursue the personal passions that make you feel truly alive. Christine Hassler, who describes herself as a "life coach" for emerging adults, is a cheerleader for this approach. She tells young people to forget about their parents' hopes for them, to give up their desperate search for "The Plan" and

"The One," and to stop jumping through society's hoops—with this last injunction directed especially at young women because, Hassler says, they are more prone than men to define themselves by externals. Her advice is to concentrate on what is inside. The secret to happiness is to get in touch with yourself and discover your own deep passions, which she defines as the core of human spirituality. "For me, spirituality means being connected to the Self. I write Self with a capital 'S' because I am referring to my higher Self. I see this higher Self as one with God, a higher power, the Universe, and the unseen energy field we are all part of.... Immeasurable blessings come from a connection to your Self, God, or the Universe—semantics are not important." Hassler instructs emerging adults to avoid being mindlessly shallow, but she also says not to waste too much time planning for the future. Seize the moment. "Unless you are breaking a legal or moral law, purposely hurting someone, or lying—forget about doing the 'right' thing. Seriously, there is no such thing as 'right' and 'wrong' in terms of what you are doing in your twenty-something years. As long as we are committed to learning from our experiences, there are no mistakes!"[37] Being authentic, according to Hassler, is the one and only pathway to meaning and personal happiness.

The Summoned Life: A third option assumes that a sense of vocation depends on more than an inner voice; it must also be based on accurate information about the world. The psychologist John Neafsey, who teaches at Loyola University in Chicago, says that the first step is to "hear the word of reality," and then to respond appropriately, which may include "a capacity to feel shame" when reality reveals one's own flaws.[38] The columnist and social commentator David Brooks says that it is ultimately unhelpful either to let passions direct life or to view life as a well-planned "project to be completed." A more helpful approach is to envision the future as "an unknowable landscape to be explored." The future will almost certainly bring calamities and opportunities that cannot possibly be foreseen in advance. A well-lived life is one that responds appropriately to all of these unpredictable occurrences. Having a strong sense of self can help. Being aware of one's passions, commitments, values, and core purpose (should a person be single-minded enough to have one) can be invaluable in facing crises, whether those crises are positive or negative in substance. But life is not only about staying firmly aligned with passions or plans; it is also about being responsive and willing to change. Brooks says, "The person leading the Summoned Life starts with a very concrete situation: I'm living in a specific year in a specific place facing specific problems and needs. At this point in my life, I am confronted with specific job opportunities and specific options. The important questions are: What are these circumstances summoning me to do? What is needed in this place? What is the most useful social role before me?"[39] The answers to these questions are not first of all about authenticity or steadfastness of purpose; they are about assessing real needs in the real world and then responding in creative ways that make the world a better place, as much as that is possible, for everyone involved. Brooks does not identify the summoned life in such terms, but his vision of life is profoundly compatible with his own religious background of Judaism. In contrast to some other religions, the Jewish tradition always "attends to the particular, not just the universal,"[40] and it cares little for sincerity or authenticity in the abstract.[41] What matters is how one lives wisely and practically within the unpredictable flux of life.

Barry Schwartz and Kenneth Sharpe, both members of the faculty at Swarthmore College, have recently written a book that explores this terrain of what they term "practical wisdom." They begin by recounting the story of a hospital custodian named Luke. Luke has just cleaned the room of one patient—a young man who was in a fight several months earlier and has been comatose ever since—when the patient's father appears and accuses him of not cleaning his son's room. Luke continues the story: "I was going to argue with him. But I don't know. Something caught me and I said, 'I'm sorry. I'll go clean the room.' . . . It was like six months that his son was here. He'd be a little frustrated, and so I cleaned it again. But I wasn't angry with him. I guess I could understand."[42] Luke had every right to defend himself, and nothing in his job description required him to respond so compassionately to an unreasonable demand. But Luke decided to do the right thing in the right way at the right time. He put aside his own sense of indignation and willingly cleaned the room again as a means of helping the patient's father through the stress of coping with his sorrow. Schwartz and Sharpe describe Luke as possessing an Aristotelian ethic, an ability to see the *telos* or deeper purpose of what it means to be a hospital worker: You care for patients and you also care for their families. But Luke's story could also be used as an illustration of what Buddhists might call "mindfulness" and Christians might call "denial of self." The summoned life in this sense is about more than personal success or authenticity; it is about living toward meaning and purpose that transcends the self.

Elements from all three visions can be braided together in a single life. Planning and perseverance, passion and authenticity, and being attuned to the needs of others can be combined, and when that happens, the result is something wonderful, what the researchers Howard Gardner, Mihaly Csikszentmihayli, and William Damon call "good work."[43] Good work is meaningful, moral, well done, rewarded, and respected. But good work is also dependent on a host of concerns beyond anyone's control, and lining up passion, performance, compassion, and pay is never easy.

Most students are simultaneously realists and idealists. They would like to lead lives of meaning and purpose, building a better world for both themselves and others, and they hope that kind of life is possible. On the other hand, they are realists, and often deflated realists at that. They feel powerless, not only about changing the world, but even about controlling their own lives. They feel like cogs being prepared to take their place in the great machine of society, and they hope there really will be a place in the machine for them. If not, they may be living in their parents' basements forever.

Colleges and universities are supposed to help students find a way through these tensions. They are in the business of providing students with knowledge and skills they can sell in the job market. This is the realistic side of higher education, and it is important and necessary. But people can get job training (or "cog training") in many places. What colleges and universities also have the opportunity to do—and many claim as their institutional calling—is something more. Harold T. Shapiro, former president of both the University of Michigan and Princeton University, defines the content of this "more" without equivocating: The ultimate test of every college or university, he says, is not "what we teach, or even what our students learn, but what kind of persons they become."[44] If Shapiro is right—and we think he is—then paying attention to matters like character and vocation (matters that are for many students inherently religious) is not something optional for colleges and universities; it is central to why they exist.

Conclusion: Religion and the Future of University Education

THE ARGUMENT OF this book is straightforward but complex. First, we point out that religion has "returned" to higher education in the last two decades; it has become much more visible. This is a simple statement of fact, but we add the qualification that the religion that has returned to university education in recent years is not the same kind of religion that dominated higher learning in America during the eighteenth and nineteenth centuries. Religion today is much more pluriform than it was in the past and much less easily distinguished from other lifestances that formerly might have been called secular. We now live in a foggy religio-secular world where many kinds of faiths (both traditionally religious and other) mingle together. This new shape of religion means that it would be virtually impossible to fence religion out of the academy even if such exclusion was preferred.

Our second assertion is that religion, as it exists within higher education today, is not an extraneous add-on to the goals and purposes of college and university learning. Colleges and universities seek to understand the world as it really is, and like it or not religion is still a significant part of our world. Religion is part of the world outside ourselves, both in the form of historic religion (traditional "organized" religion) and in the form of public religion (the religion-like ideas, values, and practices of societies). But religion is also part of the world "inside" people, taking the form of personal religion (or spirituality) that focuses on the ideals, values, and practices that ground us as human beings and make our lives meaningful. The kind of real-world, student-centered pedagogy that sets the standard for college and university education today makes paying attention to all three of these modes or varieties of religion a necessary part of any quality program of higher learning. Including religion more fully in higher education does not necessitate the adding of new courses dealing specifically with religion—though the prominence of religion in today's world might make that a reasonable thing to do. We suggest instead that religion is already implicit in many of the courses and subjects being taught, and that it makes sense to give it more attention.

Our third proposition is that giving more careful and nuanced attention to religion can be a source of revitalization for higher education as a whole. This third suggestion is less prominent in the text than the first two—it is mentioned, but not developed in detail—and it will be highlighted here. It is a bold claim. There are still many people in the academy who worry that any inclusion of religion in higher education will undermine critical thinking and liberal learning, people who believe that religion is either inherently irrational (and thus antithetical to higher learning) or insufficiently important to be a central subject of study within the framework of higher education. We disagree entirely. There is no question that, handled poorly, religion can be a disruptive force within higher education, but this is true of many other subjects as well, including politics, economics, race, class, and gender. Making an argument against religion in higher education because it is challenging would eliminate many other important topics of study as well. Religion is difficult because it is important. When the subject is handled well, discussed intelligently, and reflected upon seriously, religion (broadly construed) has the potential to enhance higher learning and open up a range of questions about the world and the human condition that otherwise might never be asked. Not all of these questions are themselves religious, at least not in the traditional sense of that term. But they are all functionally religious because they are about "things that matter."

Anyone who is interested in American higher education knows that the word "crisis" is often used to describe the contemporary scene. The list of complaints and concerns is long: Students can't write; grade inflation is a problem; the faculty tenure system seems broken; the liberal arts are in decline; nonstop partying interferes with learning; and (depending on one's point of view) colleges and universities are either giving too much or not enough attention to preparing students for the workplace. Some of these concerns are overstated, but the general picture is clear: Higher education is not living up to its promise.

One of our worries about this language of crisis in higher education is that most of the proposed solutions focus on the nuts and bolts of academic programming and policies, on things like getting rid of tenure or making the listing of courses more uniform (along the lines of the Bologna agreement in Europe) or re-configuring academic departments or developing new and more precise ways of assessing measureable learning outcomes or devising new ways to deliver the curriculum more cheaply and efficiently. Of course, every college and university must attend to these kinds of practical matters, and a failure to do so can have disastrous effects, but attending to these kinds of matters alone is not enough. Clarity, efficiency, assessment, and costs are vital concerns, but so are the less easily quantified ideals that define college and university learning at its best.

The goal of college and university learning at its best is to transform students as persons. This includes helping students gain some degree of distance on themselves and some ability to realistically evaluate their personal strengths and weaknesses, some understanding and appreciation of how people different from themselves comprehend the world, and some sense of how people and groups can work together toward making the world a better place for everyone. As Louis Menand argues in *The Marketplace of Ideas: Reform and Resistance in the American University* (2010), "It is the academic's job in a free society to serve the public culture by asking questions the public doesn't want to ask, investigating subjects it cannot or will not investigate, and accommodating voices it fails or refuses to accommodate."[1] If higher education is in crisis and somehow needs to "be saved," that salvation will require addressing these kinds of broader (some would say idealistic) human concerns alongside the other more practical matters that are currently receiving the bulk of attention.

No one doubts that colleges and universities should offer "training" to their students—instruction related to the skills and knowledge needed for landing and keeping a job—but colleges and universities have always claimed to do more than just that, and they need to do more than that today. The aim is not to juxtapose personal transformation and career preparation as if these two concerns are opposites; the goal is to affirm both. This has always been the genius of the American higher educational system: It has been both practical and reflective. At present, however, this balance is being threatened by neglect of the more broadly human and humane aspects of traditional college and university study. The current president of Harvard, Drew Gilpin Faust agrees:

> American universities have long struggled to meet almost irreconcilable demands: to be practical as well as transcendent; to assist immediate national needs and to pursue knowledge for its own sake; to both add value and question values.... Universities are meant to be producers not just of knowledge but also of (often inconvenient) doubt. They are creative and unruly places, home to a polyphony of voices. But at this moment in our history, universities may well ask if they have in fact done enough to raise the deep and unsettling questions necessary to any society.[2]

Our contention is that giving careful and nuanced attention to religion (broadly construed) can help colleges and universities revive the more reflective dimension of this double-sided, classically American vision of higher learning. This is not a new role for religion. During the colonial period and most of the nineteenth century, religion, especially as expressed in concern about character and moral development, was the glue that held the curriculum together. Over time, the relatively narrow way in which religion was defined (primarily as Protestantism) made it impossible for religion to continue to play such a role in an increasingly pluralistic America, and religion was pulled out of the curriculum and privatized. Many educators hoped that the humanities would fill the hole left by religion, raising the questions and supplying the inspiration that religion had formerly provided. But over the last few decades, the humanities, like the rest of the academic disciplines, have become so mired in minutia and so saturated with special jargon that outsiders—that is, ordinary students and faculty who are not "in the humanities"—no longer feel genuinely welcomed into their conversations and no longer find their questions particularly relevant. There are exceptions, of course, but most humanities courses are no longer attuned to the living questions of students. It seems unlikely that the humanities will reclaim the job of being the liberal-learning engine of the university any time soon.

But, as the chapters in the second half of this book demonstrate, paying careful and nuanced attention to religion—not the old religion of the past, but the pluriformity of religion as it exists on campuses and in American culture today—can raise the kinds of questions that help students reflect on who they are and who they are becoming. The religious questions discussed in this book address the hopes, dreams, fears, and concerns of students who are trying to understand twenty-first-century realities and make sense of their lives in that context. This includes questions about living in an increasingly multifaith world (religious literacy and interfaith etiquette), truth and values in the public domain (framing knowledge and civic engagement), and personal identity and purpose (convictions, character, and vocation).

To *invite* religion into the work of the university is something new—at least compared to recent history—but many colleges and universities are doing just that because they see its educational potential. Religious questions need not be esoteric or narrow. Instead, they can focus on "things that really matters," things that matter for everyone whether they describe themselves as religious, secular, spiritual, or something else. There is no hint here of a return to the past. The particularistic and paternalistic ways in which religion was construed prior to the twentieth century will not serve the purposes of learning in the twenty-first century. But religion is no longer what it once was. The religio-secular realities of life in America today are much more about questing and questioning than they are about defending or imposing the ideas and ideals of any particular religion on anyone else. It is this new mode of religion that colleges and universities are re-engaging today, and it is this new mode of religion that may allow the academy to recapture a nearly lost conversation about "things that really matter" and how these deeper concerns of life relate to the more practical skills and knowledge that colleges and universities also convey to students.

The topics discussed in this book are all in some sense inherently religious, but it is clearly not necessary to address all of these concerns religiously. In fact, many students and professors will address them nonreligiously. This being the case, why stress religion at all? Our contention is that asking questions in ways that welcome religion into the conversation will open the discussion to everyone. Asking these questions in ways that explicitly ignore religion or render it invisible will signal something very different: that only some perspectives are to be taken seriously. When particular views or topics are banished before a conversation gets past the starting gate, the discussion as a whole quickly ceases to be about real people in the real world and becomes merely "academic."

Keeping higher education open to the critical, transcendent, unruly, questing, and questioning elements of learning will be as much a measure of its success in the years ahead as any other more easily quantifiable measures of knowledge acquired or jobs obtained. Objective measurements of knowledge, skills, and job placement are important, and higher education should not shy away from them. Yet, many of the most important outcomes of higher education cannot be immediately measured. The success of a seed is not measured by how fast it germinates, but by the tree it eventually becomes. Similarly, the effects of some forms of learning may take years to flower, but the intellectual, moral, and spiritual trajectories that begin in college often shape the rest of a person's life. College and university learning should be useful, but it has always sought to be more than merely pragmatic or economically self-advancing. Our hope is that big questions of meaning and purpose, important questions of social norms and values, factual questions about science and society, and existential questions about how people with differing ideas, ideals, and life goals can live and work together for the benefit of everyone will be part of every undergraduate experience. Colleges and universities will engage these religion-infused questions in many different ways, but choosing to ignore them or pushing them to the educational margins is patently irresponsible in an age when religion remains such a visible and influential part of public and personal life.

Acknowledgments

WE ARE GRATEFUL for the opportunity to be publishing a third book with Oxford University Press; the responsiveness and wise counsel of religion editor Cynthia Read and the professionalism of her colleagues always make it a pleasure. We are also grateful for the students and colleagues at Messiah College who have been conversational partners over the years, shaping our foundational perceptions and prodding our thinking every step of the way. More recently, our thinking about higher education has been shaped significantly by our children and their spouses—all five of them accomplished scholars and dedicated university educators. We salute Kate, Anna, Brandon, Kristen, and Grant not only for their endlessly entertaining anecdotes and insights about the machinations of particular disciplines and educational institutions, but also for their intellectual integrity and genuine passion to make the world a better place.

The process of writing this book has felt like being back in school. We have learned so much from so many wonderful people, young and old, that it is impossible to name everyone who contributed to our education. Some of these individuals agreed with something we proposed and tried to help us say it better. Some disagreed and tried gently (or, on occasion, quite vehemently) to correct our thinking—and sometimes they succeeded. Some individuals simply viewed the world from an entirely different angle, and attempting to twist ourselves around mentally to get a better glimpse of their perspectives was a stretching and often exhilarating experience. Over and over again, in the midst of these conversations, we had the sense of experiencing the academy at its best: administrators, professors, students, and student-life professionals all trying to explain to us how they do their work when they are doing it well and how the process of teaching and learning can enrich lives while simultaneously enlarging knowledge of the world. We have chosen not to list the names of every individual who met with us during the research process, in part to protect privacy and in part because we feared omitting someone. We hope the people who shared their time and insights so generously with us will find their perspectives fairly represented, and we hope they know how grateful we are for their assistance. They have given us more than we can ever repay.

This book and the Religion in the Academy Project as a whole would never have been possible without the support and encouragement of the Lilly Endowment. From our very first conversation with the folks at Lilly to the end, we were told to follow our insights and instincts wherever they led us and not to get caught up in any premature attempt to summarize what we were hearing and thinking. They told us to listen, learn, and reflect, and then do it some more, and we are still a bit amazed that the Lilly Endowment provided the funding for us to do just that. It would be thoroughly inaccurate to say this was a leisurely research and writing process. We were frequently on the road, followed by processing what we had heard and then preparing for the next round. Later in the project, we were writing and rewriting, and then rewriting again. Having the freedom and financial support to do this work was an incredible gift. We are very thankful to the Lilly Endowment for its support and to Craig Dykstra, head of the religion division, and Chris Coble, our program officer, for the trust they placed in us.

We are enormously indebted to Pepperdine University, and particularly to Provost Daryl Tippens, for an invitation to be visiting scholars during the spring semester of 2010. Living in the university's Brock guest house—a delightful hideaway on the Pacific coast—freed us from routine distractions and allowed us to begin moving from the research phase to the writing phase of the project. Because there were no pre-formulated categories of interpretation at the outset, it was not an easy task to make sense of it all. We tried various alternatives. We simplified things to make the thesis more understandable, and then discovered that we needed to reintroduce complexity to keep the story honest. We had differences of opinion (and perhaps even a few arguments), but eventually we nailed down the blueprint for the book as a whole. The writing process continued for many more months, but the time at Pepperdine—away from the diversions of home and with the wonderful faculty of Pepperdine serving as a sounding board—allowed the research to jell into this book.

A great number of people contributed, including some individuals who provided feedback on portions of the manuscript. Gene Rice and Diana Akiyama were especially helpful in the early stages of writing—friends willing to read some very rough drafts and help us find our voice for the book as a whole. Others read individual chapters (or several chapters) and helped us avoid mistakes, change emphases, and rearrange the flow of arguments. These include Ken and Jo-Ann Badley, Larry Braskamp, John Corrigan, Lisa DeBoer, Marie Griffith, Chris Hoeckley, Amir Hussain, Mark Mann, Mark Noll, Dan Pals, Eboo Patel, Jerry Pattengale, Stephanie Paulsell, Sharon Daloz Parks, Shirley Roels, Sam Speers, Les Steele, Jeff Stout, Bill Sullivan, and Molly Sutphen. Lee Shulman (former president of the Carnegie Foundation for the Advancement of Teaching) and

Ann Taves (professor of religious studies at the University of California at Santa Barbara) each read the manuscript in its entirety and provided helpful suggestions along with encouragement. Finally, three individuals read all or most of the manuscript at several stages in its evolution, and we are massively indebted to them for their detailed criticism and constructive advice: Mark Edwards, former president of St. Olaf College and now senior advisor to the dean at Harvard Divinity School; Kathryn Jacobsen, professor of epidemiology at George Mason University; and Patricia Killen, provost at Gonzaga University. Quite obviously, the weaknesses and flaws that remain in this book are entirely our own.

Notes

PREFACE

1. Douglas Jacobsen and Rhonda Hustedt Jacobsen, eds., *The American University in a Postsecular Age* (New York: Oxford University Press, 2008), x–xi.

2. In addition to campus visits, structured group conversations were held in conjunction with the annual meetings of the American Academy of Religion, the Association of College and University Religious Administrators, the board meeting of the Center for the Study of Religion at Princeton, Collegium (a Catholic higher education association), the Community College Humanities Association, the Lilly Fellows Network, and the Society for Values in Higher Education. We also met with leaders from the Association of American Colleges and Universities, the Council for Christian Colleges and Universities, the Council of Independent Colleges, and Hillel: The Foundation for Jewish Campus Life.

CHAPTER 1

1. "Code of Ethics," Penn State Center for Ethics and Religious Affairs, http://studentaffairs.psu.edu/spiritual/aboutus/ethics.shtml (accessed June 30, 2010).

2. Telephone conversation, January 30, 2012.

3. Robert B. Townsend, "AHA Membership Grows Modestly as History of Religion Surpasses Culture" *AHA Today* (June 30, 2009), http://blog.historians.org/news/823/aha-membership-grows-modestly-as-history-of-religion-surpasses-culture (accessed August 2, 2010).

4. American Psychological Association, "Resolution on Religious, Religion-Based and/or Religion-Derived Prejudice" (August 2007), http://wthrockmorton.com/apa-resolution-on-religious-religion-based-andor-religion-derived-prejudice/ (accessed August 2, 2010).

5. William Barton Rogers, *The Life and Letters of William Barton Rogers*, vol. I (New York: Houghton Mifflin, 1896), 420.

6. Robert Randolph, "I am Robert Randolph. This is my Story," MIT Inventing our Future website, http://diversity.mit.edu/people/Robert-randolph (accessed April 30, 2011).

7. *Preliminary Report: Task Force on General Education* (Cambridge, MA: President and Fellows of Harvard College, 2006), 18–19.

8. Steven Pinker, "Less Faith, More Reason," *The Harvard Crimson* (October 27, 2006), http://www.thecrimson.com/article/2006/10/27/less-faith-more-reason-there-is/ (accessed March 14, 2009).

9. *Report of the Task Force on General Education* (Cambridge, MA: President and Fellows of Harvard College, 2007), 11–12.

10. Lisa Miller, "Harvard's Crisis of Faith: Can a Secular University Embrace Religion without Sacrificing its Soul?" *Newsweek* (February 22, 2010), 45.

11. *Gaudium et Spes,* Pastoral Constitution on the Church in the Modern World Promulgated by His Holiness, Pope Paul VI on December 7, 1965, http://www.vatican.va/archive/hist_councils/ii_vatican_council/documents/vat-ii_cons_19651207_gaudium-et-spes_en.html (accessed April 13, 2011).

12. Quoted in Elizabeth Redden, "Crucifixes in the Classroom," *Inside Higher Ed* (February 11, 2009), http://www.insidehighered.com/news/2009/02/11/bostoncollege (accessed July 16, 2009).

13. Ibid.

14. On this point, see Craig Calhoun, Mark Jurgensmeyer, and Jonathan Van Antwerpen, eds., *Rethinking Secularism* (New York: Oxford University Press, 2011). In the introduction to this book, the editors report that a host of activists and scholars are now "challenging established understandings of how the terms 'secularism' and 'religion' function in public life and calling into question a supposedly clear division between the religious and the secular" (p. 3). See also Arvind-Pal S. Mandair and Markus Dressler, eds., *Secularism and Religion-Making* (New York: Oxford University Press, 2011).

15. On the term "religio-secular," see Martin E. Marty, "Our Religio-Secular World," *Daedalus* (Summer 2003), 42–46.

16. Sam Harris, *The End of Faith: Religion, Terror, and the Future of Reason* (New York: Norton, 2005), 15.

17. See, for example, Alan Wolfe, *The Transformation of American Religion: How We Actually Live Our Faith* (Chicago: University of Chicago Press, 2003), and Robert Wuthnow, *After the Baby Boomers: How Twenty- and Thirty-Somethings Are Shaping the Future of American Religion* (Princeton, NJ: Princeton University Press, 2007). On the history of this alternative style of faith, see Catherine L. Albanese, *A Republic of Mind and Spirit: A Cultural History of American Metaphysical Religion* (New Haven, CT: Yale University Press, 2007); Robert C. Fuller, *Spiritual, But Not Religious: Understanding Unchurched America* (New York: Oxford University

Press, 2001); and Leigh Schmidt, *Restless Souls: The Making of American Spirituality* (New York: HarperCollins, 2005).

18. Charles Taylor, *A Secular Age* (Cambridge, MA: Harvard University Press, 2007), 5.

19. Susan Neiman, *Moral Clarity: A Guide for Grown-Up Idealists* (New York: Harcourt, 2008), 235.

20. See Daniel C. Dennett, *Breaking the Spell: Religion as a Natural Phenomenon* (New York: Viking, 2006), 170.

21. Thomas Luckmann, *The Invisible Religion: The Problem of Religion in Modern Society* (New York: Macmillan, 1967).

22. See, for example, André Comte-Spoonville, *The Little Book of Atheist Spirituality* (New York: Viking, 2007); Greg M. Epstein, *Good without God: What a Billion Nonreligious People Do Believe* (New York: HarperCollins, 2009); and Robert C. Solomon, *Spirituality for the Skeptic: The Thoughtful Love of Life* (New York: Oxford University Press, 2002).

23. Paul Tillich, *The Essential Tillich*, F. Forrester Church, ed. (Chicago: University of Chicago Press, 1999), 11–39.

24. This description of religion is similar to that proposed by Ann Taves in her 2010 presidential address to the American Academy of Religion, "'Religion' in the Humanities and the Humanities in the University," *Journal of the American Academy of Religion* 79:2 (June 2011), 287–314. Also see Ann Taves, *Religious Experience Reconsidered* (Princeton, NJ: Princeton University Press, 2009).

25. Ernest L. Boyer, "Teaching About Religion in Public Schools," *Selected Speeches, 1979–1995* (Princeton, NJ: Carnegie Foundation for the Advancement of Teaching, 1997), 119, 121, 125.

26. Anthony T. Kronman, *Education's End: Why Colleges and Universities Have Given Up on the Meaning of Life* (New Haven, CT: Yale University Press, 2007), 237.

27. Martha Nussbaum, *Not For Profit: Why Democracy Needs the Humanities* (Princeton, NJ: Princeton University Press, 2010), 6.

CHAPTER 2

1. Protestantism is an incredibly diverse movement, and not all of that diversity was present in America. For the most part, the kind of Protestantism that has flourished in North America has been of a generally Reformed character (as opposed to being, for example, Lutheran or Anglican). Protestantism has also been more populist and individually oriented in America than it has been in Europe. But Protestantism's dominance in America, even if it is a limited form of Protestantism, is beyond question, and that remains true today. In terms of percentages, 30 percent of the world's Protestants live in North America, and in terms of sheer numbers, there are more Protestants living in the United States than in any other country on earth. See Douglas Jacobsen, *The World's Christians: Who They Are, Where They Are, and How They Got There* (Oxford, UK: Wiley/Blackwell, 2011).

2 See J. David Hoeveler, *Creating the American Mind: Intellect and Politics in the Colonial Colleges* (New York: Rowman & Littlefield, 2002). A number of other colleges were started before the Revolutionary War, but only these nine were formally chartered.

3. John R. Thelin, *A History of American Higher Education* (Baltimore, MD: The Johns Hopkins University Press, 2004), 63.

4. Ibid., 90.

5. Abraham Lincoln, "Second Inaugural Address" (March 4, 1865), http://www.bartleby.com/124/pres32.html.

6. See Charles Reagan Wilson, *Baptized in Blood: The Religion of the Lost Cause, 1865–1920* (Athens, GA: University of Georgia Press, 1980).

7. See Edward L. Wheeler, *Uplifting the Race: The Black Minister in the New South, 1865–1902* (Lanham, MD: University Press of America, 1986).

8. Many scholarly books have been written on this topic. See, for example, James Tunstead Burtchael, *The Dying of the Light: The Disengagement of Colleges and Universities from their Christian Churches* (Grand Rapids, MI: Eerdmans, 1998); D. G. Hart, *The University Gets Religion: Religious Studies in American Higher Education* (Baltimore, MD: The Johns Hopkins University Press, 1999); David A. Hollinger, *Science, Jews, and Secular Culture: Studies in Mid-Twentieth-Century American Intellectual History* (Princeton, NJ: Princeton University Press, 1996); George Marsden, *The Soul of the American University: From Protestant Establishment to Established Nonbelief* (New York: Oxford University Press, 1994); William C. Ringenberg, *The Christian College: A History of Protestant Higher Education in America* (Grand Rapids, MI: Baker Academic, 2006); Jon H. Roberts and James Turner, *The Sacred and Secular University* (Princeton, NJ: Princeton University Press, 2000); Julie A. Rueben, *The Making of the Modern University: Intellectual Transformation and the Marginalization of Morality* (Chicago: University of Chicago Press, 1996); Douglas Sloan, *Faith and Knowledge: Mainline Protestantism and American Higher Education* (Louisville, KY: Westminster John Knox, 1994); Christian Smith, ed., *The Secular Revolution: Power, Interests, and Conflict in the Secularization of American Public Life* (Berkeley, CA: University of California Press, 2003); and C. John Sommerville, *The Decline of the Secular University* (New York: Oxford University Press, 2006).

9. Both the notion of secularity and the theory of secularization are complex and highly contested. A variety of definitions have been offered along with many different historical narratives of secularization. Because of how contested this field of study has become, we generally try to avoid the term other than to use "secular" as synonymous with "nonreligious." Obviously, the issue of what secularity is (if, indeed, it is one thing, which is now a matter of debate) and how it may be advancing or declining is a matter worthy of serious scholarly attention. To enter into that discussion here would, however, overwhelm the main concerns of this volume. On the issue of secularity and secularization, see Talal Assad, *Formations of the Secular: Christianity, Islam, Modernity* (Palo Alto, CA: Stanford University Press, 2003);

Peter L. Berger, ed., *The Desecularization of the World: Resurgent Religion and World Politics* (Grand Rapids, MI: Eerdmans, 1999); Steve Bruce, *Secularization: In Defense of an Unfashionable Theory* (New York: Oxford University Press, 2011); Craig Calhoun, Mark Jurgensmeyer, and Jonathan Van Antwerpen, eds., *Rethinking Secularism* (New York: Oxford University Press, 2011); Martin Marty, *The Modern Schism: Three Paths to the Secular* (New York: Harper and Row, 1969); and Charles Taylor, *A Secular Age* (Cambridge, MA: Harvard University Press, 2007).

10. On the imagery of exile, see Mark R. Schwehn, *Exiles from Eden: Religion and the Academic Vocation in America* (New York: Oxford University Press, 1993).

11. See Marsden, *The Soul of the American University*, "Introduction," 3–9.

12. See Hollinger, *Science, Jews, and Secular Culture*.

13. See Joel A. Carpenter, *Revive Us Again: The Reawakening of American Fundamentalism* (New York: Oxford University Press, 1997), and George M. Marsden, *Fundamentalism and American Culture*, 2nd edition (New York: Oxford University Press, 2006).

14. William James, *The Varieties of Religious Experience* (New York: Longmans, Green, and Company, 1915), 31.

15. Mark Noll, *A History of Christianity in the United States and Canada* (Grand Rapids, MI: Eerdmans, 1992), 365.

16. For more detailed historical descriptions, see Sloan, *Faith and Knowledge*, and Hart, *The University Gets Religion*.

17. Emphasis added. Quoted on the website of the Dwight D. Eisenhower Presidential Library and Museum, http://www.eisenhower.archives.gov/ (accessed March 26, 2010).

18. Will Herberg, *Protestant, Catholic, Jew: An Essay in American Religious Sociology* (New York: Doubleday, 1955).

19. Peter L. Berger, *The Sacred Canopy: Elements of a Sociological Theory of Religion* (Garden City, NY: Doubleday, 1967), 107, 124.

20. Peter L. Berger, *A Rumor of Angels: Modern Society and the Rediscovery of the Supernatural* (New York: Anchor, 1970).

21. Alexander W. Astin, Helen S. Astin, Jennifer A. Lindholm, Alyssa N. Bryant, Shannon Calderone, and Katalin Szelényi, *The Spiritual Life of College Students: A National Study of College Students' Search for Meaning and Purpose* (Los Angeles: UCLA Higher Education Research Institute, 2004), 5.

CHAPTER 3

1. *Gilmore Girls,* Season 6, Episode 4, "Always a Godmother, Never a God" (2006), http://www.tv.com/gilmore-girls/always-a-godmother-never-a-god-474891 (accessed February 9, 2010).

2. T. S. Eliot, "East Coker" in *Four Quartets* (New York: Harcourt, Brace, and World, 1943), 31.

3. See Mark U. Edwards, Jr., *Religion on Our Campuses: A Professor's Guide to Communities, Conflicts, and Promising Conversations* (New York: Palgrave, 2006), especially chapter four, "Disciplinary Formations."

4. See Neil Gross and Solon Simmons, "The Religious Convictions of College and University Professors" in Jacobsen and Jacobsen, eds., *The American University in a Postsecular Age*, 19–29.

5. See Elaine Howard Ecklund, *Science vs. Religion: What Scientists Really Think* (New York: Oxford University Press, 2010), 32–33.

6. See Talal Asad, *Formations of the Secular: Christianity, Islam, Modernity* (Stanford, CA: Stanford University Press, 2003), and Charles Taylor, *A Secular Age*. For critical appraisals of the views of these two scholars, see Charles Hirschkind and David Scott, eds., *Powers of the Secular Modern: Talal Asad and His Interlocutors* (Stanford, CA: Stanford University Press, 2006), and Michael Warner, Jonathan VanAntwerpen, and Craig Calhoun, eds., *Varieties of Secularism in a Secular Age* (Cambridge, MA: Harvard University Press, 2010).

7. Sam Speers, "Secularity, Spirituality, and Liberal Arts Education" (February 6, 2007), http://religion.ssrc.org/reforum (accessed April 19, 2011).

8. Richard Rorty, *Philosophy and Social Hope* (New York: Penguin, 1999), 169, 171.

9. Mother Teresa, *Come Be My Light: The Private Writings of the "Saint of Calcutta,"* Brian Kolodiejchuk, ed. (New York: Doubleday, 2007).

10. Astin et al., *The Spiritual Life of College Students*, 6.

11. The term "hot topics" is sometimes used to refer to these campus discussions. See, for example, Robert J. Nash, DeMethra LaSha Bradley, and Arthur W. Chickering, *How to Talk About Hot Topics on Campus: From Polarization to Moral Conversation* (San Francisco: Jossey-Bass, 2008).

12. Sharon Daloz Parks, *Big Questions, Worthy Dreams: Mentoring Young Adults in Their Search for Meaning, Purpose, and Faith* (San Francisco: Jossey-Bass, 2000), 5, 7.

13. Art Chickering, "Finding Purpose and Meaning in and out of the Classroom," *Peer Review* 13:1 (Winter 2011), 31.

14. Parks, *Big Questions, Worthy Dreams*, xii.

15. See Adam B. Seligman, Robert P. Weller, Michael J. Puett, and Bennett Simon, *Ritual and Its Consequences: An Essay on the Limits of Sincerity* (New York: Oxford University Press, 2008).

CHAPTER 4

1. "U.S. Religious Landscape Survey," The Pew Forum on Religion and Public Life (February 2008) http://religions.pewforum.org/pdf/report-religious-landscape-study-full.pdf (accessed April 23, 2011).

2. See Jacobsen, *The World's Christians*.

3. See Mark Juergensmeyer, ed., *The Oxford Handbook of Global Religions* (New York: Oxford University Press, 2006).

4. For a description of the "traditioning" process, see Dale T. Irvin, *Christian Histories, Christian Traditioning: Rendering Accounts* (Maryknoll, NY: Orbis Books, 1998).

5. This definition is based on Emile Durkheim, *The Elementary Forms of the Religious Life*, translated by Karen E. Fields (New York: Free Press, 1995).

6. Various states did have religious establishments. Connecticut, for example, maintained the Congregational Church as its state religion until 1818, and Massachusetts kept its established church until 1833. But the nation as a whole has never had a formal state church.

7. Robert N. Bellah, "Civil Religion in America," *Daedalus* 96:1 (1967), 1–21, http://www.robertbellah.com/articles_5.htm.

8. Robert N. Bellah, Richard Madsen, William M. Sullivan, Ann Swidler, and Steven M. Tipton, *Habits of the Heart: Individualism and Commitment in American Life* (Berkeley, CA: University of California Press, 1985), 221.

9. David Brooks, *The Social Animal: The Hidden Sources of Love, Character, and Achievement* (New York: Random House, 2011), xii.

10. See Nancy Ammerman, "Journeys of Faith: Meeting the Challenges in Twenty-First-Century America" in James L. Heft, ed., *Passing on the Faith: Transforming Traditions for the Next Generation of Jews, Christians, and Muslims* (New York: Fordham University Press, 2006), 40.

11. Ralph Waldo Emerson, *Essays, First Series*, "Self-Reliance" (1841), http://www.emersoncentral.com/selfreliance.htm (accessed July 5, 2011).

12. See George Dennis O'Brien, *The Idea of a Catholic University* (Chicago: University of Chicago Press, 2002).

13. See Marcia B. Baxter Magolda, *Authoring Your Life: Developing an Internal Voice to Navigate Life's Challenges* (Sterling, VA: Stylus, 2009).

14. Alexander W. Astin, Helen S. Astin, and Jennifer A. Lindholm, *Cultivating the Spirit: How College Can Enhance Students' Inner Lives* (San Francisco: Jossey-Bass, 2011).

CHAPTER 5

1. "U.S. Religious Knowledge Survey," The Pew Forum on Religion and Public Life (September 28, 2010), http://pewforum.org/other-beliefs-and-practices/u-s-religious-knowledge-survey.aspx (accessed August 3, 2011).

2. On the current lack of religious knowledge among American young people, see Christian Smith and Melinda Lundquist Denton, *Soul Searching: The Religious and Spiritual Lives of American Teenagers* (New York: Oxford University Press, 2005).

3. "Ann Curry Cites Wrong School's Alumni in Speech," AOL News (May 25, 2010), accessed online January 27, 2011 at http://www.aolnews.com/2010/05/25/

oops-ann-curry-cites-wrong-schools-alumni-in-speech/. On the problem of religious illiteracy and journalism in general, see Paul Marshal, Lela Gilbert, and Roberta Green Ahmanson, eds., *Blind Spot: When Journalists Don't Get Religion* (New York: Oxford University Press, 2009).

4. Omid Safi, "Good Sufi, Bad Muslims," *Sightings* (January 27, 2011), accessed online January 27, 2011 at http://divinity.uchicago.edu/martycenter/publications/sightings/.

5. Madeleine Albright, *The Mighty and the Almighty: Reflections on America, God, and World Affairs* (New York: HarperCollins, 2006), 9, 11.

6. See Daniel Burke, "Kmiec's Gospel Falls Flat at State Department," *Christian Century* (May 17, 2011), 15–16.

7. Stephen Prothero, *Religious Literacy: What Every American Needs to Know—and Doesn't* (New York: HarperCollins, 2007), 5, 6.

8. Ibid., 12–13.

9. AAR Religion in the Schools Task Force (Diane L. Moore, chair), Guidelines for Teaching about Religion in K-12 Public Schools in the United States (Atlanta, GA: American Academy of Religion, 2010), 4. Available online at http://www.aarweb.org/publications/Online_Publications/Curriculum_Guidelines/AARK-12CurriculumGuidelines.pdf (accessed August 5, 2011).

10. Warren A. Nord, "Taking Religion Seriously in Public Universities," in Douglas Jacobsen and Rhonda Hustedt Jacobsen, eds., *The American University in a Postsecular Age* (New York: Oxford University Press, 2008), 167. See also Warren A. Nord, *Religion and American Education: Rethinking a National Dilemma* (Chapel Hill, NC: University of North Carolina Press, 1995), and *Does God Make a Difference? Taking Religion Seriously in Our Schools and Universities* (New York: Oxford University Press, 2010).

11. Amanda Porterfield, "Religious Pluralism, the Study of Religion, and 'Postsecular' Culture," in Jacobsen and Jacobsen, eds., *The American University in a Postsecular Age*, 187, 191.

12. Quoted in Bobby Ross, Jr., "Beyond Believers," *Christianity Today* (March 2010), 14.

13. Robert Orsi, *Between Heaven and Earth: The Religious Worlds People Make and the Scholars Who Study Them* (Princeton, NJ: Princeton University Press, 2005), 183.

14. Charles Kimball, *When Religion Becomes Evil: Five Warning Signs* (San Francisco: HarperSanFrancisco, 2002).

15. Harold T. Shapiro, *A Larger Sense of Purpose: Higher Education and Society* (Princeton, NJ: Princeton University Press, 2005), 110.

16. "The Religious Studies Major and Liberal Education," *Liberal Education* (Spring 2009), 48–55. For more details, see http://www.aarweb.org/Programs/Department_Services/Survey_Data/Undergraduate/default.asp.

17. "The Religious Studies Major in a Post-9/11 World: New Challenges, New Opportunities," reprinted with permission of the American Academy of Religion in *Teaching Theology and Religion,* Volume 14, Issue 1 (January 2011), 44.

18. Ibid., 41.

CHAPTER 6

1. See William H. Willimon, "Arguing with Muslims," *Christian Century* (November 16, 2004), 38.

2. Numbers for the years 1900 and 1970 are based on data from David B. Barrett, George T. Kurian, and Todd M. Johnson, *World Christian Encyclopedia* (Oxford, UK: Oxford University Press, 2001). Estimates for the year 2010 are based on *U.S. Religious Landscape Survey* (Washington, DC: Pew Forum on Religion and Public Life, 2008), http://religions.pewforum.org/reports (accessed June 21, 2011). The numbers from the Pew survey do not add up to 100 percent because 1 percent of those queried either refused to name their religious identity or did not know.

3. See Christian Smith, *American Evangelicalism: Embattled and Thriving* (Chicago: University of Chicago Press, 1998).

4. See D. Michael Lindsay, *Faith in the Halls of Power: How Evangelicals Joined the American Elite* (New York: Oxford University Press, 2007).

5. Jonathan D. Sarna, *American Judaism: A History* (New Haven, CT: Yale University Press, 2004), 373. See also Steven M. Cohen and Arnold M. Eisen, *The Jew Within: Self, Family, and Community in America* (Bloomington, IN: Indiana University Press, 2000).

6. Jack Wertheimer, "Recent Trends in American Judaism," *American Jewish Year Book* (Philadelphia: Jewish Publication Society of America, 1989), 162.

7. See *Muslim Americans: Middle Class and Mostly Mainstream* (Washington, DC: Pew Research Center, 2007). See also Robert Wuthnow, *America and the Challenges of Religious Diversity*, 56–63, and Diana L. Eck, *A New Religious America*, 222–293.

8. See Geneive Abdo, *Mecca and Main Street: Muslim Life in America after 9/11* (New York: Oxford University Press, 2006).

9. See *U S. Religious Landscape Survey*. For a critique of this report, see Sempai Sensei, "Buddhism in America," http://www.bffct.net/id65.html (accessed August 30, 2010). See also Wuthnow, *America and the Challenges of Religious Diversity*, 47–56, and Diana L. Eck, *A New Religious America*, 142–221.

10. See Charles S. Prebish and Kenneth K. Tanaka, eds., *The Faces of Buddhism in America* (Berkeley, CA: University of California Press, 1998).

11. See Wuthnow, *America and the Challenges of Religious Diversity*, 38–47; see also Diana L. Eck, *A New Religious America*, 80–141. On the history of Hinduism in America, see Gurinder Singh Mann, Paul Numrich, and Raymond Williams, *Buddhists, Hindus, and Sikhs in America: A Short History* (New York: Oxford University Press, 2008).

12. Ner LeElef, "World Jewish Population," Judaism Online, http://webcache.google-usercontent.com/search?q=cache:-YzXSicDKgcJ:www.simpletoremember.com/vitals/world-jewish-population.htm+where+jews+live+US+cities&cd=1&hl=en&ct=clnk&gl=us&source=www.google.com (accessed June 22, 2011).

13. "Muslim Youth in NYC Public Schools Study" (2008), Teachers College, Columbia University, http://www.tc.columbia.edu/muslimyouthstudynyc/index.html (accessed July 9, 2011).

14. See Mark Silk, *One Nation, Divisible: How Regional Religious Differences Shape American Politics* (Lanham, MD: Rowman & Littlefield, 2008).

15. See Barry A. Kosmin and Ariela Keysar, *American Religious Identification Survey (ARIS 2008): Summary Report* (Trinity College: Hartford, CT: 2009), "Highlights," http://www.americanreligionsurvey-aris.org/reports/ARIS_Report_2008.pdf (accessed July 9, 2011).

16. "Not All Nonbelievers Call Themselves Atheists," The Pew Forum on Religion and Public Life (April 2, 2009), http://www.pewforum.org/Not-All-Nonbelievers-Call-Themselves-Atheists.aspx (accessed July 9, 2011).

17. "Faith in Flux: Changes in Religious Affiliation in the U.S.," The Pew Forum on Religion and Public Life (April 2, 2009), http://www.pewforum.org/Faith-in-Flux.aspx (accessed July 9, 2011). On Catholicism, also see Peter Steinfels, "Further Adrift: The American Church's Crisis of Attrition," *Commonweal* (October 22, 2010), 16–20.

18. Astin et al., *The Spiritual Life of College Students*, 17.

19. See Larry A. Braskamp, "The Religious and Spiritual Journeys of College Students," in Jacobsen and Jacobsen, eds., *The American University in a Postsecular Age*, 117–134.

20. See Neil Gross and Solon Simmons, "The Religious Convictions of College and University Professors" in Jacobsen and Jacobsen, eds., *The American University in a Postsecular Age*, 23–25. Faculty religiosity varies from campus to campus and from discipline to discipline. As a group, for example, faculty at community colleges tend to be more religious than faculty at research universities and elite liberal arts colleges, and faculty in professional programs and applied fields tend to be more religious than faculty in psychology and biology. Not surprisingly, faculty at church-related institutions report stronger ties to religion than those at other schools, but these numbers vary dramatically from school to school because they include institutions that range from Notre Dame and Emory to Elon and Liberty.

21. See Scott Jaschik, "Students and Faith," *Inside Higher Ed* (June 14, 2007), http://www.insidehighered.com/news/2007/06/14/religion (accessed July 11, 2011). See also Wuthnow, *After the Baby Boomers*, 107–108. In the past, higher levels of education were linked with relative loss of religious adherence; see Robert Wuthnow, *The Restructuring of American Religion* (Princeton, NJ: Princeton University Press, 1988), 170–171.

22. "Student Demographics: Attitudes and Characteristics of Freshmen at 4-Year Colleges, Fall 2009," *The Chronicle of Higher Education* 58:1 (August 27, 2010), 32.

23. Gary A. Tobin and Aryeh K. Weinberg, *Profiles of the American University, Vol. II: Religious Beliefs and Behavior of College Faculty* (Institute for Jewish and Community Research, 2007), 3.

24. These numbers are based on a compilation of data from Christian Smith and Patricia Snell, *Souls in Transition: The Religious and Spiritual Lives of Emerging Adults* (New York: Oxford University Press, 2009), and Putnam and Campbell, *American Grace*.

25. Astin et al., *The Spiritual Life of College Students*, 6.

26. All of these numbers come from Smith and Snell, *Souls in Transition*; see especially chapter 4, "Religious Affiliations, Practices, Beliefs, Experiences, and More," 103–142.

27. Ibid., 135.

28. "Trends Among First-Time Full-Time Freshmen of George Mason University: Results from the CIRP Freshman Surveys between 2000 to 2005" (Fairfax, VA: Office of Institutional Assessment, George Mason University, 2006), 5, http:// assessment.gmu.edu/Results/Freshman/2006/2005CIRPReport_Web.pdf (accessed July 14, 2011).

29. "Hillel House," Muhlenberg College website, http://www.muhlenberg.edu/main/ campuslife/hillel/ (accessed July 11, 2011). See also "Jewish Student Populations at Various Colleges and Universities," http://www.inlikeme.com/jewish-student-populations-various-colleges-universities.html (accessed July 11, 2011).

30. This conclusion is based on an analysis of campuses that have formally organized Muslim student associations. There are about 125 such schools, and most are located in the northeastern quadrant of the country. See "Muslim Student Associations: Affiliation List" (2011), http://www.msanational.org/affiliate/list (accessed July 11, 2011).

31. Beth Cousens, *Hillel's Journey: Distinctively Jewish, Universally Human* (Washington, DC: Hillel, 2007), 34.

32. Smith and Snell, *Souls in Transition*, 146.

33. See, for example, Stephen Prothero, *God Is Not One: The Eight Rival Religions That Run the World* (New York: HarperOne, 2010).

34. *Teaching for Inclusion* (Chapel Hill, NC: UNC-CH Center for Teaching and Learning, 1997), 103.

35. Na'ilah Suad Nasir and Jasiyah Al-Amin, "Creating Identity-Safe Spaces on College Campuses for Muslim Students," *Change* 38:2 (March/April 2006), 22–27.

36. "Code of Ethics," Penn State Center for Ethics and Religious Affairs, http:// studentaffairs.psu.edu/spiritual/aboutus/ethics.shtml (accessed February 4, 2012).

37. Quoted in Beckie Supiano, "A Christian College Devotes a Chapel to Many Faiths," *The Chronicle of Higher Education* (March 13, 2009), A23.

38. Henri J. M. Nouwen, *Reaching Out: The Three Movements of the Spiritual Life* (Garden City, NY: Doubleday, 1986), 99.

39. Paul J. Griffiths, "Student Teachers: Reading Augustine with Muslims," *Christian Century* (March 20, 2007), 11.

40. A. Suresh Canagarajah, "The Possibility of a Community of Difference," *The Cresset: A Review of Literature, the Arts and Public Affairs* (Easter 2010), 28.

41. Noah Cogan, "Sukkahs Speak to Religion's Presence at VC," *The Miscellany News* 145:6 (October 27, 2011), 9.

42. T. D. Snyder and S. A. Dillow, *Digest of Education Statistics 2010* (Washington, DC: National Center for Education Statistics, U.S. Department of Education, 2011), 281–282.

43. These percentages are derived from "Distribution of Institutions and Enrollments by Classification Categories," Carnegie Foundation for the Advancement of Teaching, http://classifications.carnegiefoundation.org/summary/size_setting.php (accessed February 11, 2012).

44. See Douglas Jacobsen and Rhonda Hustedt Jacobsen, "The Ideals and Diversity of Church-Related Higher Education," in Jacobsen and Jacobsen, eds., *The American University in a Postsecular Age*, 64.

45. See Robert M. O'Neil, "A Fine Legal Mess: When Student Groups Collide With Anti-Bias Policy," *The Chronicle of Higher Education* (November 27, 2009), A76.

46. Mike Mount, "Air Force Probes Religious Bias Charges at Academy," CNN News (May 5, 2005), http://articles.cnn.com/2005-05-03/us/airforce.religion_1_religious-intolerance-senior-cadets-religious-sensitivity?s=PM:US (accessed August 8, 2011). See also Brian McGrath Davis, "Air Force Academy Addresses 'Challenges to Pluralism,'" Pluralism Project, Harvard University, http://pluralism.org/research/reports/davis/afareport.php (accessed August 8, 2011).

47. Victor H. Kazanjian and the students of the Wellesley College Multifaith Council, "Beyond Tolerance: From Mono-Religious to Multi-Religious Life at Wellesley," in Victor H. Kazanjian and Peter L. Laurence, eds., *Education as Transformation: Religious Pluralism, Spirituality, and a New Vision for Higher Education in America* (New York: Peter Lang, 2000), 220.

48. Mark Eddington, "The Campus Chapel as an Interfaith Laboratory," *The Chronicle Review* (April 15, 2011), B13.

49. See Scott Jaschik, "Tests of Faith," *Inside Higher Ed* (January 12, 2006), http://www.insidehighered.com/news/2006/01/12/faith (accessed July 15, 2011).

50. Samuel Schuman, *Seeing the Light: Religious Colleges in Twenty-First-Century America* (Baltimore, MD: The Johns Hopkins University Press, 2010), 233.

51. University of North Dakota Wellness Center, http://und.edu/health-wellness/wellness/7dimensions.cfm (accessed August 6, 2011).

52. The role of religion at Yale has been the subject of discussion (and heated debate) throughout its history, perhaps most notably in William F. Buckley's *God and Man at Yale* (Chicago: Henry Regnery Company, 1951).

53. USC Casden Institute, http://casdeninstitute.usc.edu/ (accessed July 18, 2011).

54. Institute for Advanced Catholic Studies, http://www.ifacs.com/about/ (accessed July 18, 2011).

55. USC American Muslim Civic Leadership Institute, http://crcc.usc.edu/initiatives/amcli/ (accessed July 18, 2011).

56. See the center's website, http://crcc.usc.edu/.

57. See the Pluralism Project's website, http://pluralism.org/.

58. Soka University of America, "Mission and Values," http://www.soka.edu/about_soka/mission_and_values.aspx (accessed July 18, 2011).

59. Kwame Anthony Appiah, *Cosmopolitanism: Ethics in a World of Strangers* (New York: Norton, 2006), 85.

CHAPTER 7

1. Immanuel Kant, "An Answer to the Question: What Is Enlightenment?" in James Schmidt, ed., *What Is Enlightenment?: Eighteenth-Century Answers and Twentieth-Century Questions* (Berkeley, CA: University of California Press, 1996), 58–64.

2. Andrew Dickson White, *A History of the Warfare of Science with Theology in Christendom* (New York: D. Appleton, 1896).

3. For a summary of this debate, see Lisa Miller, "Is NIH Director Francis Collins Disqualified by his Faith?" *Newsweek* (August 11, 2009).

4. See Francis Collins, *The Language of God: A Scientist Presents Evidence for Belief* (Boston: Free Press, 2007).

5. Schwehn, *Exiles from Eden*, 14.

6. See Karl Mannheim, *Ideology and Utopia: An Introduction to the Sociology of Knowledge* (Whitefish, MT: Kessinger Publishing, 2008). This book was first published in German in 1929 and translated into English in 1936.

7. Thomas S. Kuhn, *The Structure of Scientific Revolutions* (Chicago: The University of Chicago Press, 1962).

8. See Arthur C. Danto, "Margins for Error: In His Final Collection, Rorty Argues for Philosophy's Irrelevance," Bookforum (September/October/November 2007), http://www.bookforum.com/inprint/014_03/850 (accessed January 26, 2012).

9. Michel Foucault, *Discipline and Punishment: The Birth of the Prison* (New York: Vintage Books, 1979), 27–28.

10. Michael Halpern, "The Costs of a Climate of Fear," *Academe* (November–December 2010), 17–19.

11. Richie Zweigenhaft, "Is this Curriculum for Sale?" *Academe* (July–August 2010), 38–39.

12. Ludwig Wittgenstein, *Culture and Value*, Peter Winch, trans. (Chicago: University of Chicago Press, 1980), 64e.

13. See Douglas Jacobsen and Rhonda Hustedt Jacobsen, *Scholarship and Christian Faith: Enlarging the Conversation* (New York: Oxford University Press, 2004).

14. Elaine Howard Ecklund, "Science on Faith," *The Chronicle Review* (February 11, 2011), B10.

15. Wayne C. Booth, *Critical Understanding: The Powers and Limits of Pluralism* (Chicago: University of Chicago Press, 1979), 340.

16. See George M. Marsden, *The Outrageous Idea of Christian Scholarship* (New York: Oxford University Press, 1997) and David K. Naugle, *Worldviews: The History of a Concept* (Grand Rapids, MI: Eerdmans, 2002).

17. See Ninian Smart, *Worldviews: Cross Cultural Explorations of Human Beliefs* (Upper Saddle River, NJ: Prentice-Hall, 1994), for a discussion that places "worldview" in a broader context.

18. Peter J. Boyer, "Fox among the Chickens," *The New Yorker* (January 31, 2011), 59.

19. Charles Colson and Nancy Pearcey, *How Now Shall We Live?* (Wheaton, IL: Tyndale House, 1999), 17.

20. Nicholas Wolterstorff, *Reason within the Bounds of Religion*, 2nd ed. (Grand Rapids, MI: Eerdmans, 1984), 15–20.

21. Alasdair MacIntyre, *Three Rival Versions of Moral Enquiry: Encyclopaedia, Genealogy, and Tradition* (Notre Dame, IN: University of Notre Dame, 1990), 222.

22. Eck, *A New Religious America*, 9.

23. Tariq Ramadan, *Western Muslims and the Future of Islam* (New York: Oxford University Press, 2004), 226–227.

24. John Henry Cardinal Newman, *An Essay on the Development of Christian Doctrine* (Westminster, MD: Christian Classics, 1968), 40.

25. Booth, *Critical Understanding*, 339.

26. Solomon, *Spirituality for the Skeptic*, 63–64. Stephen Toulmin makes a similar point in his *Return to Reason* (Cambridge, MA: Harvard University Press, 2003).

27. Austin Dacey, *The Secular Conscience: Why Belief Belongs in Public Life* (Amherst, NY: Prometheus, 2008), 17.

28. Ibid., 201.

29. Elizabeth Kamarck Minnich, *Transforming Knowledge*, 2nd ed. (Philadelphia: Temple University Press, 2005), 255.

30. Ibid., 46.

31. Wendy Doniger, *The Hindus: An Alternative History* (New York: Penguin, 2009), 48.

32. Lee S. Shulman, "Professing Understanding and Professing Faith: The Midrashic Imperative" in Jacobsen and Jacobsen, eds., *The American University in a Postsecular Age*, 216. Peter Ochs and Nancy Levene develop a similar understanding of knowledge and meaning in their edited volume *Textual Reasonings: Jewish Philosophy and Text Study at the End of the Twentieth Century* (Grand Rapids, MI: Eerdmans, 2002).

33. On this distinction, see Jeffrey Stout, *Democracy and Tradition* (Princeton, NJ: Princeton University Press, 2005), and also his "2007 Presidential Address: The Folly of Secularism," *Journal of the American Academy of Religion*, 76 (September 2008): 533–544.

34. Personal correspondence with Jeffrey Stout, September 23, 2011.

35. "25 Top Schools in America," *First Things*, No. 27 (November 2010), 14 (New York: Institute on Religion and Public Life).

36. Taylor, *A Secular Age*, 754.

CHAPTER 8

1. Not everyone agrees with this view of higher educational goals. For a contrasting opinion, see Stanley Fish, *Save the World on Your Own Time* (New York: Oxford University Press, 2008).

2. Jeffrey Stout, *Blessed Are the Organized: Grassroots Democracy in America* (Princeton: Princeton University Press, 2010), 223.

3. Quoted in Carol Geary Schneider, "Civic Learning in a Diverse Democracy," *Diversity & Democracy*, Vol. 10, No. 3 (Fall 2007), 3.

4. National Task Force on Civic Learning and Democratic Engagement, *A Crucible Moment: College Learning and Democracy's Future* (Washington, DC: Association of American Colleges and Universities, 2012), vii.

5. Cliff Zukin, Scott Keeter, Moly Andolina, Krista Jenkins, and Michael X. Delli Carpini, *A New Engagement?: Political Participation, Civic Life, and the Changing American Citizen* (New York: Oxford University Press, 2006), 154.

6. John Saltmarsh and Matthew Hartley, eds. *"To Serve a Larger Purpose": Engagement for Democracy and the Transformation of Higher Education* (Philadelphia: Temple University Press, 2011), 6.

7. Robert N. Bellah, "Civil Religion in America," *Daedalus* 96:1 (Winter 1967), 1–21.

8. "Higher Education for American Democracy" (1947), quoted in Geoffrey Galt Harpham, *The Humanities and the Dream of America* (Chicago: University of Chicago Press, 2011), 162.

9. "Report of the Commission on the Humanities" (1964), quoted in Harpham, 165.

10. Anne Colby, Thomas Ehrlich, Elizabeth Beaumont, and Jason Stephens, *Educating Citizens: Preparing America's Undergraduates for Lives of Moral and Civic Responsibility* (San Francisco: Jossey-Bass, 2003), 11.

11. John Saltmarsh, "The Civic Promise of Service Learning," *Liberal Education* (Spring 2005), 50–55.

12. Martha C. Nussbaum, "Radical Evil in Liberal Democracies: The Neglect of the Political Emotions" in *Democracy and the New Religious Pluralism*, Thomas Banchoff, ed. (New York: Oxford University Press, 2007), 184–186.

13. Ibid., 185.

14. Bellah, *Habits of the Heart*. See especially chapter two, "Culture and Character: The Historical Conversation."

15. Vanessa Bing and Rosemary Talmadge, "Speaking of Religion: Facilitating Difficult Dialogues," *Diversity and Democracy*, Vol. 11, No. 1 (Winter 2008), 13.

16. James Davison Hunter, *Culture Wars: The Struggle to Control the Family, Art, Education, Law, and Politics in America* (New York: Basic Books, 1992).

17. James Davison Hunter, *To Change the World: The Irony, Tragedy, and Possibility of Christianity in the Late Modern World* (New York: Oxford University Press, 2010), 263, 281.

18. Barry Checkoway, "Renewing the Civic Mission of the American Research University," *Journal of Higher Education*, 2001, 72(2), 127. Quoted in Barbara Jacoby, ed., *Civic Engagement in Higher Education: Concepts and Practices* (San Francisco: Jossey-Bass, 2009), 8.

19. See description on "Great Nonprofits" at http://greatnonprofits.org/reviews/profile2/interfaith-youth-core (accessed March 8, 2011).

20. Eboo Patel, "Religious Diversity and Cooperation on Campus," *Journal of College & Character*, Vol. IX, No. 2 (November 2007), 5.

21. Ibid.

22. Zukin et al., *A New Engagement?*, 188–190, 195.

23. Paul R. Loeb, "5 Minutes with Paul Loeb," *The Chronicle of Higher Education* 57:28 (March 18, 2011), A27.

24. "'Service Learning' Becomes the New Standard at Tulane U," *The Chronicle of Higher Education,* reported by Katherine Mangan (February 21, 2010), A16.

25. See the Bloch School website at http://www.bloch.umkc.edu/business-civic-engagement/index.aspx (accessed February 19, 2011).

26. Widener University advertisement in *The Chronicle of Higher Education* (April 8, 2011), A61.

27. John Saltmarsh, Matt Hartley, and Patti Clayton, "Democratic Engagement White Paper" (Boston: New England Resource Center for Higher Education, 2009), http://futureofengagement.files.wordpress.com/2009/02/democratic-engagement-white-paper-2_13_09.pdf (accessed February 23, 2011).

28. Robert D. Putnam and David E. Campbell, *American Grace: How Religion Divides and Unites Us* (New York: Simon and Schuster, 2010), 444, 446, 448, 454–455, 464.

29. Putnam and Campbell, *American Grace*, 467, 477.

30. Robert Wuthnow, *Saving America: Faith-Based Services and the Future of Civil Society* (Princeton, NJ: Princeton University Press, 2004), 102.

31. Kim Severson, "For Some Helping with Disaster Relief Is Not Just Aid, It's a Calling," *The New York Times* (May 9, 2011), http://www.nytimes.com/2011/05/09/us/09baptist.html?_r=2&ref=kimseverson (accessed May 16, 2011).

32. Jennifer A. Lindholm and Helen S. Astin, "Understanding the 'Interior' Life of Faculty: How Important is Spirituality?" in Michael D. Waggoner, ed., *Sacred and Secular Tensions in Higher Education* (New York: Routledge, 2011), 57.

33. Alexander W. Astin, Helen S. Astin, and Jennifer A. Lindholm, *Cultivating the Spirit: How College Can Enhance Students' Inner Lives* (San Francisco: Jossey-Bass, 2011), 70.

34. Additional corroboration is found in a 2007 survey of 24,000 undergraduate students drawn from twenty-three colleges and universities that was conducted by researchers at the University of Michigan's Center for the Study of Higher and Postsecondary Education. They found that 30.9 percent of "students who report regularly praying or meditating (54 percent of all students surveyed) were consistently more likely to strongly agree about all aspects of contributing to a larger community" in comparison to the 20 percent of students who do not pray or meditate. Eric L. Dey, Cassie L. Barnhardt, Mary Antonaros, Molly C. Ott, and Matthew A. Holsapple, *Civic Responsibility: What is the Campus Climate for Learning?* (Washington, DC: Association of American Colleges and Universities, 2009.)

35. "Service Statistics 2008: Highlights and Trends from Campus Compact's Annual Membership Survey," 2 (accessed April 12, 2011 at www.compact.org).

36. See Kosmin and Keysar, *ARIS 2008*, 14.

37. Christopher D. Stedman, "Youth Voices: Why Interfaith Work Must Happen on College Campuses," *Journal of College and Character* 12:1 (February 2011), http://journals.naspa.org/jcc/ (accessed March 8, 2011).

38. Belle S. Wheelan, quoted in Reginald Stuart, "Influential Lumina Foundation Drives Higher Education Change, Innovation," *Diverse: Issues in Higher Education* (August 18, 2010), http://diverseeducation.com/article/14047c4/influential-lumina-foundation-drives-higher-education-change-innovation.html (accessed January 26, 2012).

39. Quoted in Beth McMurtrie and Karin Fischer, "Campus Officials: Globalization is Inevitable, Whatever the Path," *The Chronicle of Higher Education* (February 26, 2011), A32.

40. See Martha C. Nussbaum and Joshua Cohen, eds., *For Love of Country?* (Boston: Beacon, 2002).

41. Bron Taylor, *Dark Green Religion: Nature Spirituality and the Planetary Future* (Berkeley, CA: University of California Press, 2010).

42. See Kwame Anthony Appiah, *Cosmopolitanism: Ethics in a World of Strangers* (New York: Norton, 2006).

CHAPTER 9

1. Blaise Pascal, *Pascal's Pensée*, W. F. Trotter, trans. (New York: E. P. Dutton, 1958), 78.

2. See Erik Erikson, *Childhood and Society* (New York: Norton, 1950); James Fowler, *Stages of Faith* (New York: Harper, 1981); Carol Gilligan, *In a Different Voice: Psychological Theory and Women's Development* (Cambridge, MA: Harvard University Press, 1982); Robert Kegan, *The Evolving Self: Problems and Process in Human Development* (Cambridge, MA: Harvard University Press, 1982); Lawrence Kohlberg, *The Psychology of Moral Development* (San Francisco: Harper and Row, 1981); and Jean Piaget, *The Psychology of the Child* (New York: Basic Books, 1969).

3. William G. Perry, Jr., *Forms of Intellectual and Ethical Development in the College Years: A Scheme* (New York: Holt, Rinehart, and Winston, 1970).

4. Tim Clydesdale, *The First Year Out: Understanding American Teens After High School* (Chicago: University of Chicago Press, 2007), 2, 4, 44–45.

5. Ibid., 170–180.

6. Parks, *Big Questions, Worthy Dreams*, 10.

7. Neiman, *Moral Clarity*, 8.

8. Anouar Majid, "Educating Ourselves into Coexistence," *Diversity and Democracy*, Vol. 11, No. 1 (Winter 2008), 5.

9. Quoted in Parks, *Big Questions, Worthy Dreams*, 63.

10. Quoted in Peter W. Marty, "Love that Changes Minds," *Christian Century* (February 23, 2010), 14.

11. Mark C. Taylor, *Field Notes from Elsewhere* (New York: Columbia University Press, 2009), 117–118. This is the same Mark C. Taylor who has more recently published *Crisis on Campus: A Bold Plan for Reforming Our Colleges and Universities* (New York: Knopf, 2010).

12. Ibid., 280.

13. Ibid., 118.

14. Wendy Doniger, "Thinking More Critically About Thinking Too Critically," *Criterion,* Vol. 46, No. 3 (Fall 2008/Winter 2009), 15.

15. Parker J. Palmer, *The Courage to Teach: Exploring the Inner Landscape of a Teacher's Life* (San Francisco: Jossey-Bass, 1998), 2.

16. R. Eugene Rice, "Faculty Priorities," in *The American University in a Postsecular Age,* Douglas Jacobsen and Rhonda Hustedt Jacobsen, eds., (New York: Oxford University Press, 2008), 111.

17. "Freedom in the Classroom," report of the AAUP's Committee A on Academic Freedom and Tenure (June 2007), http://www.aaup.org/AAUP/comm/rep/A/class.htm.

18. Parks, *Big Questions, Worthy Dreams,* 166.

19. See Rice, "Faculty Priorities," 110.

20. Quoted in Steven Meyers, "Do Your Students Care Whether You Care about Them?," *College Teaching* 57:4 (Fall 2009), 206.

21. We borrow the notion of "mentoring communities" from Sharon Parks, *Big Questions, Worthy Dreams.*

22. Salvatore Scibona, "Where I Learned to Read," *The New Yorker* (June 13 & 20, 2010), 14.

CHAPTER 10

1. For the full text of this commencement talk, see "'You've Got to Find What You Love,' Jobs says," Stanford University News, http://news.stanford.edu/news/2005/june15/jobs-061505.html (accessed October 12, 2011).

2. Quoted in Christian Smith with Kari Christoffersen, Hilary Davidson, and Patricia Snell Herzog, *Lost in Transition: The Dark Side of Emerging Adulthood* (New York: Oxford University Press, 2011), 106.

3. Astin et al., *The Spiritual Life of College Students,* 5.

4. Quoted in Ernest L. Boyer, *Selected Speeches, 1979–1995* (Princeton, NJ: Carnegie Foundation for the Advancement of Teaching, 1997), 31.

5. "Estimated Median Age at First Marriage, by Sex: 1890 to the Present," U.S. Census Bureau, www.census.gov (accessed July 28, 2011).

6. See Jeffrey Jensen Arnett, *Emerging Adulthood: The Winding Road from the Late Teens through the Twenties* (New York: Oxford University Press, 2004), 3, 219.

7. Alan Wolfe, *Moral Freedom: The Search for Virtue in a World of Choice* (New York: W. W. Norton, 2001).

8. The Cheesecake Factory analogy is from Christine Hassler, *20 Something Manifesto: Quarter-Lifers Speak Out about Who They Are, What They Want, and How to Get It* (Novato, CA: New World Library, 2008), 7.

9. Catherine Rampell, "Many with New College Degree Find the Job Market Humbling," *New York Times* (May 18, 2011), http://www.nytimes.com/2011/05/19/business/economy/19grads.html (accessed October 13, 2011).

10. Martin Handford, *Where's Waldo?* (Somerville, MA: Candlewick Press). The first book in the series was published in 1987.

11. See Mary Kelleher, "Study: Americans Seek Soul-Mate Spouse," http://abcnews.go.com/US/story?id=93078&page=1 (accessed August 6, 2011).

12. William Damon, *The Path to Purpose: Helping Our Children Find Their Calling in Life* (New York: Free Press, 2008), 59–60.

13. Christian Smith et al., *Lost in Transition,* see "Introduction."

14. Charlie Szold, "College Culture Needs Overhaul," *The Eagle* (February 4, 2009), http://www.theeagleonline.com/opinion/story/college-culture-needs-overhaul/ (accessed May 17, 2011).

15. See the "One in Four" website, http://www.oneinfourusa.org/statistics.php. Accurate statistics about rape on campus, like statistics about alcohol, are hard to acquire. Various reporting sites have differing interests in making the rates of rape seem either higher or lower.

16. Donald L. Hilton Jr., quoted in "Five Questions about Pornography" by Emily R. Breslow, *The Harvard Crimson* (April 7, 2011).

17. John Christoffersen, "Feds investigate sex harassment complaints at Yale," TODAY News (April 1, 2011), http://www.msnbc.msn.com/id/42381332/ns/us_news-life/t/feds-investigate-sex-harassment-complaints-yale/ (accessed January 27, 2012).

18. Donna Freitas, *Sex and the Soul: Juggling Sexuality, Spirituality, Romance, and Religion on America's College Campuses* (New York: Oxford University Press, 2008).

19. Stephanie Paulsell, "Friendship and Intimacy" in Dorothy C. Bass and Susan R. Briehl, *On Our Way: Christian Practices for Living a Whole Life* (Nashville, TN: Upper Room, 2010), 80.

20. Shaun Gallagher, *How the Body Shapes the Mind* (New York: Oxford University Press, 2005), 247.

21. See Elizabeth Kiss and J. Peter Euben, eds., *Debating Moral Education: Rethinking the Role of the Modern University* (Durham, NC: Duke University Press, 2010), 17.

22. "AAC&U Announces National Initiative on Fostering Personal and Social Responsibility in Today's College Students," http://www.aacu.org/press_room/press_releases/2006/CoreCommitmentsInitiative.cfm (accessed May 20, 2011). Also see Caryn McTighe Musil, "Educating Students for Personal and Social Responsibility: The Civic Learning Spiral" in Barbara Jacoby, ed., *Civic Engagement*

in Higher Education: Concepts and Practices (San Francisco: Jossey-Bass, 2009), 49–68.

23. "Carolinian Creed," University of South Carolina, http://www.sc.edu/words/item.php?wid=29 (accessed January 27, 2012).

24. "Southern Oregon University Raider Creed," http://www.assou.net/raider-creed.html (accessed August 8, 2011).

25. "University Creed," University of Mississippi, http://www.olemiss.edu/info/creed.html (accessed August 8, 2011).

26. Frederick Buechner, *Wishful Thinking: A Theological ABC* (New York: Harper & Row, 1973), 95.

27. Dorothy C. Bass, "Living a Whole Life: An Introduction" in Dorothy C. Bass and Susan R. Briehl, *On Our Way: Christian Practices for Living a Whole Life* (Nashville, TN: Upper Room, 2010), 11.

28. "Ignatian Center for Jesuit Education," Santa Clara University, http://www.scu.edu/ignatiancenter/partners/discoverhistory/plan.cfm (accessed July 6, 2011).

29. "First Year Experience," Guilford College, http://www.guilford.edu/academics/academic-support/first-year-experience/ (accessed July 6, 2011).

30. Center for Vocation, Faith and Service, Hastings College, http://www.hastings.edu/igsbase/igstemplate.cfm/SRC=DB/SRCN=/GnavID=108 (accessed July 30, 2011).

31. Office of Religious Life, Denison University, http://www.denison.edu/offices/religiouslife/lillyprogram.html (accessed July 30, 2011).

32. "Answering the Call," the Center for Faith and Vocation, Butler University, http://www.butler.edu/faith-vocation/calling/overview/ (accessed July 6, 2011).

33. "The well-planned life" and "the summoned life" are terms borrowed from "The Summoned Self," an opinion piece written by David Brooks that appeared in *The New York Times* (August 2, 2010).

34. Clayton M. Christensen, "How Will You Measure Your Life?," *Harvard Business Review* (July/August 2011), 48.

35. Ibid., 49, 51.

36. Robert K. Greenleaf, *The Power of Servant Leadership*, Larry C. Spears, ed. (San Francisco: Berrett-Koehler, 1998), 70.

37. Christine Hassler, *20 Something, 20 Everything: A Quarter-Life Woman's Guide to Balance and Direction* (Novato, CA: New World Library, 2005), 10–11, 41, 130.

38. Neafsey, *A Sacred Voice Is Calling*, 64–65.

39. David Brooks, "The Summoned Self."

40. Jonathan Sacks, *The Dignity of Difference: How to Avoid the Clash of Civilizations* (New York: Continuum, 2002), 25.

41. See Seligman, Weller, Puett, and Simon, *Ritual and Its Consequences*.

42. Barry Schwartz and Kenneth Sharpe, *Practical Wisdom: The Right Way to Do the Right Thing* (New York: Riverhead, 2010), 14.

43. Howard Gardner, Mihaly Csikszentmihayli, and William Damon, *Good Work: When Excellence and Ethics Meet* (New York: Basic Books, 2001).

44. Harold T. Shapiro, *A Larger Sense of Purpose: Higher Education and Society* (Princeton, NJ: Princeton University Press, 2005), 90.

CONCLUSION: RELIGION AND THE FUTURE OF
UNIVERSITY EDUCATION

1. Louis Menand, *The Marketplace of Ideas: Reform and Resistance in the American University* (New York: W. W. Norton & Company, 2010), 158.

2. Drew Faust Gilpin, "The University's Crisis of Purpose," *The New York Times* (September 6, 2009).

Index

Note: page numbers in italics refer to figures.

AAC&U. *See* Association of American Colleges and Universities
AAR. *See* American Academy of Religion
academic excellence, standards of, 104
    academic freedom, religion as perceived threat to, 32–33
ACURA. *See* Association of College and University Religious Affairs
advocacy, as style of teaching, 133–34
    age of faculty, and views on religion in academia, 33–34
Ailes, Roger, 98
Albright, Madeleine, 61–62
alcohol use, as campus problem, 143–45
AMCLI. *See* American Muslim Civic Leadership Institute
American Academy of Religion (AAR), 65, 71
American Association of University Professors, 133–34
American Grace: How Religion Divides and Unites Us (Putnam and Campbell), 117, 118

American Historical Association, new attention given to religion, 6
American Muslim Civic Leadership Institute (AMCLI), 91
American Psychological Association, new attention given to religion, 6–7
Americans United for Separation of Church and State, 84
American University, student partying at, 143
The American University in a Postsecular Age (Jacobsen and Jacobsen), viii, 47
Amherst College, in Protestant era, 18
Amin, Jasiyah Al-, 79–80
Amish
    and political engagement, 113
    rumspringa tradition, 142
anonymity, as style of teaching, 132–33
Appiah, Kwame Anthony, 91
Aristotelian ethic, 151
Arizona State University, enrollment, 83
Arnett, Jeffrey, 139
Asian religions, increasing presence in U.S., 27
Assad, Talal, 34

Association of College and University
    Religious Affairs (ACURA),
    142–43
Association of American Colleges and
    Universities (AAC&U), 108,
    145–46
Association of American Universities,
    23
Astin, Alexander, 55
Astin, Helen, 55
atheists
    new complexity of religious beliefs and,
        100
    as percent of U.S. population, 76
Augsburg College, 119
Ave Maria University, viii
authentic life, 149–50

Bass, Dorothy C., 147
Baxter Magolda, Marcia B., 55
Baylor University, PTEV and, 146
beliefs. *See* religious beliefs
Bellah, Robert N., 53, 110, 112
Berger, Peter L., 26
Bible and civil religion, 112
Bible colleges, establishment of, 20
Big Questions, Worthy Dreams (Parks),
    43–44
big questions, as trail marker for
    discussion of religion, 43–45,
    47, 48
Blair, Tony, 91
Bloch School of Management, University
    of Missouri, 116
Bologna agreement, 154
Booth, Wayne, 98, 101
Boston College, 9–11
Bowdoin College, 18
Boyer, Ernest L., 14
Brigham Young University, viii,
    86–87
Brooks, David, 54, 150–51

Brown University, viii, 18, 143
Bryan, William Jennings, 22
Bucknell University, 34
Buddhism
    in U.S., 74, 75, 76
    mindfulness in, 151
    number of followers, 49
Buechner, Frederick, 147
Butler University, 148

cafeteria Catholicism, 54
Calhoun, Craig, 162
California State University Bakersfield,
    viii
calling. *See* vocation
Campbell, David E., 117, 118
Campus Compact, 118–19
campus-wide spiritual needs, meeting of,
    85–86
Canagarajah, Suresh, 82
Carleton College, 143
Carnegie Foundation for the Advancement
    of Teaching, 14, 111
Carolinian Creed (University of South
    Carolina), 146
Casden Institute for the Study of the
    Jewish Role in American Life
    (at USC), 90
Catholic higher education in U.S.,
    9–10, 20
Catholics
    leaving church, 77
    as percentage of U.S. population,
        74, 75
    religious privatization and, 21
    views on proselytizing, 78
Center for Ethics and Religious Affairs
    (CERA, at Penn State), 3–4
Center for Muslim-Jewish Engagement
    (at USC), 90–91
Center for Religion and Civic Culture
    (at USC), 91

Center for the Study of Higher and
    Postsecondary Education,
    (at University of Michigan), 176
CERA. *See* Center for Ethics and
    Religious Affairs
chapel services, required attendance at,
    87
Chapman University, 80–81
character education, 137–52
    college years as moral holiday, 142–45
    destructive behavior, colleges' failure to
        address, 143–45
    displacement by scholarly research
        paradigm, 22–23
    good life, three visions of, 149–51
    institutions' renewed interest in,
        145–48
    institutions' rhetoric *vs.* reality, 141–43,
        152
    lack of guidance for students in,
        139–41
    as natural site of engagement with
        religion, *56*
    in Protestant era, 18–19, 20
Chickering, Art, 44
Chinese traditional religion, 11
Christensen, Clayton, 149
Christianity
    denial of self in, 151
    as percentage of U.S. population,
        74, 75
    and religious literacy, 64, 70–71
    subdivisions of, 49
Christians
    American, confidence of, 32
    monist style in, 102–3
    number of, 49
    percent of Americans identifying as, 49
    perception of U.S. religious climate,
        74–75
Church of Jesus Christ of Latter Day
    Saints (Mormons), 78, 86–87

churches, lack of support for emerging
    adults, 139
church-related colleges
    accommodation of minority religious
        groups, 87
    and examination of convictions,
        125–26
    model of religious management at,
        86–87
    religion as threat to academic freedom,
        33
    religious diversity at, 79
CIC. *See* Council of Independent
    Colleges
civic, definition of, 121
civic engagement, 107–22
    and college/university public relations,
        108, 116
    as community service, 109
        and historic religion, engagement
            with, 116–20, 176
        increasing student interest in, 115
        issues faced by, 109
        varieties of service, 116
    efforts to revitalize, 108–9
    focus of, as point of contention,
        120–22, *121*
    as goal of education, 108, 111–12, 114
    as goal of faculty, 107
    as site of engagement with religion, *56*
    as political activism, 109
        as civic religious practice, 110–12
        declining support for, 109, 111, 115
        and historic religion, engagement
            with, 112–14
        resurgence of after Sept. 11th attacks,
            111
    public religion as motive for, 107–8
    religious motivation for, 107–8,
        112–14, 121–22
civil religion, 53. *See also* public
    religion

Civil Rights Movement, as public
    religion, 110
Civil War
    divided loyalties in, 122
    and fracturing of American
        Protestantism, 19
Clinton, William J., 37
Clydesdale, Tim, 125–26
Coble, Christopher, viii–ix
college attendance
    benefit from, 155–57
    in era of religious privatization, 24
    increases in, 24, *25*
    in Protestant era, 18–19
College of William and Mary, *18*, 86
Collins, Francis, 93, 95
colonial colleges, 17–18, *18*
Colson, Charles, 98
Columbia University, *18*
Commission on Higher Education,
    Truman Report (1947), 110
common good, contested character of,
    120
community colleges, establishment of, 110
community service, as form of civic
    engagement, 109
    current issues within, 109
    and historic religion, engagement with,
        116–20, 176
    increasing student interest in, 115
    and interfaith encounters, 82
    varieties of, 116
consumerism, 141
control beliefs, 98
convictions, 123–36. *See also* religious
    beliefs
    difficulty of hiding in
        classroom, 130
    styles of managing in classroom,
        132–34
    mentoring relationships and, 135–36
    as site of engagement with religion, *56*

personal religion and, 55
student questioning and modification of
    crisis necessary for, 124, 130
    critical *vs.* transcendent forms of,
        129–32
    importance of, 126, 136
    intermingling of with academic life,
        123–24
    as purpose of college experience, 123,
        124–26
Cornell University, 143
Council of Independent Colleges (CIC),
    147
critical unsettling of convictions, 129–31
Csikszentmihayli, Mihaly, 151
Culture Wars (Hunter), 113
Curry, Ann, 61

Dacey, Austin, 102
Damon, William, 141, 151
dark green religion, 121
Dartmouth University, *18*
Dawkins, Richard, 52
Deep South, religious climate in, 76
denial of self, in Christian ethics, 151
Dennett, Daniel, 52
Denison University, 143, 148
Department of Education, and civic
    engagement, 108–9
developmental theories
    on development in college, 124–25
    on emerging adults' moral
        development, 139–40
difficult dialogues, as trail marker for
    discussion of religion, 41–43,
    47, *48*
DiIulio, John, viii
disaster relief, organized religion as
    vehicle for, 118
"Diversity, Democracy, and Liberal
    Learning" initiative (AAC&U),
    108

diversity, religious, 74, *75. See also*
    pluriformity of contemporary
    religion
  changing demographics, 74, *75*
  of college students, increase in, 77–79
  as invisible, 79
  perceptions of by religious groups, 74–76
  and religious privatization, 24
divinity schools, in history of higher
    education, 17–18
dogmatism, and framing of knowledge,
    93, 96, 97
Doniger, Wendy, 103, 131
Duke, Benjamin, 23
Duke University, 23, 73, 85, 146
Dunn, Jack, 10

Eck, Diana, 68, 100
Ecklund, Elaine, 34
ecozoic loyalties, and focus of civic
    engagement, *121,* 121–22
*Educating Citizens: Preparing America's
    Undergraduates for Lives of Moral
    and Civil Responsibility* (2003),
    111
"Education as Transformation: Religious
    Pluralism, Spirituality, and
    Higher Education" conference
    (Wellesley College; 1998), 6
Edwards, Mark, viii
Eisenhower, Dwight D., 25–26
emerging adults, 139–41
Emerson, Ralph Waldo, 55
Emory University, 143
employment. *See* job training
Enlightenment, and U.S. public religion,
    51
enrollment figures for U.S. colleges,
    82–83
epistemological pluralism, 27–29
  ethics as academic field of study, 28–29
  ethnic denominational colleges, 19–20

Euthyphro (Plato), 104
evangelical Protestant colleges,
    life-changing learning at, 126
evangelical Protestantism, resurgence of,
    26, 27
evangelical Protestants
  and civic engagement, 118
  and interfaith dialogue, 81
  as monists, 98
  perception of religious climate, 75
  and Princeton religion department, 104
  views on proselytizing, 78
evil religions
  Kimball on, 68
  problems with designation of, 69
evolution, theory of, and American
    Protestantism, 21–22
expressive individualism, and civil
    religion, 112

factual literacy in religion, 62–65
faculty
  and civic engagement, 107
  convictions of
    silence about, 127–28
    difficulty of hiding, 130
    styles of managing in classroom,
        132–34
  monist thinking in, 97, 100
  pluralist thinking in, 100–1
  religious illiteracy among, 42
  religious self-identification, 77, *78,* 170
  views on religion, factors in, 32–34
Faith and Globalization Initiative (at
    Yale), 91
familiarity, as form of religious literacy,
    62, 62–63, 65–68
Farmer, Ronald L., 80–81
Faust, Drew Gilpin, 155
feminist thought, on knowledge, 95, 102
First Things (periodical), 105
The First Year Out (Clydesdale), 125–26

Ford Foundation, and difficult dialogues, 42
foreign policy, religious illiteracy and, 61–62
formation, and information in the classroom, 128–29
Forms of Intellectual and Ethical Development in the College Years (Perry), 124–25
Foucault, Michel, 95
framing knowledge. *See also* monist style of thought; pluralist style of thought
  contemporary, complexity of, 94–96
  definition(s) of, 93
  as distinctive responsibility of academia, 92
  and historic religion, 102–3
  as liberation and limit, 103
  monist style of, 96–100
  of others, acceptance of as prerequisite for productive debate, 93, 99–100, 105–6
  pluralist style of, 100–2
  in postmodern context, 96
  as site of engagement with religion, *56*
free market model of campus religious management, 83, 88
Freitas, Donna, 144
fundamentalists, 21–22
Furman University, 143
future of education, religion and, 153–57

Gandhi, Mahatma, 129
Gardner, Howard, 151
George Mason University, 78
George Washington University, 79
German university model, U.S. adoption of, 22–23
G.I. Bill, and college attendance, 24
Gilmore Girls (TV series), 31
Global Perspective Institute, 108

good life, three visions of, 149–51
good work, definition of, 151
Graham, Billy, 61
Great Awakening, 12, 76
great books curriculum, 24
Greenleaf, Robert K., 149
Griffiths, Paul, 81
Guilford College, 96, 148

Habits of the Heart (Bellah *et al.*), 54, 112
Hankins, Barry, 67
Harris, Sam, 11–12, 52
"Harvard's Crisis of Faith" (Miller), 9
Harvard University
  founding of, *18*
  interfaith etiquette, teaching of, 91
  introduction of "culture and belief" course requirement, 8–9
  model for campus religious management, 85
  as pace-setting university, 21
  Pluralism Project, 91
  religious diversity at, 79
Hassler, Christine, 149–50
Hastings College, 148
Herberg, Will, 26
HERI. *See* Higher Education Research Institute
Heschel, Abraham Joshua, 138–39
higher education. *See also* religion in higher education
  crisis in, 154
    engagement with religion as solution for, 155–57
    inadequacy of current approach to, 154–55
  purpose of, spiritual components of, 14–15
  student expectations for, 80
  university system of
    history of, 141–42
    U.S. adoption of, 22–23

U.S. system of, as both practical and reflective, 155

Higher Education Research Institute (at UCLA), 30, 38

Hillel, 79

Hinduism
increasing number of courses on, 71
limited U.S. knowledge about, 76

Hindus
as percent of U.S. population, 74, *75*
numbers of, globally, 49
perception of U.S. religious climate, 76
pluralist thinking in, 103

historic religion, 49–50. *See also* religions
and civic engagement
through community service, 116–20, 176
through political activism, 112–14
as communal, 49, 50
and four trail markers, 47, *48*
as motive for civic engagement, 107
natural intersections with higher learning, *56*
as object of personal loyalty, 122
as subcategory of religion more broadly construed, 47

historically Black colleges and universities, 19, 119

A History of the Warfare of Science with Theology (White), 92–93

Hitchens, Christopher, 52

homogeneous model of campus religious management, 87–88, 88–89

honor codes, and character education, 146

hook-up culture, on campus, 144–45

Hope College (Michigan), 20

hospitality model of religious accommodation, 10–11, 81

hospitality of institution, as central to interfaith etiquette, 10–11, 89

House of Representatives model of campus religious management, 83–84, 88

Hoveyda, Amir, 10

humanities
as academic replacement for religion, 14, 156
and National Endowment for the Humanities, 110
specialized language of, 156

Hunter, James Davison, 113

immigration law, and Asians in U.S., 75

individualism, as Protestant value, 17, 22, 77

industrialization, and practical focus of higher education, 19

industrial philanthropists, and higher education, 23–24

information, and formation in the classroom, 128–29

Institute for Advanced Catholic Studies (at USC), 90

interfaith etiquette, 73–91
definition of, 74
in face-to-face encounters, 43, 79–82
formal codes of, 80
hospitality of institution as central to, 89
institutional structures and, 82–89
as natural site of engagement with religion, *56*
for real world, teaching of, 89–91

Interfaith Youth Core (IFYC), 82, 114

internationalism
as educational goal, 155
and focus of civic engagement, 120–22, *121*

invisible religion, 13

Islam. *See also* Muslims
global variation in beliefs, 49
increasing number of courses on, 71

Islam. *See also* Muslims (*Cont.*)
   and monist thinking, 103
   subdivisions of, 49
Islamic Revolution in Iran, 26

James, William, 22, 34, 101
Jewish colleges, establishment of, 20
Jewish students
   interfaith encounters, 73–74, 79–80
   at U.S. universities, 79
   views on proselytizing, 78
Jews
   as percent of U.S. population, 74,
     75, 75
   perception of U.S. religious climate, 75
   pluralist thinking in, 103–4
job training, 138, 140, 155, 157
Jobs, Steve, 137, 138, 149
John Paul II (pope), 10
Johns Hopkins University, 21–23
Judeo-Christian nation, U.S.
   transformation into, 26
Jurgensmeyer, Mark, 162

Kant, Immanuel, 92
Kanter, Martha, 120
Kennedy, John F., 12
Kimball, Charles, 68–69
King, Martin Luther, Jr., 110
Kirschner, Dan, 10
knowledge. *See* framing knowledge
knowledge and power, Foucault on, 95
Kroc Institute for International Peace
   Studies (at Notre Dame), 91
Kronman, Anthony T., 14–15
Kuhn, Thomas, 95

Laemmle, Susan, 90
LaGuardia Community College, 112
Lewinsky, Monica, 37
Lilly Endowment, viii, 146
Lindholm, Jennifer, 55

Loeb, Paul, 115
Los Angeles, religious diversity in, 76
Luckmann, Thomas, 13
Lumina Foundation, 120
Luther, Martin, 147

Macalester College, 34
MacIntyre, Alasdair, 99–100
The Madonna of 115th Street (Orsi), 68
Majid, Anouar, 129
Mannheim, Karl, 95
The Marketplace of Ideas (Menand), 155
Marsden, George, 21, 26
Massachusetts Institute of Technology
   (MIT), viii, 7–8
   medieval universities, subjects of study
   in, 46
Mellow, Gail O., 112
melting pot, U.S. as, and religious
   privatization, 25–26
Menand, Louis, 8–9, 155
mentoring communities, 135–36
mentoring of students, 134–36
Mill, John Stewart, 111
Miller, Lisa, 9
mindfulness, in Buddhism, 151
Minnich, Elizabeth, 102
monist style of thought, 96–98
   and Christianity, 102–3
   as common style in academia, 97, 100
   and Islam, 103
   pluralists' contempt for, 97–98
   potential dogmatism of, 97
Moral Clarity (Neiman), 13
moral freedom, 139–40
Moral Majority, 26
Mormons. *See* Church of Jesus Christ of
   Latter Day Saints
Morrill Land Grant Act of 1862, 19
Mother Teresa, 38
Muhlenberg College, 79
multiculturalism, 28–29, 95

Muslims. *See also* Islam
number of, 49
as percent of U.S. population, 74, 75, 75
perception of U.S. religious climate, 75
public distrust of, after Sept. 11th
attacks, 75
Muslim students
at Brigham Young University, 86–87
and interfaith dialogue, 81
interfaith encounters, 73–74, 79–80
Muslim Student Union (MSU), 74

Nasir, Na'ilah Suad, 79–80
National Endowment for the
Humanities, 110
National Institutes of Health (NIH),
93, 95
National Science Foundation, 110
Native Americans, and Protestant era, 17
Neafsey, John, 150
Neiman, Susan, 13, 128
Network for Vocation in Undergraduate
Education (NetVUE),
146–47
New Atheists, and U.S. public religion,
52
New England, religious climate in, 76
Newman, John Henry (cardinal), 100
Newsweek magazine, 9
New York City, religious diversity in, 76
New Yorker magazine, 98
Noll, Mark, 23
nonreligious Americans ("nones")
movement in and out of category, 77
as percent of U.S. population, 74, 75, 76
nonreligious students
increase of, 77, 78
views on proselytizing, 78
Nord, Warren A., 66
normal schools, 19
Not for Profit (Nussbaum), 14–15
Notre Dame University, 146

Nouwen, Henri, 81
Nussbaum, Martha, 14–15, 111–12

Obama, Barack, 93, 109
O'Brien, George Dennis, 55
one-party rule model of campus religious
management, 86–87, 88–89
open source movement, 102
organized religion, U.S.
as historic religion, 49–50
history of flux in, 76–77
loosening hold of, 76, 77–78
and civic engagement, 117–18
Orsi, Robert, 68

Pacific Lutheran University, viii, 147
Pacific Northwest, religious climate in, 76
Palmer, Parker, 132
Parks, Sharon Daloz, 43–44, 126
Pascal, Blaise, 123
Pasquerilla Spiritual Center (at Penn
State), 3–4, 88
Patel, Eboo, 82, 114
Paterno, Joe, 3, 4
Paterson, David, 61
Pennsylvania State University (Penn
State)
formal code of interfaith ethics, 80
Pasquerilla Spiritual Center at, 3–4, 88
Pepperdine University, viii, 146
Perry, William G., 124–25
personal religion, 53–56
definition of, 53–54
and four trail markers, 47, 48
interpersonal dimension of, 55
natural intersections with higher
learning, 56
secular forms of, 55–56
as subcategory of religion broadly
construed, 47
vs. public religion, 54–55
Pinker, Steven, 9

Plato, 104
pluralist style of thought, 96–98,
   100–102
  characteristics of, 101
  contempt for monist thinking in,
    97–98
  and Hinduism, 103
  and Judaism, 103–4
pluriform era in higher education, 16, *17*,
  27–30
pluriformity of contemporary religion, 7,
  153. *See also* diversity, religious
  and blurring of definition of religion, 7
  confusion engendered by, 31
  growth of individualized spirituality
    and, 27
  increased cultural diversity and, 27
  and role of religion in education,
    156–57
  and student expectations about college
    education, 30
political activism as form of civic
    engagement, 109
  as civic religious practice, 110–12
  declining support for, 109, 111, 115
  and historic religion, engagement with,
    112–14
politics
  new visibility of religion in, 12–13
  need to distinguish from religion in
    classroom discussions, 42–43
Porterfield, Amanda, viii, 67
positivist paradigm of scholarship, 94–95
postmodernist views on knowledge,
  95–96
practical focus of education
  German university model and, 22–23
  industrialization and, 19
  and job training, 154–55
  practical wisdom, 151
Pratt Institute, 79
The Princeton Review, 3

Princeton University
  ACURA and, 143
  founding of, *18*
  model for campus religious
    management, 85
  as pace-setting university, 21
  religion department, religiously neutral
    stance of, 104–5
privatization of religion, 16, *17*, 20–26,
  31
professional studies, growth of, 27, 28
  and growth of ethics as field of study,
    28–29
professors. *See* faculty
Program for the Theological Exploration
    of Vocation (PTEV), 146–48
proselytizing, student opinions about, 78
Protestant, Catholic, Jew (Herberg), 26
Protestant era, in U.S. higher education,
  16, *17*, 17–20
Protestantism, American
  beliefs as focus on, 48
  characteristics of, 17, 163
  core beliefs of, 20
  education, role of, 17–18, 19
  fracturing of, in Civil War, 19
  fundamentalist-moderate split in,
    21–22
  individualism in, 17, 22, 77
  and public religion, 51
Prothero, Stephen, 63–64
PTEV. *See* Program for the Theological
    Exploration of Vocation
public religion, 50–53
  and academia, complex relation
    between, 53
  blending of secular and sacred in, 51
  and civic engagement, 107–8, 110–12
  as commitment to American way of
    life, 110–11
  contested nature of, 51–53
  definition of, 50–51

focus of, as point of contention,
  120–22, *121*
and four trail markers, 47, *48*
natural intersections with higher
  learning, *56*
Nussbaum on, 111–12
as subcategory of religion broadly
  construed, 47
in the U.S., 51, 53
vs. personal religion, 54–55
public square model of religious
  accommodation, *vs.* hospitality
  model, 10–11
Publishers Weekly, 68
purpose in life, 138–41, 149
Putnam, Robert D., 117, 118

Ramadan, Tariq, 100
Rand, Ayn, 96
Randolph, Robert, 8
Reagan, Ronald W., 111
religion
  blurring of concept, 7, 11–12, 31
  characteristics of, *vs.* spirituality, 37–39
  as component of identity, 50
  contemporary. *See* pluriformity of
    contemporary religion
  definition of, 4–5, 7, 13–14, 22
  three subcategories of, 47–49 (*See
    also* historic religion; personal
    religion; public religion)
  as unavoidable topic of study, vii,
    14–15, 29–30, 63, 153–54
religion, higher education's reengagement
    with
  and critique of religion, 5–6, 68–70
  educational benefits from, 5, 154, 156–57
  and the future of American higher
    education, 153–57
  increased academic interest in, 6–7
  pluriformity of contemporary religion
    and, 156–57

resistance to, 9, 32–33, 35–36, 92–93
self-awareness necessary for, ix
religion in higher education
  asking good questions about, 46–47,
    50, 53, 56
  history of, 16–30
    pluriform era, 16, *17*, 27–30
    Protestant era, 16, *17*, 17–20
    religious privatization era, 16, *17*,
      20–26
  natural points of intersection, 56, *56*
religion of humanity, 111–12
religions. *See also* historic religion
  basic sameness of, as commonly held
    myth, 79–80
  global, size of, 49, 74, *75*
  internal complexity of, 49
religious differences, efforts to ignore,
  79–80
religious exclusivity, decline of, 27, 78
religious extremists, 6, 11–12
religious identity
  institutional, denial of, as
    counterproductive, 89
  as integral to self, 50
  personal, interfaith encounters as way
    of exploring, 81
religious literacy, 59–72
  definition of, 65
  lack of, 42, 59–62
  levels of,
    facts, 62–65
    familiarity, 62–63, 65–68
    assessment, 62–63, 68–70
  as site of engagement with religion, *56*
  teaching of, 60–61, 70–72
Religious Literacy (Prothero),
  63–64
religious practice
  as mode of religion, 48
  in personal religion, 55
  required participation in, views on, 40

religious privatization era in higher
　　education, 16, *17*, 20–26
　and discussion of religion, atrophied
　　skill in, 31, 35
　and exclusion of personal religion from
　　academia, 56
　factors contributing to, 21–24
　humanities as replacement for religion,
　　156
　and religious tolerance, 21
　vs. secularization, 21
Religious Right
　and political engagement, 113
　and religion, modern persistence of, 26
religious tolerance. *See also* inclusive
　　environment
　increasing support for, 78, 79, 80
　at MIT, 8
　programs focusing on, 89–91
　religious privatization and, 21
　students' commitment to, 34
Rethinking Secularism (Calhoun,
　　Jurgensmeyer and Van
　　Antwerpen), 162
Rockefeller, John D., 23
Rogers, William Barton, 7
Rorty, Richard, 35–36, 95
A Rumor of Angels (Berger), 26
rumspringa, 142–45
Rutgers University, *18*

St. Olaf College, 19–20
Santa Clara University, 147–48
sapere aude ("dare to know"), 92–93
Schneider, Carol Geary, 146
Schuman, Samuel, 87
Schwartz, Barry, 151
Scibona, Salvatore, 135–36
scientism, 97
Scopes, John, 21
Scopes trial (1925), 21–22
Second Great Awakening, 12
Second Vatican Council, 9, 27, 50

The Secular Age (Taylor), 105
secularists, 11–12, 26, 92–93, 104
　secularity, as contested notion, 34–35
secularization
　of education, 9–10, 21
　theories of, 164–65
　of U.S. culture, impact on education, 26
Seeing the Light (Schuman), 87
seminaries, in history of higher
　　education, 17–18
Senate model of campus religious
　　management, 84–85, 88
separation of church and state, 17, 83
September 11th terrorist attacks
　and distrust of Muslims, 75
　and perceived importance of religion,
　　6, 68
　and management of campus-wide
　　spiritual needs, 86
　and resurgence of civic engagement, 111
Sex and the Soul (Freitas), 144
sexual practices on campus, 143–45
Shapiro, Harold T., 69, 152
Sharpe, Kenneth, 151
Shulman, Lee, viii, 103
signature truth, 55
Smith, Bob, 4
Smith, Christian, 141
Smith, Huston, 8
Social Gospel movement, 22
Soka University, viii, 91
Solidarity movement, and modern
　　persistence of religion, 26
Solomon, Robert C., 101
Soni, Varun, 90
soul mate, students' search for, 140–41,
　　149–50
soul of higher education, Nussbaum on,
　　14–15
The Soul of the American University
　　(Marsden), 21
specialization, in positivist paradigm of
　　scholarship, 94

Speers, Sam, 35
"spiritual GPS," 54
spirituality
    in classroom discussions, 36–39
    defined, 7, 37–38
    high student interest in, 30
    and organized religion, 12
    and personal religion, 54
    versus religion, 36–39
Stanford, Leland, 23
Stanford University, 23, 142–43
state church model of campus religious
        management, 85–86, 88–89
Stedman, Chris, 119
Stout, Jeffrey, 107–8
The Structure of Scientific Revolutions
        (Kuhn), 95
student(s). *See also specific groups and topics*
    convictions, questioning and
        modification of
        crisis necessary for, 124, 130
        critical *vs.* transcendent forms of,
            129–32
        importance of, 126, 136
        inevitability of, 128–29
        intermingling of with academic life,
            123–24
        as purpose of college experience, 123,
            124–26
        developmental theories on, 124–25,
            139–40
    mentoring of, 134–36
    religious self-identification, 77–78, *78*
    and spirituality, high levels of interest
        in, 30
    views on religion discussion in
        classroom, 34
student-centered learning
    religion as necessary component in, 29,
        30, 153
    turn toward, 27–28, 29
Sukkah City project (Vassar
        College), 82

summoned life, as good life, 150–51
Swarthmore College, 151

tao, 11
Taves, Ann, 162
tawhid (oneness), in Islamic thought,
        103
Taylor, Charles, 13, 34, 105
Taylor, Mark C., 130–31
teaching, as act of interpretation, and
        objectivity, 40–41
teaching about religion. *See also* trail
        markers for discussion of religion
    history of, 155–56
    potential problems in, 15, 154
    potential rewards of, 15, 154, 155–57
    students' interest in, personal reasons
        for, 41
    vs. teaching religion
        course content and, 64
        subcategories of religion and,
            47, 48
        as tactic, 39–41
terrorist attacks of September 11th. *See*
        September 11th terrorist attacks
Thomas Aquinas College, 105
tikkun olam, 117
Tillich, Paul, 13
To Change the World (Hunter), 113
trail markers for discussion of religion,
        36–45
    big questions, 43–45
    difficult dialogues, 41–43
    limitations of, 45
    relation to subcategories of religion,
        47, 48
    spirituality *vs.* religion, 36–39
    teaching about *vs.* teaching religion,
        39–41
transactional interfaith dialogues,
        82
transcendent unsettling of convictions,
        131–32

transparency, as style of teaching, 133
Truman, Harry S., 110
Truman Report (1947), 110
Tufts University, 79
Tulane University, 116

University of California, Irvine, 73–74
University of California, Los Angeles
    (UCLA), Higher Education
    Research Institute, 30, 38
University of Chicago, 23, 143
University of Denver, 143
University of Miami, viii
University of Michigan, 21, 176
University of Mississippi, 146
University of Missouri, Bloch School of
    Management, 116
University of North Carolina, Program
    in the Humanities and Values, 66
University of Notre Dame, 86, 88
University of Pennsylvania, *18*, 79
University of Phoenix, 82–83
University of South Carolina, 146
University of Southern California
    (USC), viii, 89–90
University of Southern Oregon, 146
university system
    history of, 46, 141–42
    U.S. adoption of, 22–23
U.S. Air Force Academy, viii, 84
utilitarianism and civil religion, 112

Van Antwerpen, Jonathan, 162
The Varieties of Religious Experience
    (James), 34
"Varieties of Secular Experience:
    Pedagogy, Politics, and Meaning
    in the Liberal Arts" (2008
    conference), 34–35

Vassar College, viii, 34–35, 82
Virginia Tech, 86
vocation
    definition of, 147–48
    as meaning and purpose of life, 137–38
    as site of engagement with religion, 56
    and PTEV, 146–48
    as religious calling, 147–48
    and versions of the good life, 149–51

Wake Forest University, 146
Walters, Barbara, 37
Weber, Max, 94
Wellesley College, 6, 84–85
well-planned life, as good life, 149
"What is Enlightenment" (Kant), 92
Wheaton College (IL), 61, 87, 105
Wheaton College (MA), 61
When Religion Becomes Evil (Kimball),
    68–69
White, Andrew Dickson, 92–93
Wild Hope program (Pacific Lutheran
    University), 147
Williams College, 18, 34
Willimon, William, 73
Wittgenstein, Ludwig, 96
Wolfe, Alan, 139–40
Wolterstorff, Nicholas, 98
women's colleges, founding of, 19
worldviews/world views, 98–100
Wuthnow, Robert, viii, 117, 118

Yale University
    Faith and Globalization Initiative, 91
    founding of, *18*
    model for campus religious
        management, 89
    as pace-setting university, 21
    as sexually hostile environment, 144

136 Y... lifelong learner, the interplay of convictions
* → kn (formation + informat) = central concern
email address

Intell. literacy: Xnity, H'ism — internal lit
Internal literacy: B'ism. Islam — internal lit

move toward some org of class
priorities — env'ism, ecozoic loyalties
+ Univ loyalties.

autobio of the girl?
integrate into classes where they work
on their projects + you letters — ops
for prais. as in Danger p. 131

students lead discussions — need to help
them learn how. need to require
writing responses so they have some
help forming discussion